HOW TO READ

ISLAMIC CALLIGRAPHY

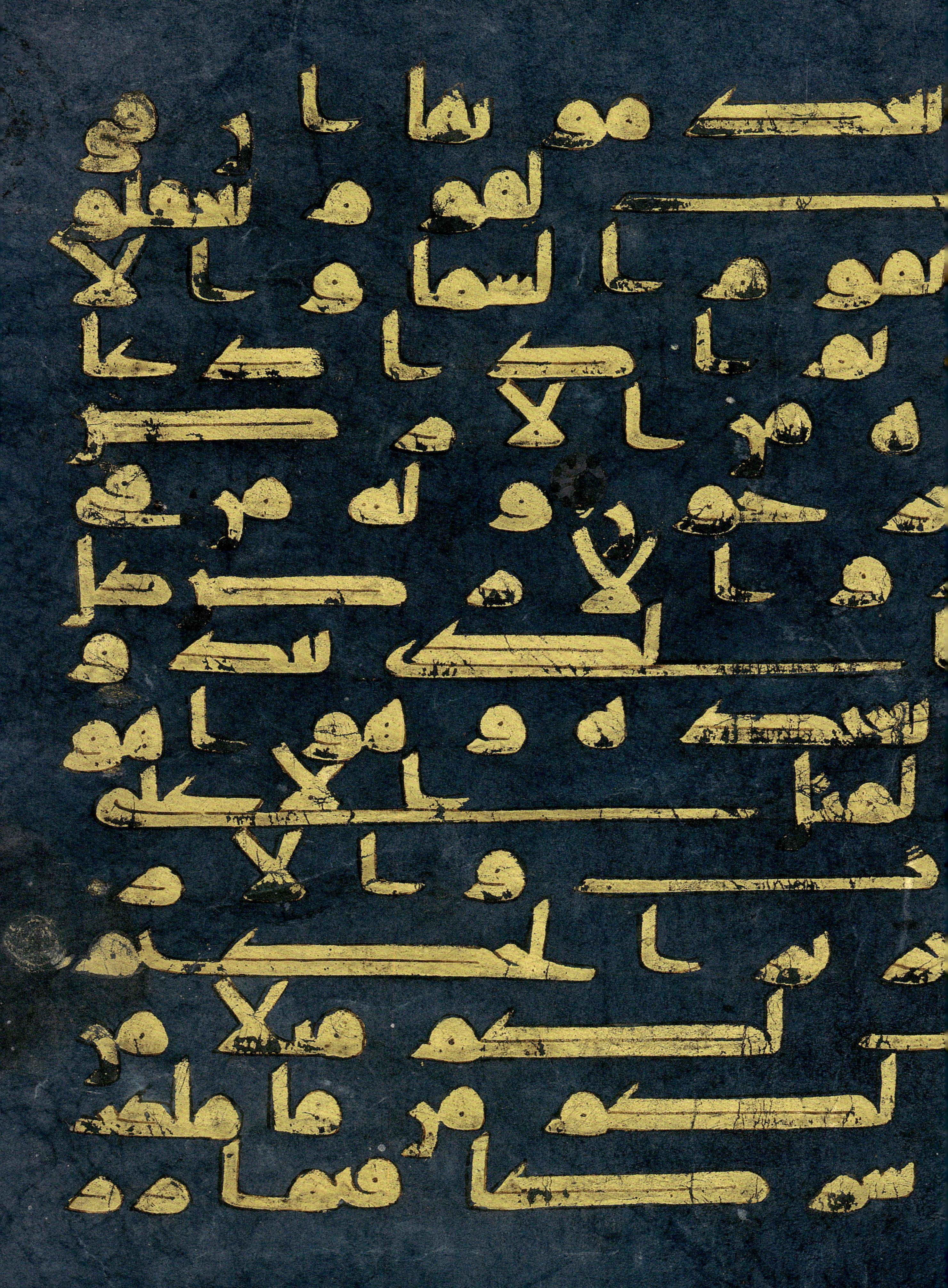

HOW TO READ

ISLAMIC CALLIGRAPHY

Maryam D. Ekhtiar

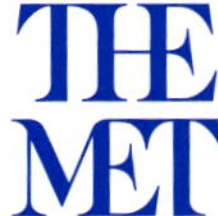

The Metropolitan Museum of Art, New York
Distributed by Yale University Press, New Haven and London

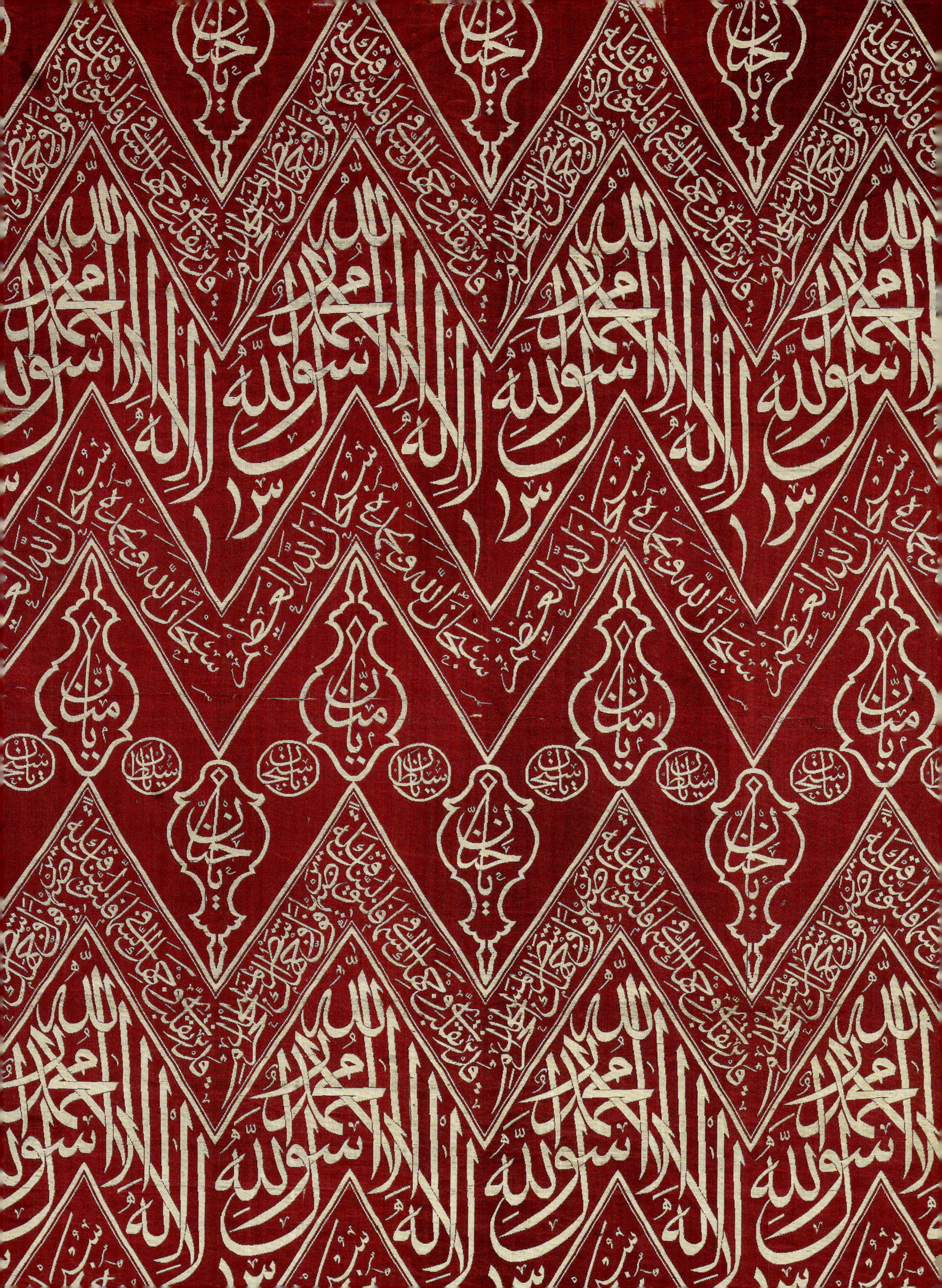

لا اله الا الله محمد رسول الله
يا حنان
يا منان
سبحان الله وبحمده سبحان الله العظيم

CONTENTS

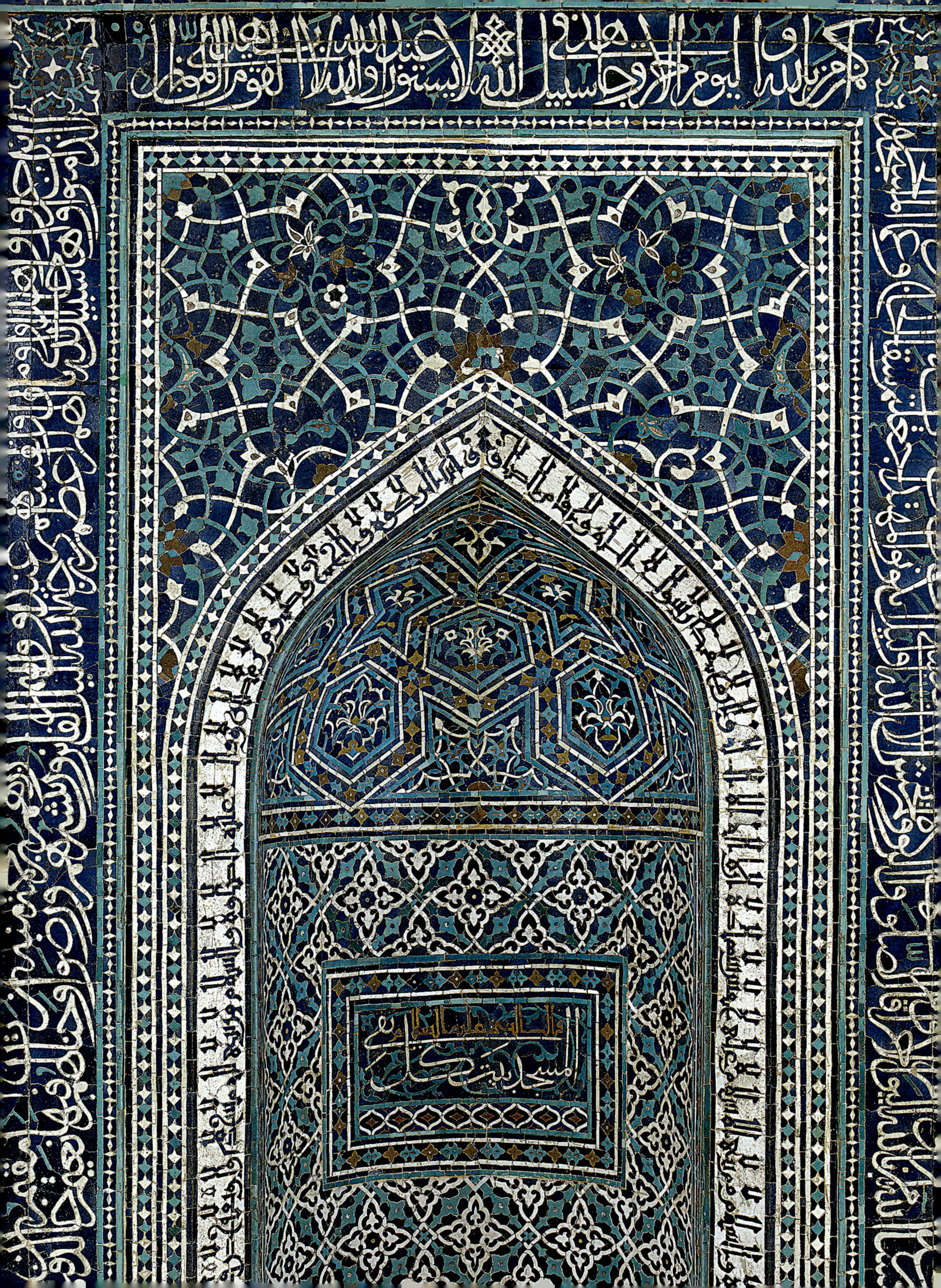

FOREWORD

The Met's comprehensive collection of Islamic calligraphy spans the dawn of the Islamic era to the present day, and includes works in media ranging from paper to stone, wood to textiles, and even arms and armor. Not only are they stunning works of art in their own right, but they also chart the development of this art form through the centuries and across continents, illustrating the vital role of the written word in Islamic culture. The literal meaning of *calligraphy* is "beautiful writing," but its importance in the Islamic world goes far beyond this basic definition. The Arabic script's intimate connection with the holy Qur'an imbues it with a spiritual force that transcends its function as a carrier of meaning and language. Present in both the religious and the secular spheres, Arabic writing can act as a signifier of faith, an object of devotion, and even as a talisman.

How to Read Islamic Calligraphy is the eighth book in The Met's How to Read series. These richly illustrated volumes introduce general readers to works in the Museum's vast collections, helping them look closely at techniques and materials and learn about their histories and meanings. Some of the works presented here came into The Met's collection as early as the nineteenth century, while others are more recent acquisitions that have never before been published or studied. Maryam D. Ekhtiar, Associate Curator in the Department of Islamic Art, examines this complex and multifaceted art form to encourage a deeper understanding and appreciation of calligraphic works in the context of the cultures in which they were created and experienced. Her illuminating text will no doubt inspire you, newly equipped with the skills and knowledge necessary to "read" them, to explore the many outstanding examples of Islamic calligraphy on view in The Met's galleries.

Daniel H. Weiss
President and CEO, The Metropolitan Museum of Art

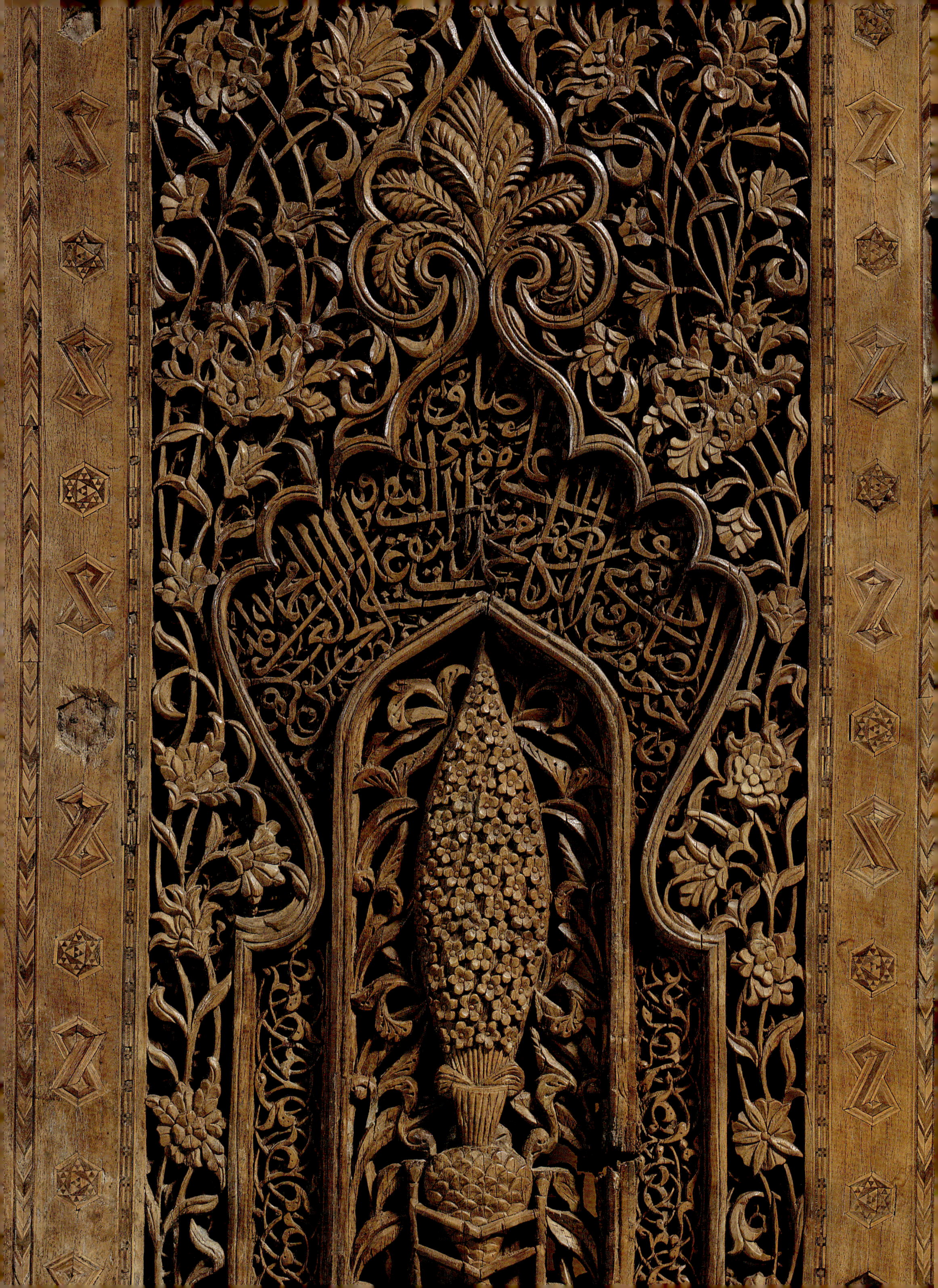

ACKNOWLEDGMENTS

This book is the result of several years of research and writing that would not have come to fruition without the involvement, support, and assistance of a number of people, both within and outside The Metropolitan Museum of Art. In the Department of Islamic Art, I would like to thank Sheila R. Canby, Patti Cadby Birch Curator in Charge, and Navina Najat Haidar, Curator, for encouraging me to write this book and supporting me throughout the process, as well as Deniz Beyazit, Associate Curator, Annick Des Roches, Collections Manager, Douglas C. Geiger, Supervising Technician, and Charles Dixon, Senior Technician. Ria Breed, Research Assistant, ensured that all the object information was correct, and Jean F. Tibbetts, Assistant for Administration, was always willing to help and facilitate as needed. A number of interns and volunteers assisted me at various stages of the process, namely Zamara Choudhary, Farah Abushullaih, and, in particular, Ana-Sofia Meneses, who was instrumental in keeping the project on track and managing the images and bibliography; I cannot thank her enough.

Outside the Museum, I am most grateful to Professor Priscilla P. Soucek of the Institute of Fine Arts, New York University, who read the manuscript and made invaluable comments and suggestions. I benefited immensely from her expertise and insight. I also thank epigraphist and language consultant Abdullah Ghouchani for coming to the rescue on several occasions when I was not able to decipher a Persian or Arabic inscription.

In The Met's Publications and Editorial Department, I thank my editor, Marcie M. Muscat, for helping me shape this book. Her patience and understanding of the material made the editing phase of the project feel seamless. I also thank Jessica Palinski, Image Acquisition Specialist, for sourcing the many images in the book, and Christopher Zichello, Production Manager, for ensuring their stunning quality. I am grateful to Mark Polizzotti, Publisher and Editor in Chief, for his unwavering support from the start, as well as to Gwen Roginsky, Associate Publisher and General Manager, Peter Antony, Chief Production Manager, and Michael Sittenfeld, Senior Managing Editor.

In the Imaging Department, for their work photographing objects in the Museum's collection, I thank Barbara J. Bridgers, Head of Imaging, Anna-Marie Kellen, Associate Chief Photographer, and Katherine Dahab and Eileen Travell, Senior Photographers. Of course, these works would not have looked their best if not for the efforts of conservators Yana van Dyke, Paper Conservation, Jean-François de Lapérouse, Objects Conservation, and Janina Poskrobko, Textile Conservation. Their preparation of the objects for photography and investigations into their materials and techniques were instrumental to my own understanding of them.

Maryam D. Ekhtiar
Associate Curator, Department of Islamic Art,
The Metropolitan Museum of Art

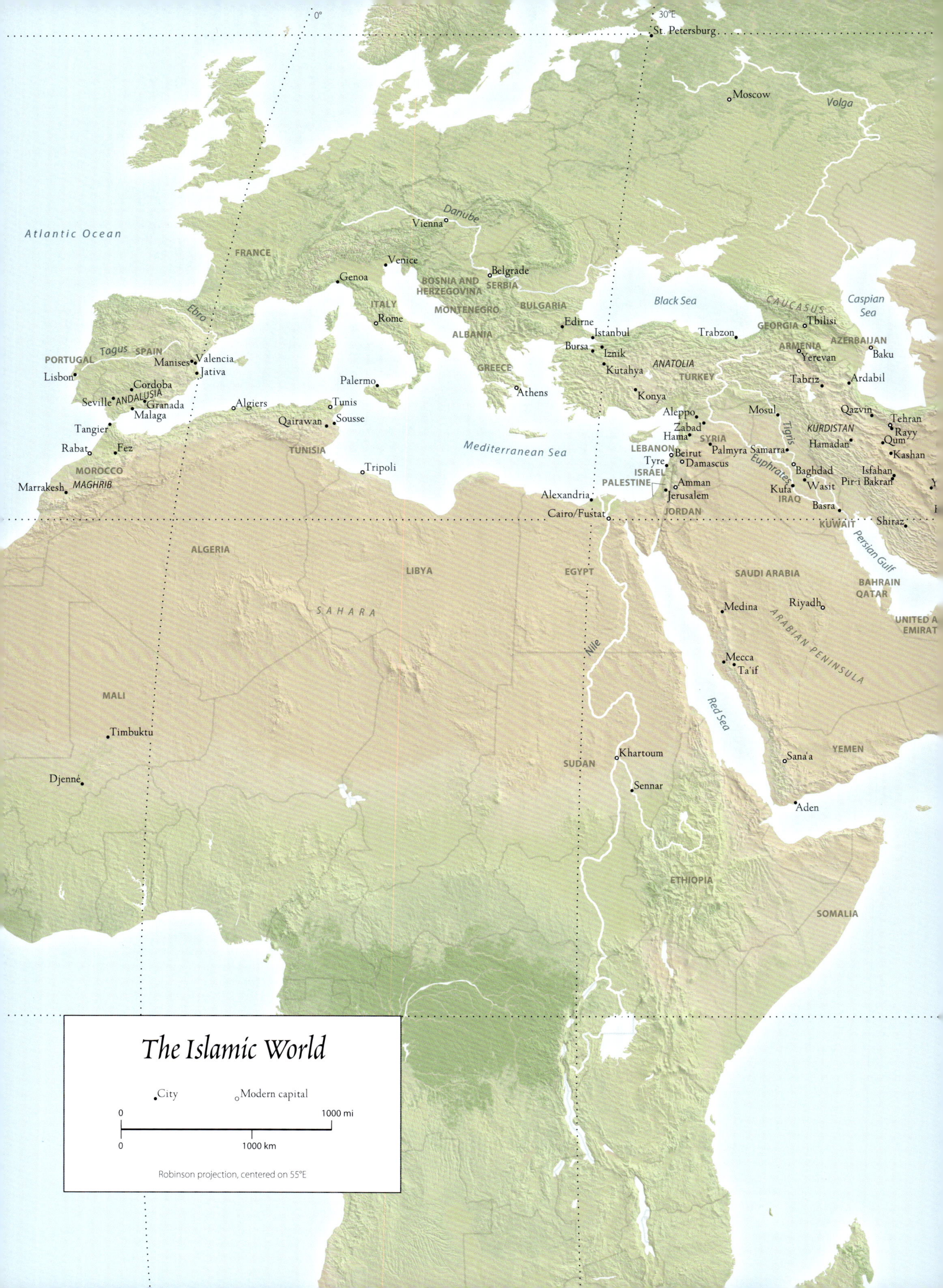
The Islamic World
City
Modern capital
0
1000 mi
0
1000 km
Robinson projection, centered on 55°E
0°
30°E
St. Petersburg
Moscow
Volga
Atlantic Ocean
Danube
Vienna
FRANCE
Venice
Genoa
Belgrade
BOSNIA AND HERZEGOVINA
SERBIA
ITALY
MONTENEGRO
BULGARIA
Black Sea
Caspian Sea
CAUCASUS
Rome
ALBANIA
Edirne
Istanbul
Trabzon
GEORGIA
Tbilisi
Ebro
Tagus
SPAIN
PORTUGAL
Lisbon
Manises
Valencia
Jativa
Cordoba
Seville
ANDALUSIA
Granada
Malaga
Tangier
Rabat
Fez
MOROCCO
MAGHRIB
Marrakesh
Bursa
Iznik
Kütahya
ANATOLIA
TURKEY
ARMENIA
Yerevan
AZERBAIJAN
Baku
GREECE
Athens
Konya
Tabriz
Ardabil
Palermo
Algiers
Tunis
Qairawan
Sousse
TUNISIA
Tripoli
Mediterranean Sea
Aleppo
Zabad
Hama
SYRIA
LEBANON
Beirut
Tyre
Damascus
Palmyra
ISRAEL
PALESTINE
Amman
Jerusalem
JORDAN
Mosul
Tigris
Euphrates
Samarra
Baghdad
Wasit
Kufa
IRAQ
Basra
KUWAIT
Qazvin
Tehran
Rayy
Qum
Kashan
KURDISTAN
Hamadan
Isfahan
Pir-i Bakran
Shiraz
Persian Gulf
Alexandria
Cairo/Fustat
ALGERIA
LIBYA
EGYPT
SAHARA
SAUDI ARABIA
BAHRAIN
QATAR
UNITED ARAB EMIRATES
Medina
Riyadh
ARABIAN PENINSULA
Mecca
Ta'if
Nile
Red Sea
MALI
Timbuktu
Djenné
SUDAN
Khartoum
Sennar
Sana'a
YEMEN
Aden
ETHIOPIA
SOMALIA

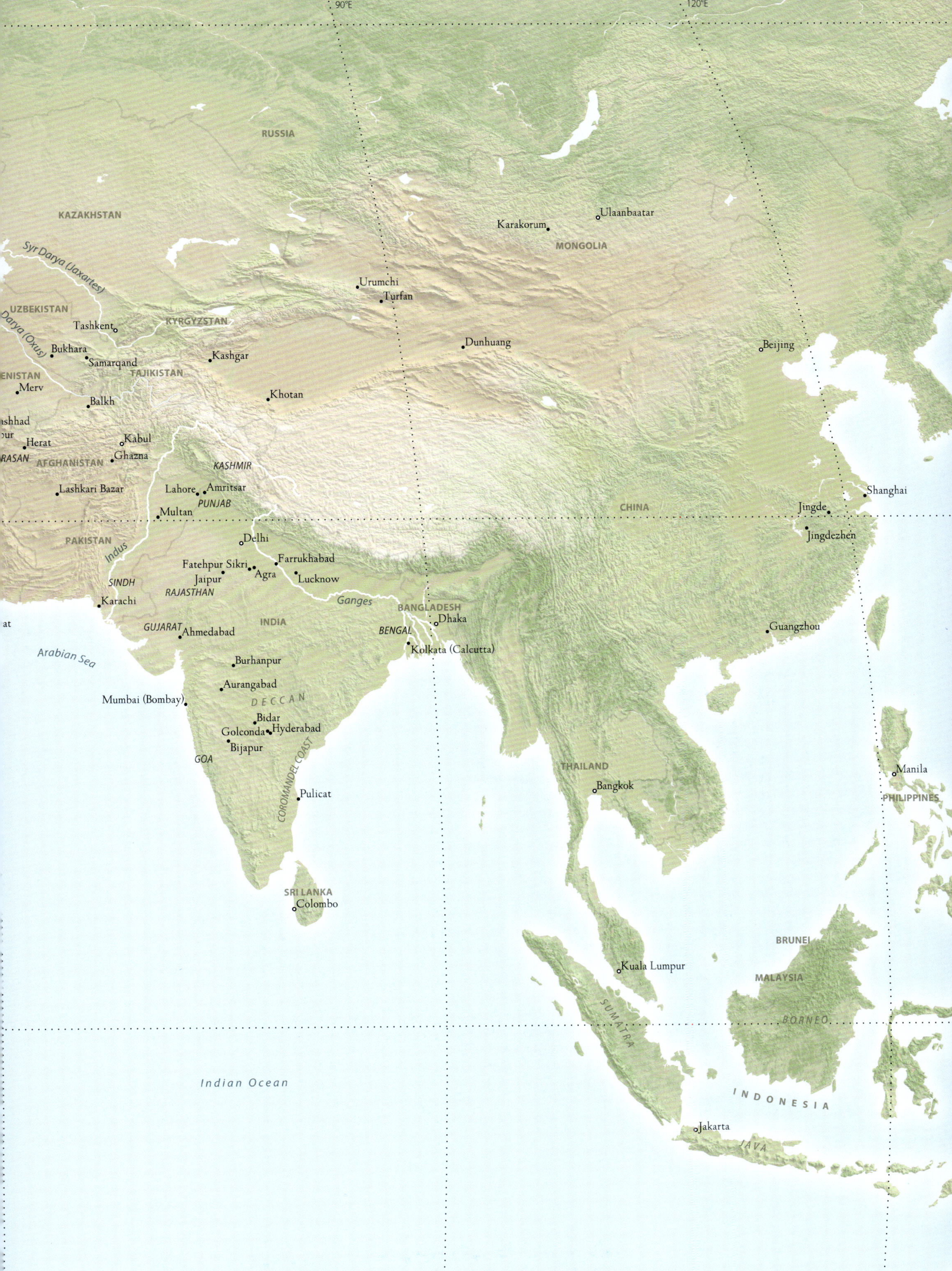

90°E
120°E
RUSSIA
KAZAKHSTAN
Syr Darya (Jaxartes)
UZBEKISTAN
Darya (Oxus)
Tashkent
KYRGYZSTAN
Bukhara
Samarqand
TAJIKISTAN
ENISTAN
Merv
Balkh
ashhad
Herat
RASAN
AFGHANISTAN
Kabul
Ghazna
Lashkari Bazar
Kashgar
Khotan
KASHMIR
Lahore
Amritsar
PUNJAB
Multan
PAKISTAN
Indus
SINDH
Karachi
Urumchi
Turfan
Dunhuang
Karakorum
Ulaanbaatar
MONGOLIA
Beijing
Shanghai
Jingde
Jingdezhen
CHINA
Delhi
Fatehpur Sikri
Agra
Farrukhabad
Lucknow
Jaipur
RAJASTHAN
Ganges
BANGLADESH
Dhaka
BENGAL
Kolkata (Calcutta)
INDIA
GUJARAT
Ahmedabad
Arabian Sea
Burhanpur
Aurangabad
Mumbai (Bombay)
DECCAN
Bidar
Golconda
Hyderabad
Bijapur
GOA
COROMANDEL COAST
Pulicat
SRI LANKA
Colombo
Guangzhou
THAILAND
Bangkok
Manila
PHILIPPINES
BRUNEI
MALAYSIA
Kuala Lumpur
BORNEO
SUMATRA
INDONESIA
Jakarta
JAVA
Indian Ocean

NOTE TO THE READER

Transliterations are based on the system used in the *International Journal of Middle Eastern Studies*. *'Ayn* and *hamza* are marked, but except when quoting a source or citing a title, we have omitted macrons, dots, hooks, and other diacritical marks.

Dates are given in the Gregorian calendar unless an object carries a precise *hijri* date, in which case dates are given in both eras. English translations of the Qur'an are taken from Arthur J. Arberry's *The Koran Interpreted* (1966).

Dimensions are given in the following sequence: height precedes width precedes depth. When necessary, the abbreviations H. (height), L. (length), W. (width), and Diam. (diameter) are given for clarity. Unless specified, given diameters are the maximum, and dimensions for manuscript illustrations are for a single folio.

Definitions of certain Arabic, Persian, and Turkish words are given in the Glossary on pages 153–54, and date ranges for important empires and dynasties appear on page 155.

In lieu of in-text citations in the form of footnotes, sources consulted in the preparation of this book have been aggregated by chapter, ordered by date of publication, and presented on page 147, with a full bibliography following. The author acknowledges all the scholars who, owing to the constraints of this format, may not be cited here by name, but whose work in the field of Islamic art and calligraphy was instrumental to the present endeavor.

HOW TO READ

ISLAMIC CALLIGRAPHY

قريبا هو الذي ارسل رسوله بالهدى و
دين الحق ليظهره على الدين كله
وكفى بالله شهيدا
محمد رسول الله والذين
معه اشداء على الكفار رحماء بينهم ترا
هم ركعا سجدا يبتغون فضلا
من الله ورضونا سيماهم في وجو
ههم من اثر السجود ذلك مثلهم في ا
لتورية ومثلهم في الانجيل كزرع اخر
ج شطاه فازره فاستغلظ فا
ستوى على سوقه يعجب الزراع ليغيظ
بهم الكفار وعد الله الذين امنوا وعملوا
الصلحت منهم مغفرة واجرا عظيما

INTRODUCTION

Handwriting is jewelry fashioned by the hand from the pure gold of the intellect. It is also brocade woven by the calamus *with the thread of discernment.*

—Hisham b. Hakam (d. early 9th century), quoted in the treatise on penmanship of Abu Hayyan al-Tawhidi (d. after 1009–10)

Calligraphy has been referred to as the sacred symbol of Islam, the most characteristic expression of the Islamic spirit, and a key achievement of Islamic civilization. References to its importance abound in the Qur'an and the Hadith (the sayings and traditions of the Prophet Muhammad). From as early as the tenth century, calligraphers, scribes, poets, religious leaders, statesmen, and philosophers have expounded on the virtues of good handwriting and the centrality of the written word in all aspects of Islamic life. The subject has captured the attention of modern scholars, as well, who continue to work toward unraveling its exceptional nuances and complexities.

Perhaps most importantly, however, Islamic calligraphy has mesmerized viewers through the centuries with its sheer beauty, sophistication, and variety. It can appear in myriad forms and styles, ranging from elegant, refined, and eminently readable to decorative, abstract, and barely legible. One of its most unique features is its pervasive use as a mode of ornament to embellish architecture and objects in a multitude of media—paper, parchment, ceramic, stone, glass, ivory, metal, and textiles (figs. 1–4). Indeed, no other culture has explored the decorative and creative possibilities of the written word as extensively as Islam. Calligraphy is the thread that binds the art of regions as far west as Spain and North Africa and as far east as the Indian subcontinent. As such, the art form reaches well beyond its fundamental function as a vehicle for written communication.

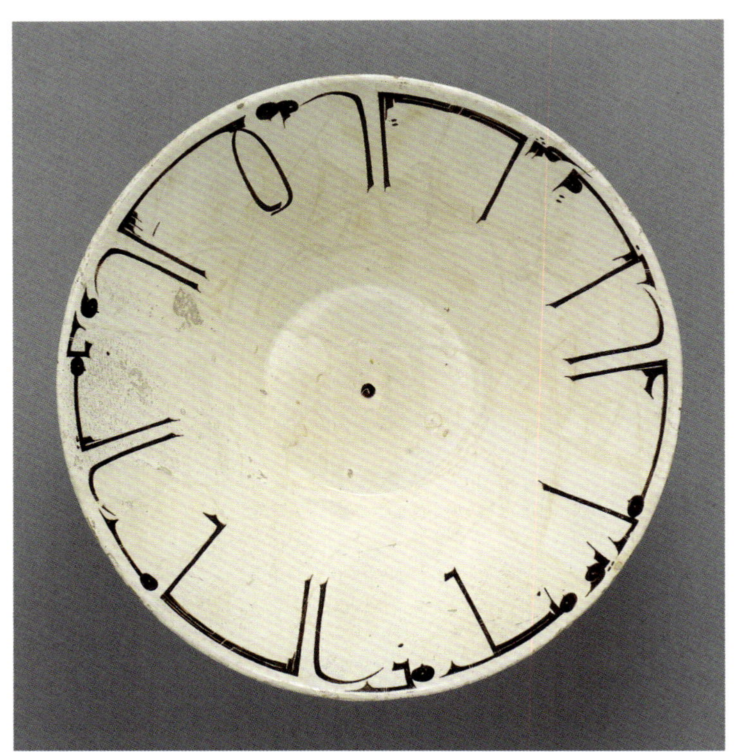

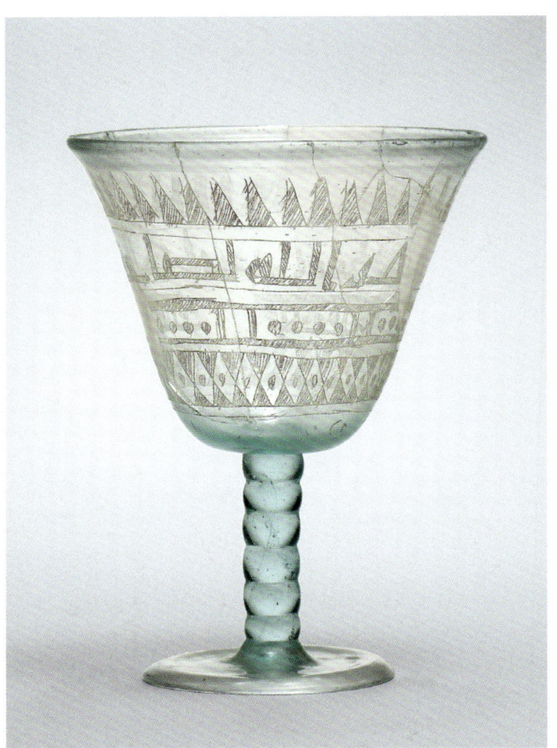

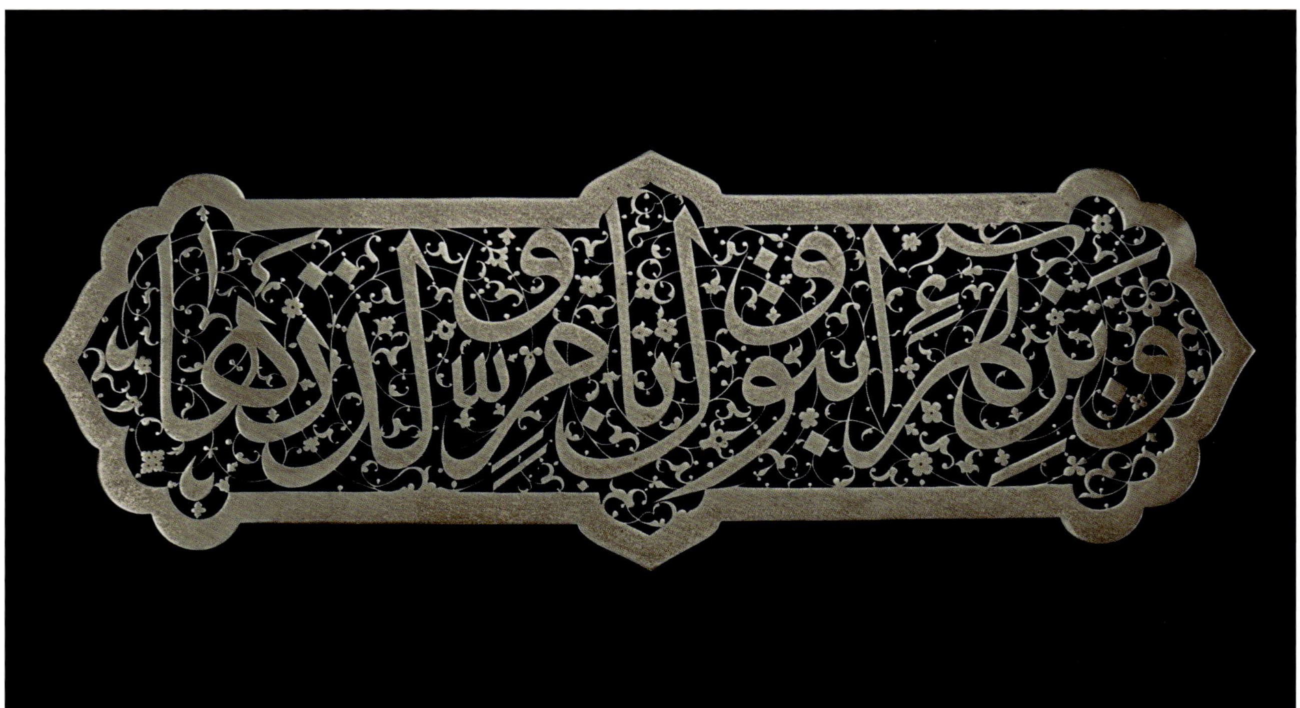

Clockwise from top left: Fig. 1. Bowl with Arabic inscription. Iran, Nishapur, Samanid, 10th century. Earthenware; white slip with black-slip decoration under transparent glaze, Diam. 18 in. (45.7 cm). Rogers Fund, 1965 (65.106.2). Fig. 2. Goblet. Probably Iraq or Syria, 8th–9th century. Glass, bluish green; blown, applied solid stem and blown foot; scratch-engraved, H. 4 5/8 in. (11.7 cm); Diam. of rim 3 9/16 in. (9 cm). Purchase, Joseph Pulitzer Bequest, 1965 (65.173.1). Fig. 3. Pierced calligraphic plaque. Iran, probably late 17th century. Steel; forged and pierced, 6 1/2 x 15 in. (16.5 x 38.1 cm). Rogers Fund, 1987 (1987.14)

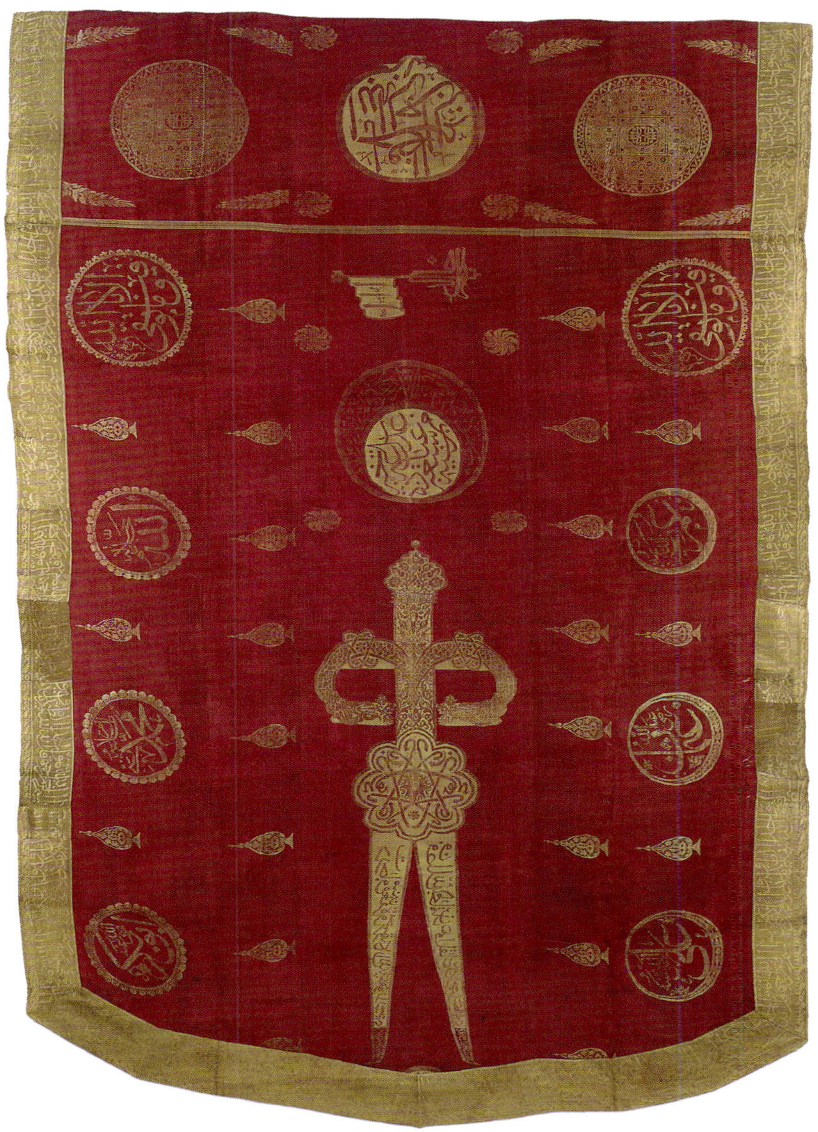

Fig. 4. Banner. Turkey, probably Istanbul, Ottoman, dated A.H. 1235/A.D. 1819–20. Silk, metal-wrapped thread; lampas, brocaded, 115¾ x 85½ in. (294 x 217.2 cm). Fletcher Fund, 1976 (1976.312)

The vital role and enduring presence of calligraphy in the lives of Muslims of all social classes is largely intertwined with the origins of the Muslim faith. Because the Divine Revelation was conveyed to the Prophet Muhammad in Arabic and compiled into Islam's holy book, the Qur'an, Muslims regard the Qur'an as the literal word of God. As a visual manifestation of God's message, the language in its written form was thus afforded an exalted status: not only did copying the Qur'an become an act of devotion, but all forms of writing in Islamic culture took on a sacred aura. The cultivation of calligraphy distinguished Islam from other faiths that relied on figural modes of depiction, and the increasing use of Islamic calligraphy as a form of ornament can be attributed to its role as a signifier of the new faith during the first few centuries of the Islamic era.

Calligraphers and Their Tools

The supremacy of calligraphy in the hierarchy of Islamic arts naturally meant that calligraphers became the most highly esteemed artists in Islamic culture. Words penned in a master's hand were regarded as a lasting vestige epitomizing the essence of their maker. In the words of the Persian poet Sa'di: "In short since in no mundane thing I see; / the signs impressed of perpetuity; This picture shall my sole memorial be, / Perhaps hereafter for the pious task; / Some man of prayer for me too grace shall be." Most calligraphers were well educated, and some came from the upper echelons of society. It was not uncommon for rulers to receive extensive training from the most talented masters and to become accomplished scribes in their own right. While most calligraphers traditionally were male, royal and elite women also studied the art form, which is today practiced widely by both men and women.

Training to become a calligrapher was a long, rigorous process involving the transfer of skills from master to apprentice and from one generation to another, often within the same family (fig. 5). To become a master calligrapher and acquire a formal license, a student had to train for years by copying his master's models to perfect his skills, instill discipline, and strengthen his hand. This entailed hours of practice known as *mashq* (see fig. 49 and cat. 39). Calligraphers were encouraged to suppress all other desires in order to achieve the mental and physical discipline required to be a scribe. According to Sultan 'Ali Mashhadi, the master of the *nasta'liq* script, "you will abandon peace and sleep, even from your tender years." He went on to stress the importance of keeping one's undivided focus on faithfully copying a master's example: "Collect the writing of the masters, throw a glance at this and at that. For whomever you feel a natural attraction, besides his writing, you must not look at others. So that your eye should become saturated with his writing; and because of his writing each of your letters should become like a pearl."

The quality of the calligrapher's tools and materials was of utmost importance. As part of their training, calligraphers learned how to prepare pens, inks, and paper.

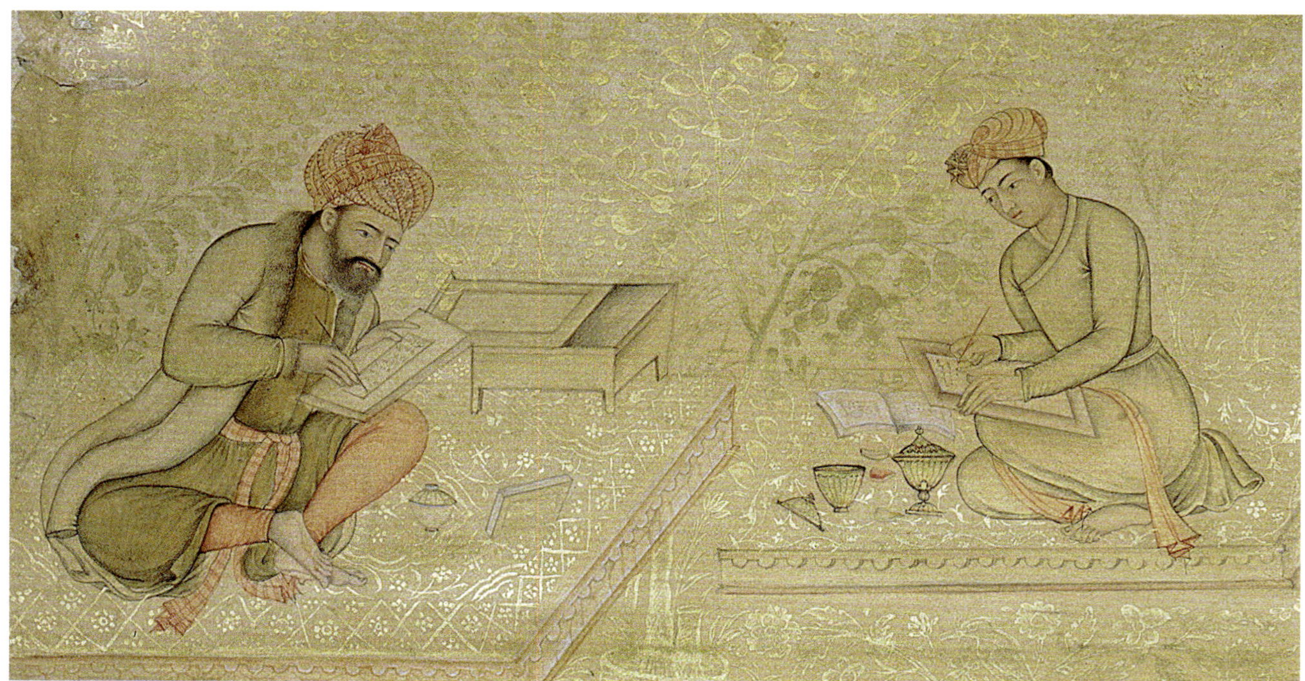

Fig. 5. Detail of folio from the Gulshan Album. India, Mughal, A.H. 1269/A.D. 1853. Ink, opaque watercolor, and gold on paper. Staatsbibliothek zu Berlin–Prussian Cultural Heritage

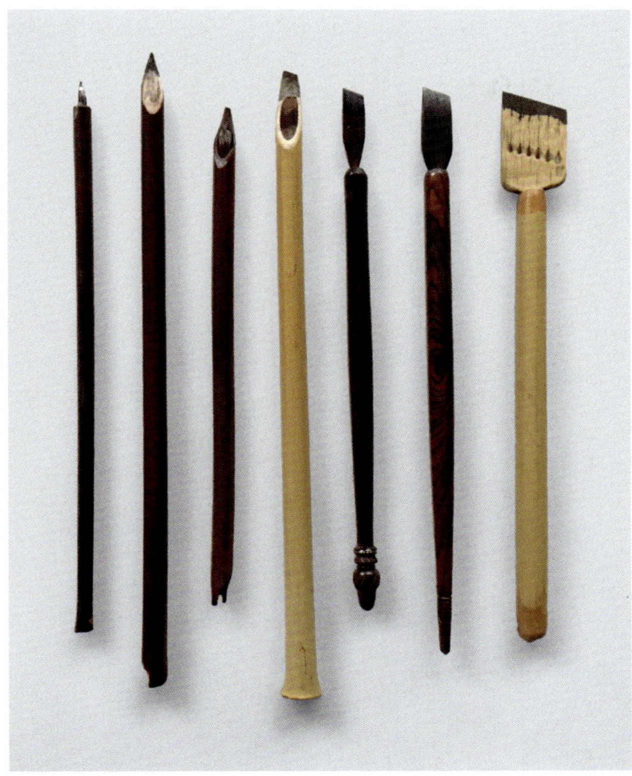

Fig. 6. Reed pens of different sizes

Pens (*qalam* or *calamus*) were fashioned from reeds due to their flexibility and durability (fig. 6). The dry, hollow reeds were cut to form a flat tongue, which was then split parallel to the pen, creating a reservoir for the ink. Finally, the tip of the tongue was cut at an oblique angle. Different scripts required reed pens with nibs of varying widths and cut at different angles. Thus, an accomplished calligrapher would need several. Inks were made of natural materials such as soot, ox gall, gum Arabic, or plant essences. Before paper was introduced to the Islamic lands from China in the mid-eighth century, texts were written on papyrus and parchment (animal skins). Parchment continued to be used widely in the Near East, North Africa, and Spain until the fourteenth century. By virtue of the status of calligraphy as an art form, the tools associated with it—shears, knives, inkwells, and pen boxes—were often elaborately decorated and sometimes made of precious materials (fig. 7).

The Arabic Alphabet: Structure and Scope

The Arabic alphabet consists of eighteen primary letter forms (*rasm*), mostly consonants and long vowels, that with the help of dots (*i'jam*) and diacritical (accent) marks express twenty-eight phonetic sounds (fig. 8). These basic forms represent the earliest and most elemental visual manifestation of the Arabic language. Short vowels, represented by a set of marks written above or below the letters, aid in pronunciation and usually appear only in the Qur'an, where correct recitation is of utmost importance, and in texts for novice readers. There is no distinction between upper- and lowercase letters, though the shapes of letters usually vary depending on whether they are in an initial, medial, or final position of a word. Arabic is written and read from right to left.

With the spread of Islam to many regions, from Spain and North Africa in the West to India and Southeast Asia in the East, a number of languages adopted the Arabic alphabet, even if their linguistic and grammatical structures bore little resemblance to it. These include Persian (Farsi), an Indo-European language spoken in Iran and various parts of Central Asia, such as present-day Afghanistan and Tajikistan; Kurdish, spoken in parts of Iran, Iraq, Syria, and Turkey; and Urdu, spoken in present-day Pakistan and parts of India. In each of these cases, Arabic was adapted to suit local linguistic and phonetic requirements. For example, Persian includes sounds that do not exist in Arabic, thus necessitating the incorporation of four additional letters into the original Arabic alphabet. And in Urdu, specifically tailored diacritical marks were added to reflect the phonetics of that language. Historically, Turkish of the Seljuq and Ottoman periods, an era spanning the eleventh to the early twentieth century, also used the Arabic script, but in 1928, under Mustafa Kemal Atatürk (1881–1938), it was replaced with one based on the Latin alphabet.

Although Arabic has always been the dominant language of Islamic epigraphy, inscriptions in Persian and Turkish are known in certain areas and time periods. Poetic verses in Persian, the literary language of the Eastern Islamic Lands, can be seen on buildings dating from the thirteenth century onward. In these regions different scripts were used to convey different types of text within the same inscription, for example, a foundational text

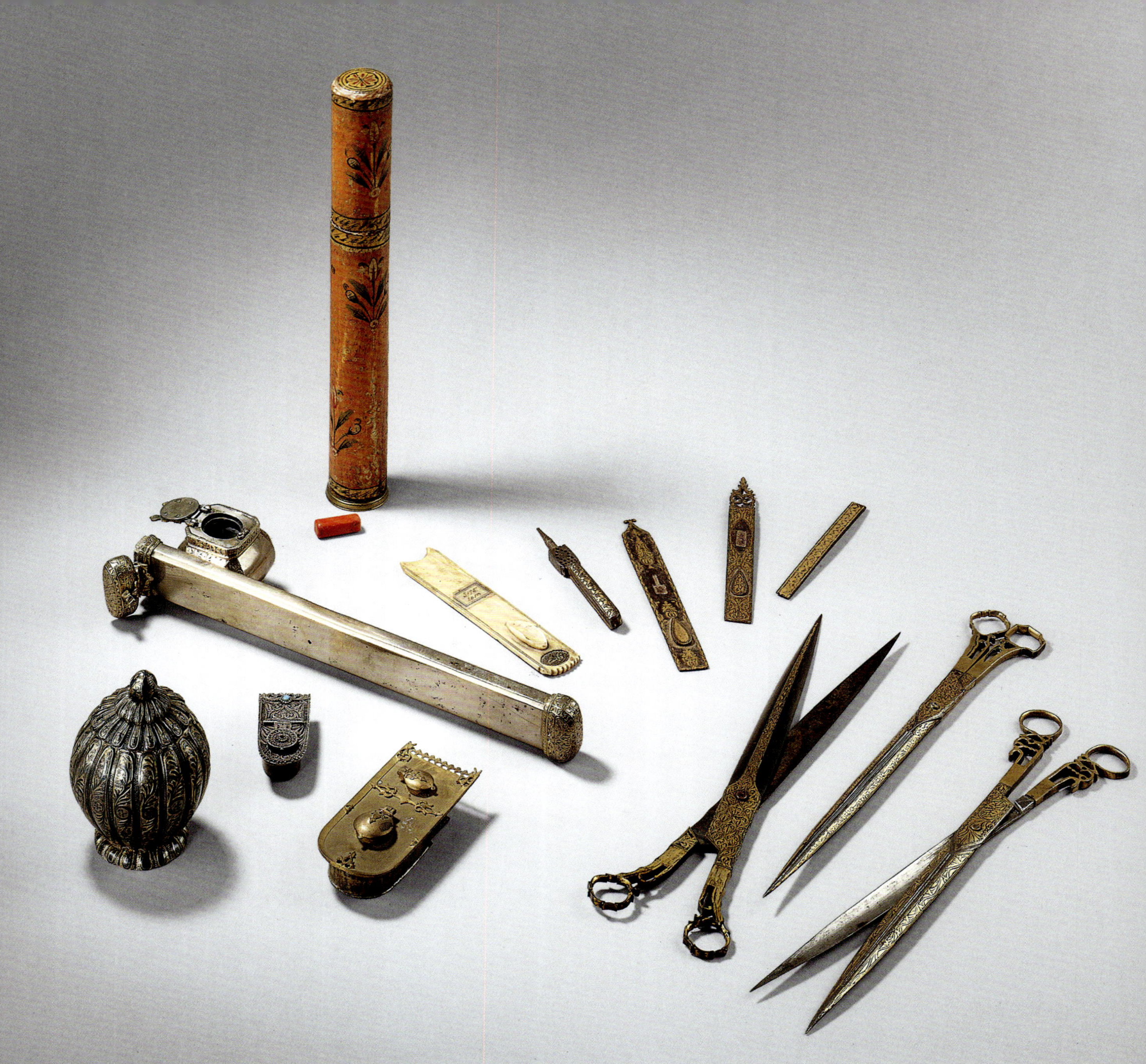

Fig. 7. Calligrapher's tools. Turkey, Ottoman, 18th–19th century. Aga Khan Museum, Toronto (AKM622)

might be written in *naskh*, and the poetic verses in floriated *kufic*.

The Multifaceted Role of Calligraphy

By the ninth century, as the shapes of Arabic letters and words became increasingly refined, decorative, and eventually more abstract and even pictorial in nature, inscriptions began to appear in diverse contexts, often as one component of a larger program of ornament. This expansion of the uses of calligraphy naturally led to its assignment of more complex roles and meanings, both literal and symbolic. For instance, accomplished penmanship came to be seen as an indicator of sound character, moral rectitude, and clarity of judgment. According to Sultan 'Ali Mashhadi's treatise on calligraphy, "He who knows the soul, knows that purity of writing proceeds from purity of the heart. Writing is the distinction of the pure." Calligraphy also became a symbol of power, legitimacy, political control,

alif	ا	za	ز	qaf	ق
ba	ب	sin	س	kaf	ك
ta	ت	shin	ش	lam	ل
tha	ث	sad	ص	mim	م
jim	ج	dad	ض	nun	ن
ha	ح	ta	ط	ha	ه
kha	خ	dha	ظ	waw	و
dal	د	ain	ع	ya	ي
dhal	ذ	ghain	غ		
ra	ر	fa	ف		

Fig. 8. The Arabic alphabet

and effective administration. Looking at a beautifully written document, the Abbasid caliph al-Ma'mun (r. 813–33) declared, "How wonderful is the *calamus*! How it weaves the fine cloth of royal power, embroiders the ornamental borders of the garment of the ruling dynasty, and keeps up the standard of the caliphate." More recently, Annemarie Schimmel, one of the world's leading authorities on Islamic calligraphy, noted, "The written word is a talisman, and the process of writing is a magic art connected not only with the master's technique, skill, and art, but also with his spiritual character."

On a more literal level, calligraphic inscriptions can also contain a wealth of practical information. They are often the most direct and reliable source documenting the date and place of an object's manufacture; the name of the artist, craftsman, and/or patron; and the object's function or intended purpose. As such, they provide extraordinary insight into the world in which the work was produced. One fascinating example, a porcelain pen rest from sixteenth-century China, is inscribed with the Persian word *khama-dan*, or "pen-holder," which not only discloses its purpose but also underscores the eminence of Muslims, many of whom were Central Asian eunuchs, at the Zhengde court and their role in promoting vibrant trade between Ming China and the great Muslim empires of the era (see cat. 14).

Inscriptions might include Qur'anic verses and other religious phrases, or laudatory or benedictory expressions praising a ruler or owner. Some even act as the "voice" of an object as they address or speak to the owner/viewer, inviting him or her into a conversation. Such inscriptions might take the form of poetic verses of a mystical nature that express the yearning of the beloved to unite with the divine in a language of puns and metaphors. A fine example is an engraved brass lampstand from Iran in The Met's collection (fig. 9). It is inscribed with verses that liken the beloved to the flame of a candle and the lover to a moth—a metaphor for the human soul's desire to reunite with the Beloved, or God. It says: "I remember one night as my eyes would not sleep / I heard a moth speaking with a candle / Said the moth: 'Because I am a lover, it is [only] right that I should burn / [But] why should you weep and burn yourself up?'" Similarly, objects could sometimes take on human features and embody lifelike qualities, such as the signed, carved ivory pyxis dating to about A.D. 966 from Madinat al-Zahra, near Cordoba, Spain (fig. 10). Its inscription addresses its viewer/owner in the first person "The sight I offer is of

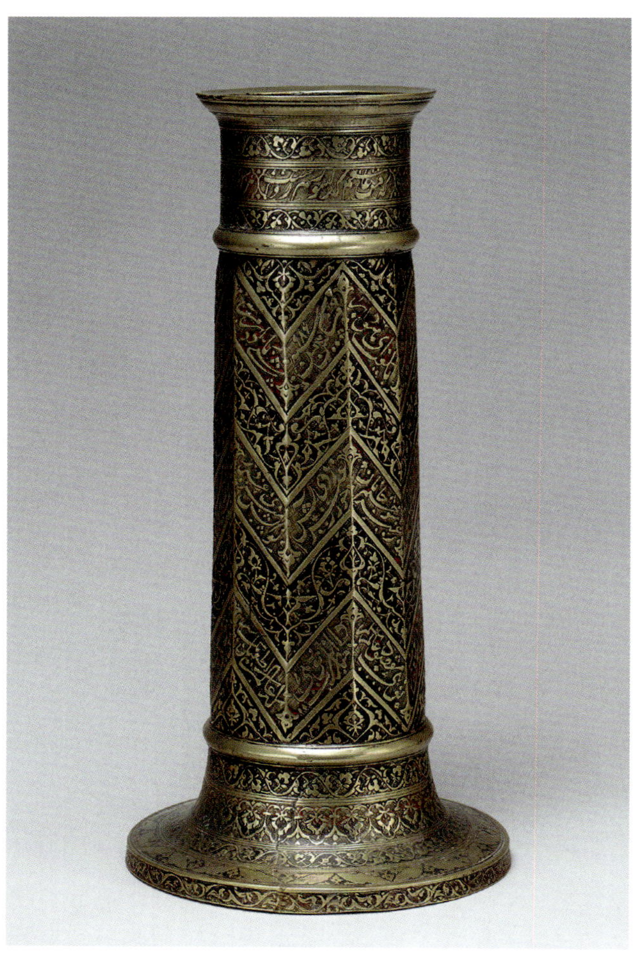

Fig. 9. Lampstand. Iran, dated A.H. 986/A.D. 1578–79. Brass; cast, engraved, and inlaid with black and red pigment, H. 13¼ in. (33.7 cm); Diam. of base 6⅝ in. (16.8 cm). Rogers Fund, 1929 (29.53)

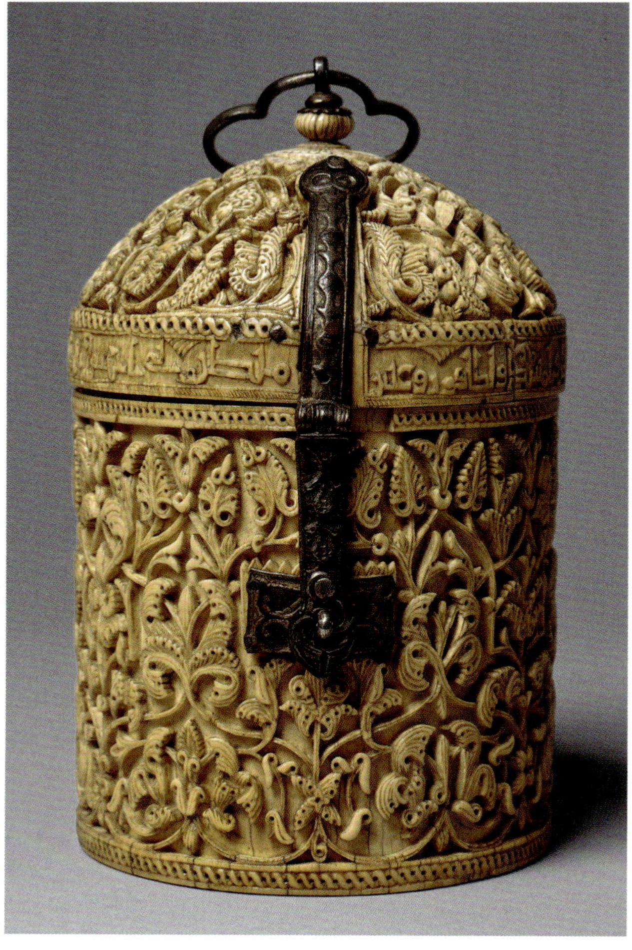

Fig. 10. Ivory pyxis. Spain, Madinat al-Zahra (Cordoba), ca. 966. Ivory; chased and nielloed silver-gilt mounts, some polychromy, H. 6⁵⁄₁₆ in. (16 cm); Diam. 4 in. (10.1 cm). Hispanic Society of America, New York (D752)

the fairest, the firm breasts of a delicate maiden. Beauty has invested me with splendid raiment that makes a display of jewels. I am a receptacle for musk, camphor, and ambergris." Here, the container, which was likely made as a gift for a court lady, tells us its function and makes direct connections between its shape and the sensuality of a woman's body.

The practice of inscribing architectural surfaces with monumental writing is not exclusive to Islam but, rather, has precedent in ancient Greece and Rome. However, no culture has explored the use of writing in buildings as extensively as Islam. Found on mosques, minarets, tombs, Sufi lodges, madrasas (religious schools), palaces, and pavilions, architectural inscriptions could be prayers or passages from the Qur'an, Hadith, or other religious texts; foundational or endowment texts, which often included the date of a building's construction and the name(s) of its supporter(s); epitaphic, benedictory, or dedicatory texts glorifying the authority of a ruler; or poetry. A fine example in The Met's collection, a carved stone panel from Gaur, in present-day Bangladesh, announces its purpose as a dedicatory inscription for a mosque with a phrase from the Hadith: "The Prophet—God's blessing and peace upon him—said: 'He who builds a mosque for God, God will build for him a palace the like of it in Paradise'" (fig. 11). Further clarifying the panel's purpose, the inscription, which is in a variant of *tughra* and consists of bow-and-arrow forms, goes on to tell who built the mosque and during whose reign it was erected: "In the reign of the Sultan Ala al-Dunya wa'l din Abu'l Muzaffar Husain Shah al-Sultan, may God prolong his rule and sovereignty. Shahzada Daniyal, may his glory endure, built this congregational mosque on the tenth of Dhu'l-Hijja in the year A.H. 905 [July 7, 1500]."

Another category of inscription comprises Qur'anic and other pious phrases with perceived talismanic properties; they often call on the Prophet and other influential religious personages to protect against harm, danger, and illness. For example, an elaborately decorated cuirass covered with Qur'anic inscriptions was intended to guide a warrior safely through battle (see cat. 26), while an Ottoman silk tomb cover woven with Qur'anic verses associated with burial addresses the deceased directly and bestows him or her with blessings, or *baraka* (see cat. 28). Similarly, in mystical circles Arabic letters were thought to have symbolic and esoteric meanings. The "science of letters" (*'ilm al-huruf*) is based on the notion that every creature derives its origins from a divine word and that the Arabic language facilitates access to and power over God's creations. In these systems, which include *abjad*, each letter of the alphabet is given a numerical value and, through alphanumeric computations, is thought to reveal profound, even divine truths.

It is important to remember that inscriptions are rarely viewed or experienced in isolation. They are integral elements of an overall decorative program that may include vegetal, floral, geometric, and figural designs and must be "read" with that in mind. The repertoire of decorative inscriptions is vast and has engaged generations of scholars with questions relating to the forms of objects and the interplay of text and representation. As we will discover in the following chapters, Arabic writing is extraordinarily versatile, with the power to adapt to a vast array of aesthetic, cultural, and sociopolitical contexts. Inscriptions are, therefore, repositories of information beyond the letters and words they represent; they carry the history, culture, and social and moral codes of their creators, patrons, and onlookers. Reading and interpreting these inscriptions are vital to understanding the role, function, and meaning of both buildings and objects from Islamic lands, underscoring the vital importance of the written word to all aspects of Islamic life and culture.

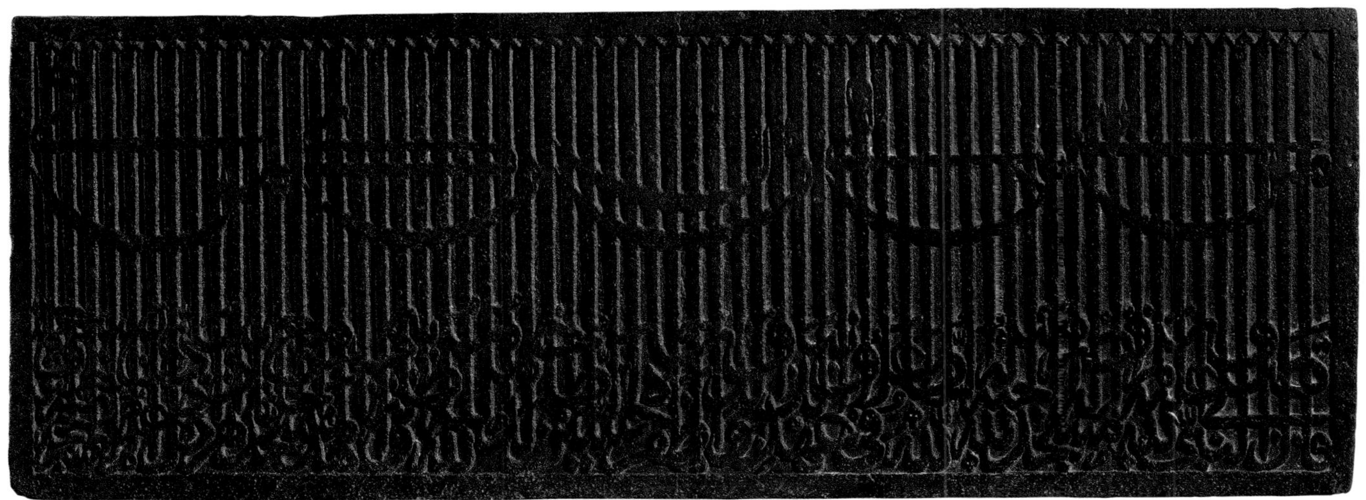

Fig. 11. Dedicatory inscription from a mosque. India, Bengal, dated A.H. 905/A.D. 1500. Gabbro; carved, 16⅛ x 45$\frac{5}{16}$ x 2¾ in. (41 x 115.1 x 7 cm). Purchase, Gift of Mrs. Nelson Doubleday and Bequest of Charles R. Gerth, by exchange, 1981 (1981.320)

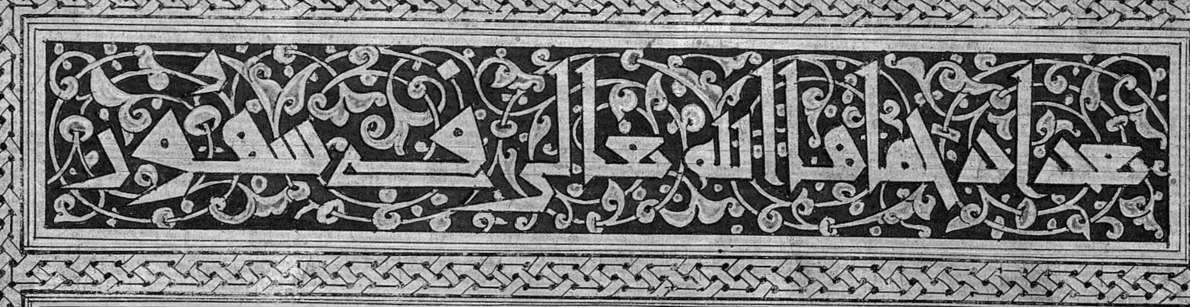

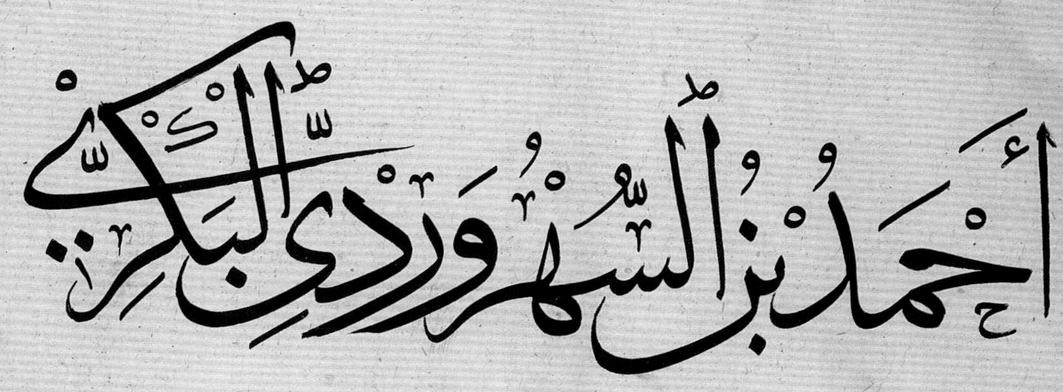

حامداً لله ومصلياً على نبيه

محمد وآله وصحبه ومسلماً

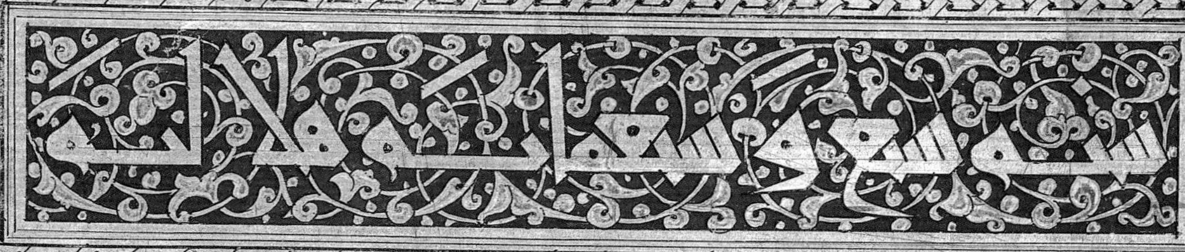

THE ARABIC SCRIPT

ORIGINS, DEVELOPMENT, AND VARIATIONS

The close associations between the practice of writing and the regions that comprise the Islamic world can be traced to about 3500–3000 B.C., when the Sumerians in Mesopotamia are credited with having invented cuneiform, a system of writing made up of basic signs, to keep track of their business dealings and to document trade transactions. This system evolved in complexity and proliferated throughout the Near East in the form of numerous alphabetic writing systems, including Aramaic, Phoenician, Hebrew, Nabatean, and Arabic, laying the groundwork for the supremacy of the written word throughout the Islamic world.

The Arabic letters as we know them began to assume their forms in the fourth century A.D. and by the sixth century had become relatively fixed. The exact origins of Arabic writing have been a subject of debate for decades, but epigraphic evidence suggests that the earliest recognizable examples, dating to 512 and 568, were found in the area between Arabia and Syria, at Zabad (see map on pp. 10–11). The most widely held argument is that the Arabic letters derive from the Nabatean Aramaic script (fig. 12), although other lines of thought trace its origins to the Syriac alphabet (fig. 13). The Arabic alphabet borrowed from Nabatean its composition of mostly consonants, as well as one of its most distinctive and enduring characteristics, the use of ligatures to connect letters at the baseline. The earliest dated evidence of Arabic cursive are documents on papyrus in a "utilitarian style" from the 640s and graffiti found on rocks,

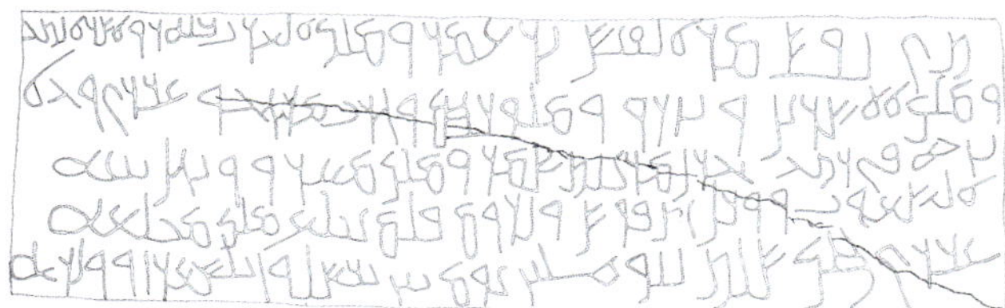

Fig. 12. Epitaph of Imru' al-Qays ("King of All the Arabs"). Syria, al-Nemara, A.D. 328. Drawing by Christian Robin and Maria Gorea

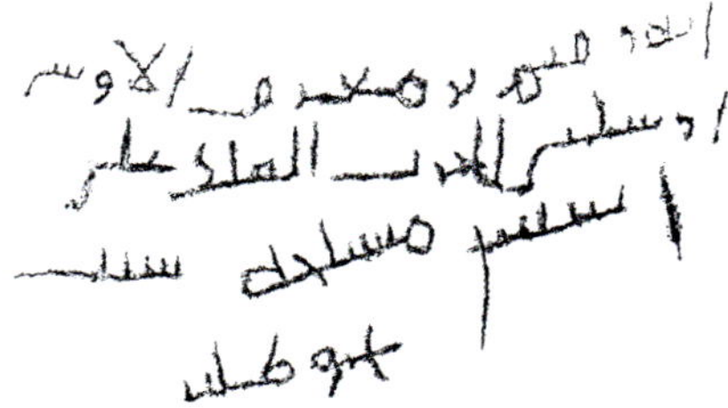

Fig. 13. Graffito inscription. Syria, Jabal Usays (southeast of Damascus), A.D. 529. Drawing by Farah Dabbous

such as the foundation text scratched on a rock near Ta'if, in the Hijaz (in present-day Saudi Arabia), recording the construction of a dam by the Umayyad caliph Mu'awiyya in 677–68. Epigraphic coins, or dinars, are also reliable evidence of a formal standard style of writing, as are architectural inscriptions, such as those encircling the ambulatory of the Dome of the Rock in Jerusalem, dated A.H. 72/A.D. 691–92 (fig. 14). As we will see, a rich variety of scripts developed over the centuries and across regions throughout the Islamic world.

Kufic Script

The rise of the *kufic* script in the late seventh to early eighth century and its subsequent widespread proliferation was a major development in the history of Islamic calligraphy (fig. 15). The earliest dinar coins dating to A.H. 76/A.D. 696–97 bear Qur'anic verses in an early formalized variation of *kufic* (see cat. 1). Although *kufic* is named after Kufa, a city and intellectual hub in southern Iraq, the term refers to a category of angular scripts that includes many variations, not necessarily a place of

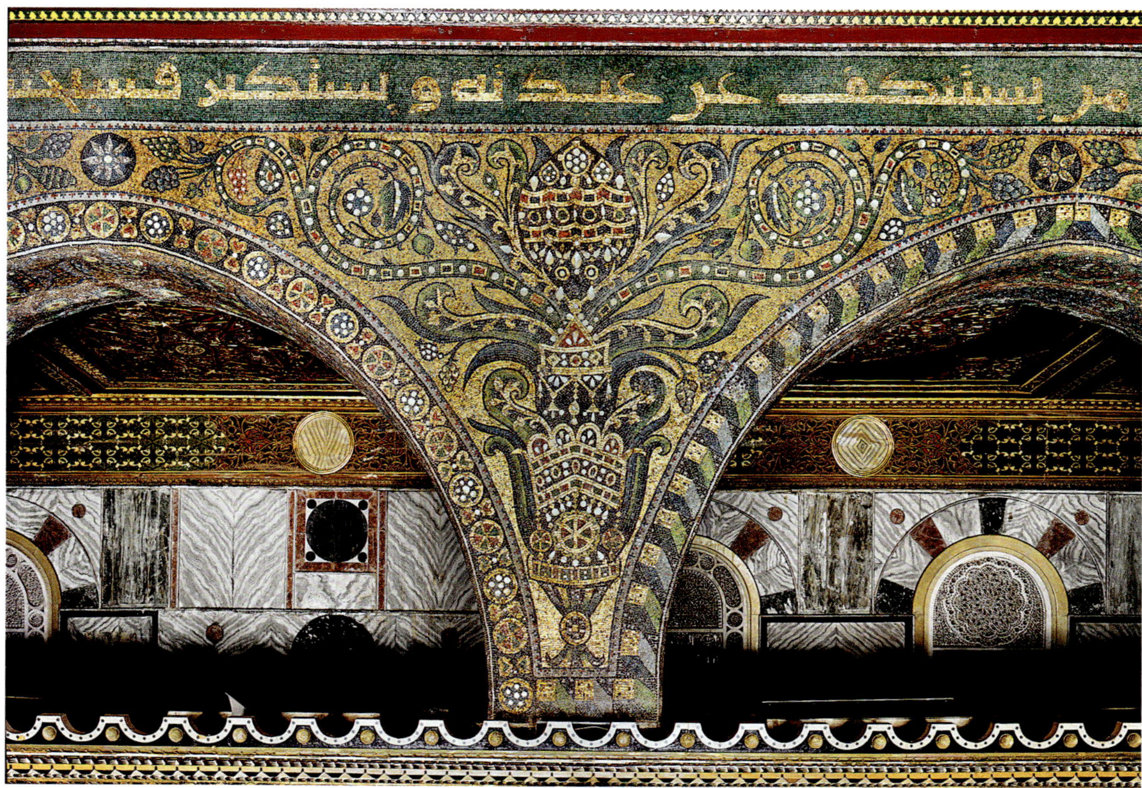

Fig. 14. Ambulatory of the Dome of the Rock, Jerusalem, with an inscription in *kufic*, A.H. 72/A.D. 691–92

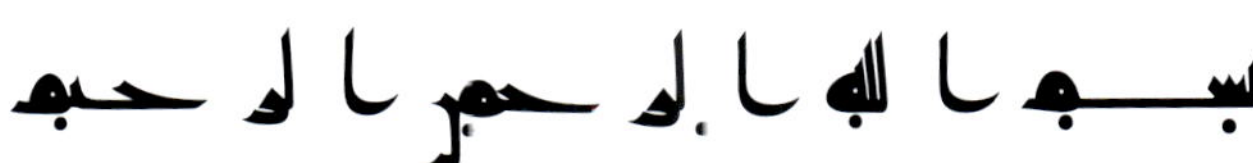

Fig. 15. Diagram of the *kufic* script

Floriated *kufic*

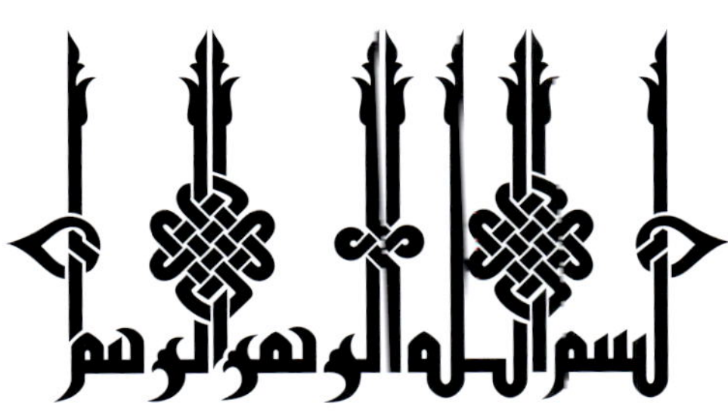

Knotted/plaited *kufic*

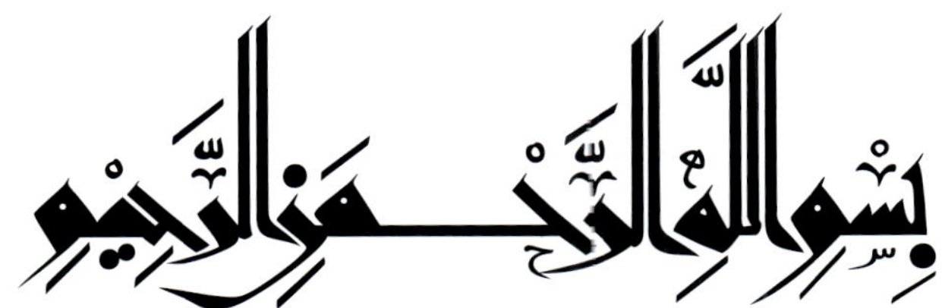

"New-style" script

Fig. 16. Variations of the new-style script

production. *Kufic* followed precise rules that prescribed carefully calibrated letters with a new sense of geometric proportion and regularity. As such, it supplanted *hijazi*, an unofficial script used to transcribe the earliest Qur'ans onto parchment (see pp. 70–72 and figs. 30, 31), as the preferred script for copying the holy book, and it enjoyed this status until about the mid- to late tenth century.

Kufic Qur'ans from the eighth to the tenth century were largely penned on parchment and came in vertical, square, and oblong formats. However, by the second half of the eighth century, oblong Qur'ans with only a few lines per page became standard. *Kufic* is generally distinguished by its clarity, generous spacing, and the horizontal extension of letters along the baseline. The majority of early *kufic* Qur'ans on parchment were composed of quinions, quires of five folios that were stacked with the flesh side up and sewn along the center crease into a single volume. Most volumes were bound in leather and housed in chests, while in some rare instances individual folios were deliberately left unbound and placed in wood or leather boxes.

The New-Style Script and the Introduction of Paper

Several important developments occurred in the ninth and tenth centuries that changed the course of Islamic calligraphy. Paper, which came to the Islamic world from China along the Silk Road in the mid-eighth century, became a universal support for documents, records, letters, edicts, and manuscripts. Paper had certain advantages over papyrus and parchment: it was not as sensitive to fluctuations in humidity and could not be easily forged. Nevertheless, parchment remained the preferred support for Qur'an manuscripts until after the tenth century, when it became obsolete in all but Spain and North Africa, where it continued to be used well into the fourteenth century. The availability and widespread use of paper in the ninth century coincided with an extraordinary rise in literacy and an efflorescence in the arts of the book, as well as the dissemination of knowledge in many different fields.

The tenth century also saw a movement away from *kufic* to a group of more readable, efficient cursive scripts, as well as a shift in page format from horizontal to vertical. One script in particular that had emerged in the late ninth century was traditionally referred to as eastern *kufic* or broken *kufic*. More recently, however, scholars have preferred the term "new Abbasid style" or "new style" for this script, claiming that variations of it were used in both the eastern and the western reaches of the Islamic world. New-style script is characterized by the extreme verticality of the shafts of the letters, razor-sharp angularity, a marked contrast between thick and thin strokes, and the consistent use of diacritical and vocalization marks (fig. 16). The compactness of the script coupled with the newly vertical page format made it possible

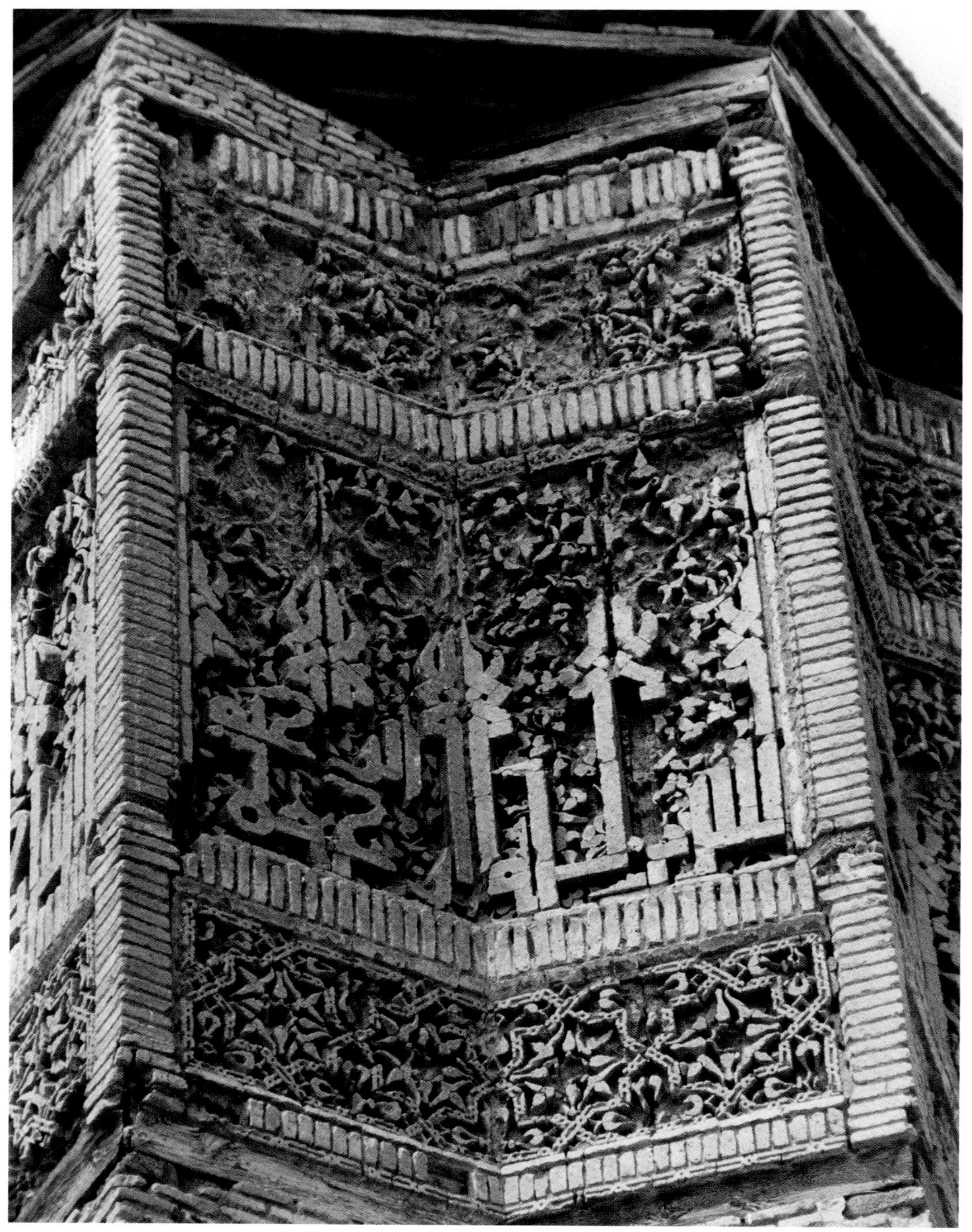

Fig. 17. Epigraphic frieze on the east face of the minaret of Mas'ud III, Ghazna, Afghanistan, early 11th century

to fit many more lines on a page and, thus, the entire text of the Qur'an into a single volume.

Used for a variety of secular and religious purposes, the new-style script opened ample possibilities for innovation and ornamentation in a range of media. Decorative variations of the script were applied to objects and architectural surfaces in Iran, Central Asia, Anatolia, and beyond (fig. 17). By the thirteenth century, however, the new-style script had been supplanted by proportional, rounded cursive scripts that were more versatile, efficient, and legible. Like *kufic*, the new-style script was eventually relegated to the decorative realm, such as illuminated *sura* headings, titles, and frontispieces.

Proportional Scripts

The theory of "proportional script" (*al-khatt al-mansub*), whereby the shapes of letters could be carefully calibrated and controlled through a series of ratios, was first advanced by the Abbasid vizier and calligrapher Abu 'Ali Muhammad ibn Muqla (886–940), who together with master calligraphers Ibn Bawwab (Abu al-Hasan Ali b. Hilal, d. 1022) and Yaqut al-Musta'simi (d. 1298) is credited with broadening the scope of Islamic calligraphy and elevating Arabic scripts to new heights. These three individuals became models of character and fine penmanship for generations of calligraphers who followed. In fact, the transmission of their scripts and styles to their pupils and beyond served as the basis for studying Islamic calligraphy from the tenth century onward, demonstrating the singular importance of the master-pupil relationship in the acquisition of calligraphic skill.

Ibn Muqla developed his proportional writing system around two basic shapes: a circle with the diameter of the letter *alif* and a rhomboid dot created by one stroke of the nib of a reed pen (fig. 18). From these geometric principles, he introduced and canonized the six classical proportional scripts, known as *al-aqlam al-sitta*, or "six pens": *naskh, thuluth, muhaqqaq, rayhan, tawqi'*, and *riqa'* (fig. 19). These six were sometimes presented as complementary pairs of large and minute, such as *thuluth–naskh*, *muhaqqaq–rayhan*, and *tawqi'–riqa'* (fig. 20). Each script or pair of scripts was suited to a particular purpose. For example, *naskh* was ideal for copying ordinary books and small Qur'ans, while *muhaqqaq* and *thuluth* suited large Qur'ans. *Thuluth* was frequently used to decorate portable objects and architectural surfaces, as well. *Rayhan,*

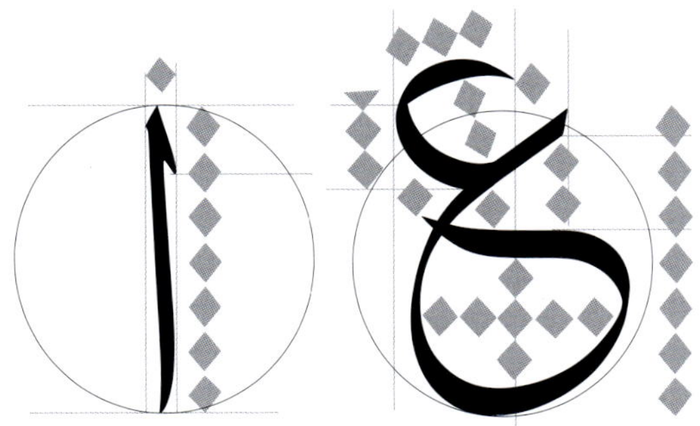

Fig. 18. Proportional rendering of the letters *alif* and *'ayn*

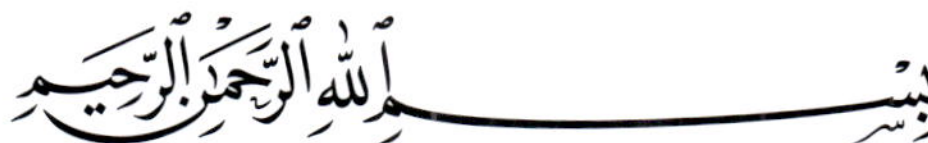

naskh

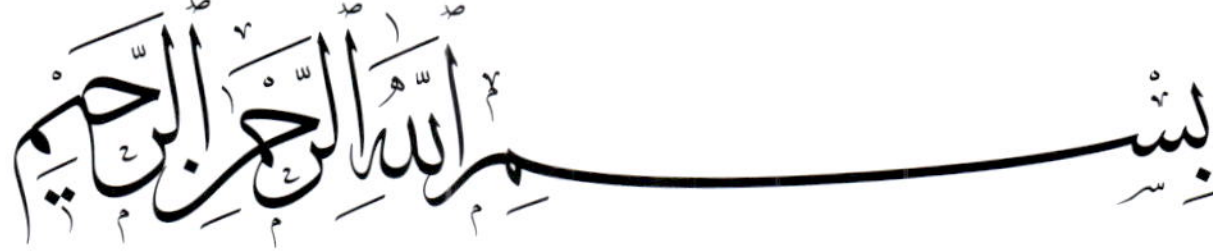

thuluth

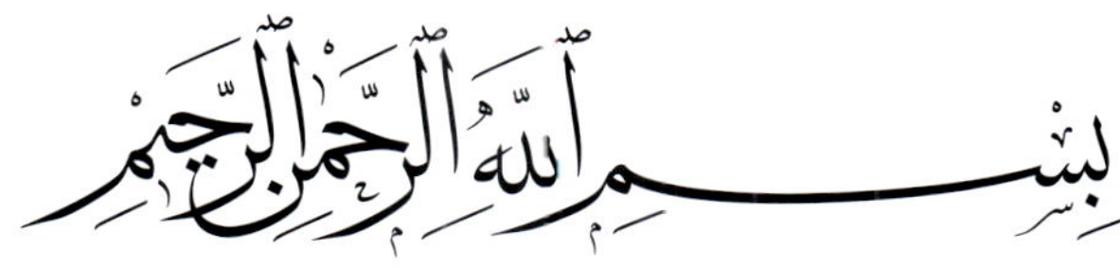

muhaqqaq

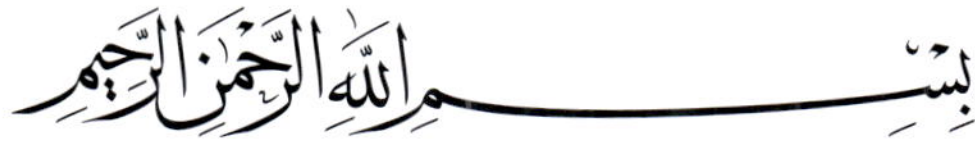

rayhan

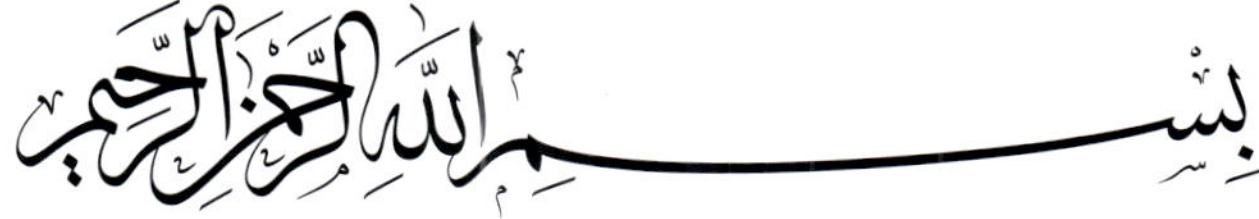

tawqi'

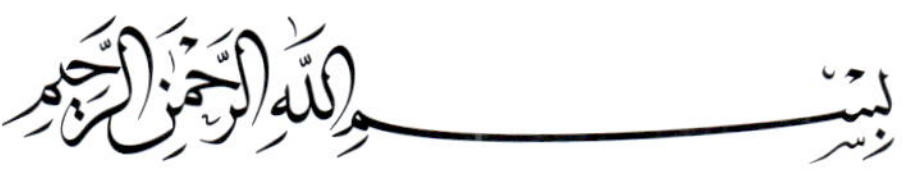

riqa'

Fig. 19. Diagram of the "six pens"

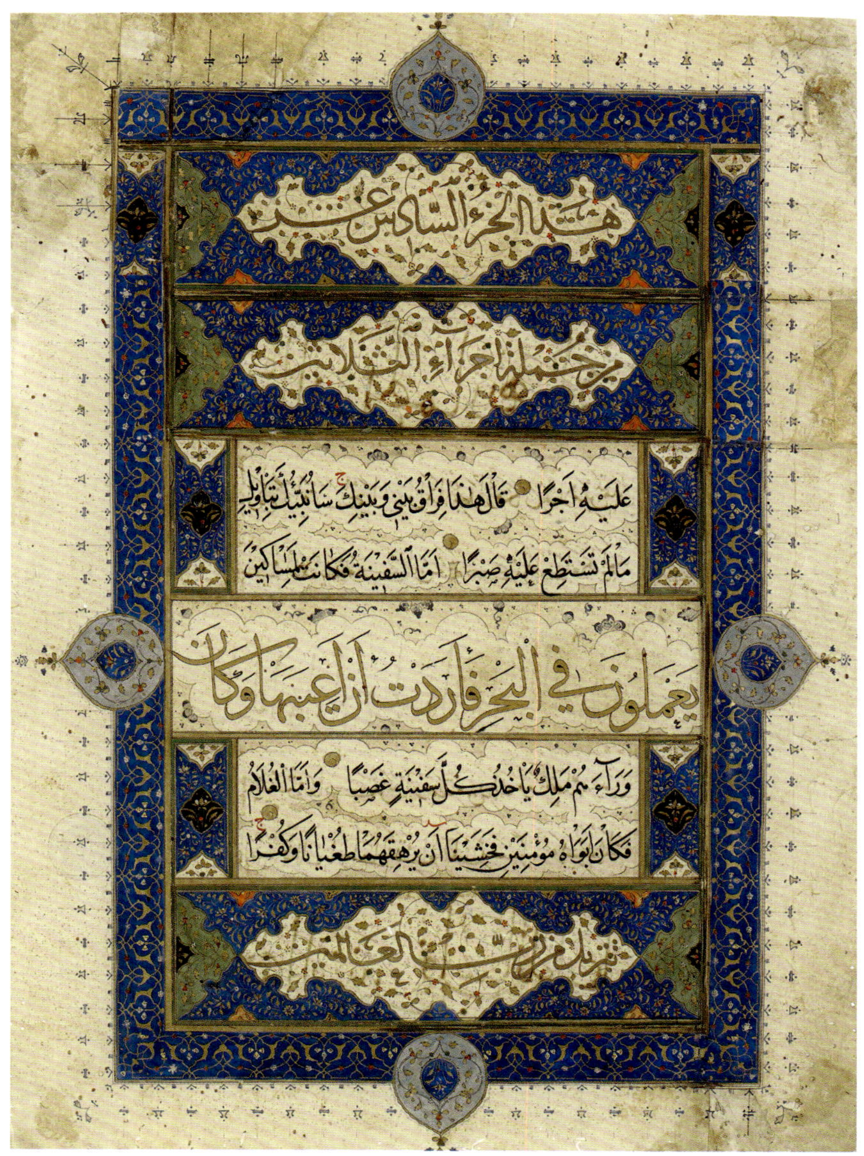

Fig. 20. Folio of calligraphy combining *naskh, thuluth,* and *tawqi'* scripts. Calligrapher: Zayn al-Abidin ibn Muhammad al-Shirazi (ca. 1480–ca. 1520), Iran, Shiraz, A.H. 888/A.D. 1483. Ink, color, and gold on paper, 16¼ x 12 in. (41.2 x 30.6 cm). Ashmolean Museum, University of Oxford (EA2012.71)

tawqi', and *riqa'* were preferred for chancellery documents or colophons, or to embellish book covers and carpet pages (see cat. 6). *Rayhan* is a smaller variant of *muhaqqaq*, and *tawqi'* and *riqa'* are characterized by the unusual connection of letters that are not linked in other scripts, such as the *dal* and the *alif.*

Ibn Bawwab is credited with perfecting Ibn Muqla's system, adding an aesthetic dimension that brought elegance and grace to the geometric canon. The only extant example in his hand is a small Qur'an copied in Baghdad in 1000–1001 (Chester Beatty Library, Dublin, MS 1431). Written in a clear and bold *naskh* script, the text is noted for the compact spacing of the letters and words and a dense overall layout of the page. In the late thirteenth century, Yaqut al-Musta'simi further perfected the system put forth by Ibn Muqla and Ibn Bawwab. His achievements were described by the sixteenth-century Iranian chronicler Qadi Ahmad, who credits Yaqut as being the first to cut the nib of the reed pen at an angle. This innovation naturally resulted in the refinement and linear variability of letters. Prioritizing elegance and aesthetics over precision, Yaqut trained many renowned calligraphers of the fourteenth century, who in turn instructed a large number of fifteenth-century calligraphers; one in particular, Ahmad ibn al-Suhrawardi al-Bakri (active 1301/2–28), is most notable. A fine example of calligraphy by his hand is a colophon that includes his name (see cat. 5).

Chancellery Scripts

The oldest surviving Arabic texts from the Islamic era were written on papyrus and date to a few decades after the *hijra*, the Prophet Muhammad's flight from Mecca to Medina in A.D. 622. They are not religious texts but documents, official and unofficial correspondence concerning administrative matters. Found in Heracleopolis, in Egypt, the earliest specimens are tax receipts and orders for the delivery of goods, which attests to the important role of written Arabic in utilitarian, nonreligious contexts.

By the medieval period, the position of secretary (*katib* or *munshi*) had become increasingly vital to the administrative hierarchy. In addition to serving as scribes, *katib*s were often counselors of rulers and princes and tasked with enforcing the supremacy of the pen as an instrument of power. As such, they were expected to be honest, loyal, and of impeccable demeanor. The stringent protocol of chancellery correspondence required *katib*s to have a knowledge of grammar, the Qur'an, and other religious texts, and skill in composing both prose and poetry. They had to be master calligraphers with a full command of the materials and techniques of the craft, such as the pen, ink, supports, and pigments. They had to be eloquent communicators capable of composing and/or responding to letters and crafting the salutation, invocation, and honorific expressions and conclusions of official correspondence. And since the appearance of written texts was deemed just as important as content, the *katib* had to make sure that the aesthetics and presentation of letters, decrees, documents, and records were of the highest order.

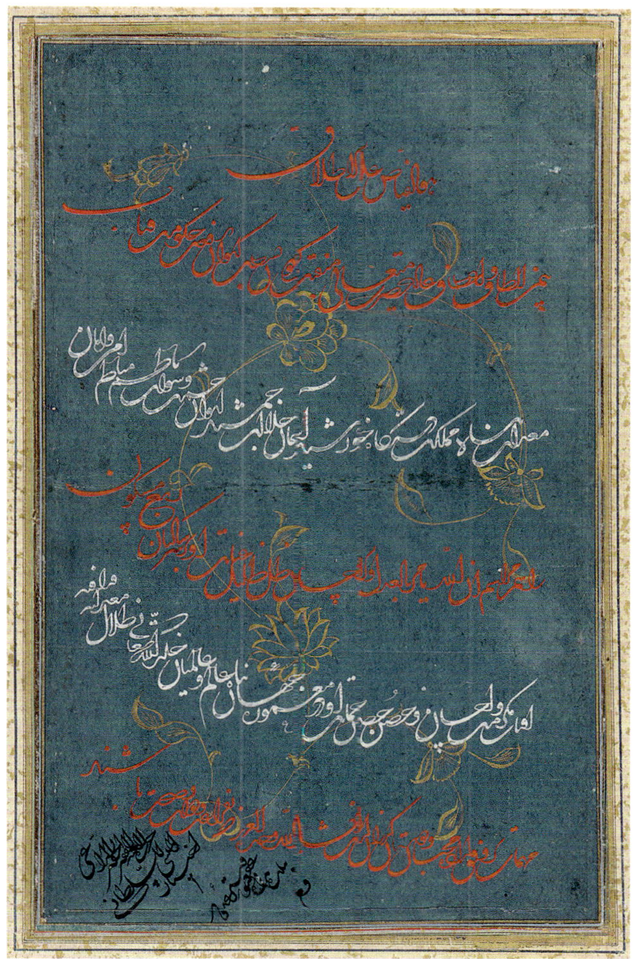

Fig. 21. Folio of calligraphy in *ta'liq* script. Calligrapher: Kamal al-Din Ikhtiyar (d. 1566–67). Iran, Safavid, ca. 1540–50. Ink, opaque watercolor, and gold on colored paper, 9⅝ x 6$^{5}/_{16}$ in. (24.5 x 16 cm). Freer Gallery of Art, Washington, D.C. (F1929.65)

The earliest administrative letters were written in cursive. Through the centuries, however, several chancellery scripts emerged specifically for administrative use, namely, *naskh*, *tawqi'*, *rayhan*, *ta'liq*, and *ghubar* (for pigeon post). Later, in Iran and Ottoman Turkey, a few new scripts evolved to fulfill administrative purposes, most notably *shikasta*, *shikasta-nasta'liq*, *tughra*, and *divani*. Many of them were purposefully difficult to read so as to disguise the message and make it accessible to only a select group of individuals. As with the scripts discussed above, each chancellery script had its leading practitioners and masters.

Ta'liq, which means "hanging" or "suspended," evolved over a long period in Iran beginning in the late thirteenth century, later spreading to Ottoman Turkey and the Indian subcontinent. It shares common features with a few of the proportional scripts, such as *riqa'* and *tawqi'*, in its exaggerated descending loops, connected letters and ligatures, and tendency for upward-sloping words at the end of a line (fig. 21). *Ta'liq* was used mainly for official decrees, documents, deeds, endowments, diplomatic correspondence (see cat. 10a), and *ziyaratnama*s (letters of recommendation issued by a shrine to pilgrims), but seldom for poetry or religious texts.

Shikasta, or "broken," script originated and developed in Iran after the sixteenth century. Like *ta'liq*, it

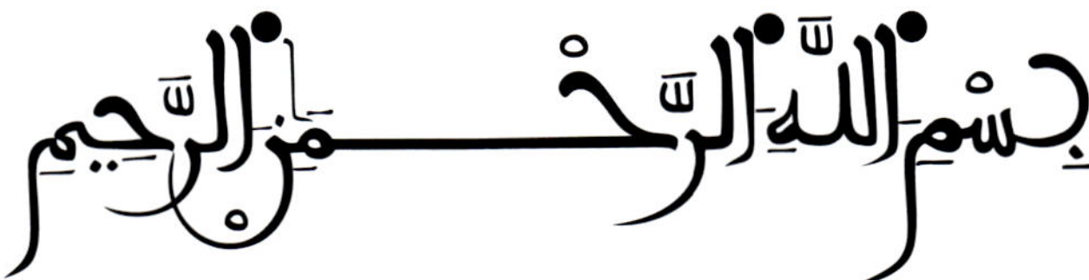

Fig. 22. Diagram of the *maghribi* script

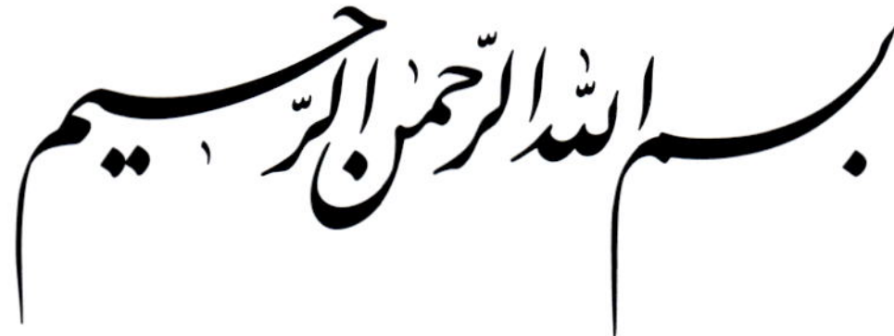

Fig. 23. Diagram of the *nasta'liq* script

contains unconventional ligatures between letters that do not traditionally connect and was thus deemed suitable for increasing speed in executing texts. A skilled calligrapher, for example, could complete a word with one stroke, without lifting the pen. Perhaps best described as the Persian equivalent of shorthand, *shikasta* prioritized irregularity and movement over horizontal regularity. Words undulate in fluid motions, and lines are positioned at various angles, creating an airy, free-flowing effect (see cat. 10b).

The main chancellery scripts of the Ottoman empire were *tughra* and *divani*. The Ottoman *tughra* can be defined as the calligraphic insignia of the sultan. It is not his signature, since it is not written by his hand, but functions somewhat like a logo representing his authority. *Tughra*s crowned official documents such as *firman*s (royal decrees) in scroll format, endowment papers, and correspondence, as well as coins and other objects. The earliest *tughra*s were unembellished, but by the early sixteenth century and reign of Sultan Süleyman the Magnificent (r. 1520–66), they became increasingly elaborate and decorative (see cat. 8).

Regional Scripts: *Maghribi* and *Nasta'liq*

Scripts have their own histories and geographic parameters; some were used widely, while others remained local to a particular region. For example, *maghribi* was developed and used primarily in Spain and North Africa (fig. 22), while *nasta'liq*, an elegant and lyrical script originating in Iran and Central Asia, spread eastward to Mughal India and westward to Ottoman Turkey (fig. 23).

As the favored script for Persian poetry, *nasta'liq*—referred to as the "bride of scripts"—was especially popular in Iran from the fifteenth century onward. According to legend, it was invented by Mir 'Ali Tabrizi (active late 14th century) after 'Ali ibn Abi Talib, cousin and son-in-law of the Prophet Muhammad and the first Shi'i Imam, appeared to him in a dream. 'Ali, who is traditionally regarded as the first calligrapher in Islam, commanded him to create letters that resemble the wings of flying geese. Scholars, however, maintain that *nasta'liq* developed in the second half of the fourteenth century in the cities of Shiraz and Tabriz as a gradual merging of *naskh* and *ta'liq*. As discussed above, *naskh* was noted for its clarity and balance and used for copying small Qur'ans and other texts, while *ta'liq* was prized for its efficiency and used for documents, edicts, and official correspondence. Hence, the fusion of the two combined the evenness and legibility of *naskh* with the sweeping gestural strokes of *ta'liq*.

Mir 'Ali's fame was matched in the next generation by that of his pupil Ja'far al-Tabrizi, the head of Prince Baisunghur's scriptorium at Herat (Afghanistan) from 1419 to 1433. One of Ja'far's own acolytes went on to train the *nasta'liq* master Sultan 'Ali Mashhadi (ca. 1440–1520), who wrote an influential treatise on penmanship and the spiritual dimensions of the calligrapher's practice. Sultan 'Ali himself trained several pupils who would go on to become masters of *nasta'liq* in their own right, namely Sultan Muhammad Nur (b. 1472; active 1490–1540), who was known for writing in a minute hand (*khafi*) (fig. 24); and Mir 'Ali Haravi (1476–1544), whose work was particularly prized at the Mughal court in India. Several well-known Mughal-era albums, including The Met's celebrated Shah Jahan Album, contain signed examples by Mir 'Ali's hand (see cat. 12b).

In the late sixteenth and early seventeenth centuries, Mir 'Imad al-Hasani (1552–1615) emerged as the undisputed

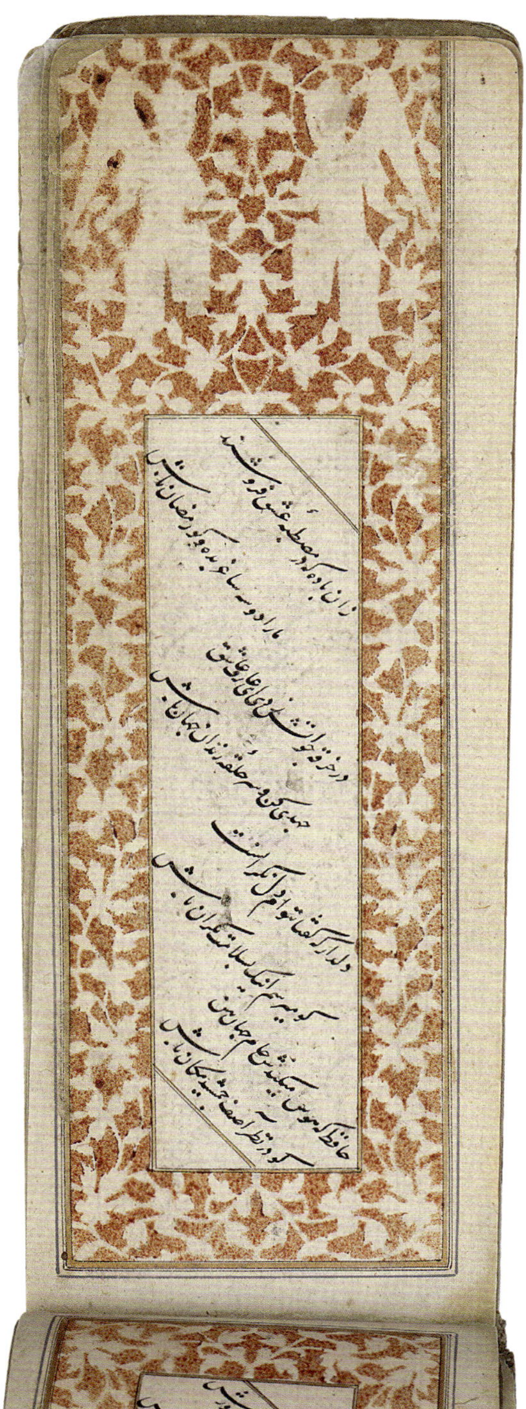

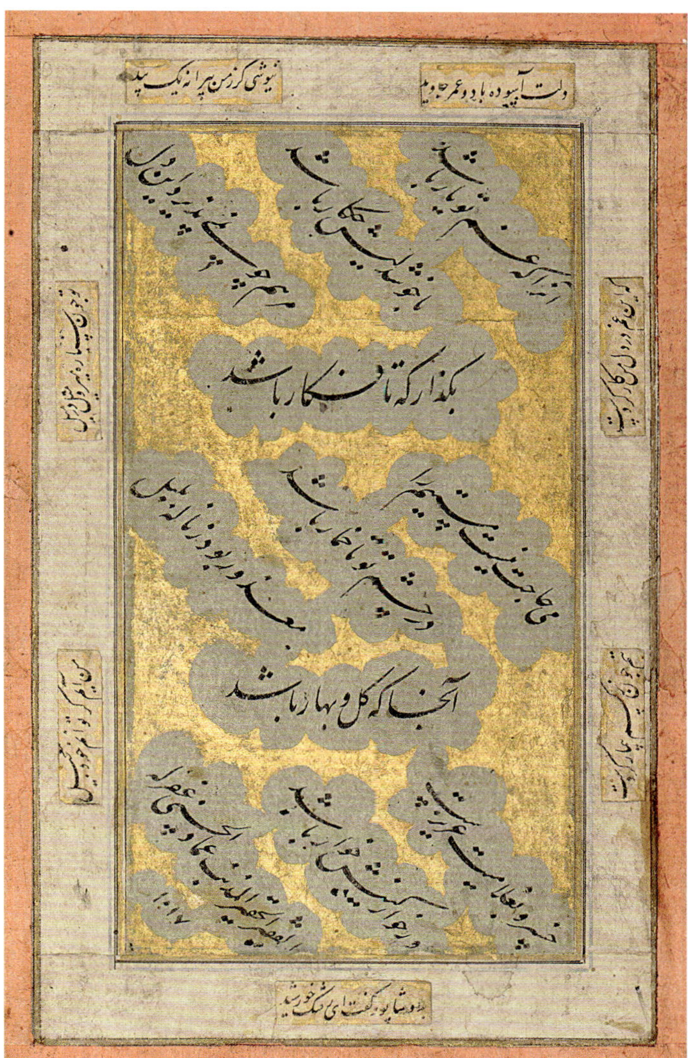

Left: Fig. 24. Anthology of Persian poetry in oblong format (*safina*). Calligrapher: attributed to Sultan Muhammad Nur (b. 1472; active 1490–1540). Present-day Afghanistan, Herat, Timurid, dated A.H. 905/A.D. 1499–1500. Ink, watercolor, and gold on paper; leather binding, 8¼ x 3 in. (21 x 7.6 cm). Purchase, Rogers Fund, Louis E. and Theresa S. Seley Purchase Fund for Islamic Art, and Persian Heritage Foundation Gift, 1997 (1997.71)

Above: Fig. 25. Folio of calligraphy by the master of *nasta'liq* Mir 'Imad al-Hasani (1552–1615). Iran, dated A.H. 1017/A.D. 1608–9. Ink, opaque watercolor, and gold on paper, 11¼ x 7½ in. (28.6 x 19.1 cm). Rogers Fund, 1946 (46.126.3)

master of *nasta'liq* (fig. 25). His hand became a model for countless calligraphers during his lifetime and for centuries afterward. He was chief calligrapher at the Safavid court of Shah 'Abbas I (r. 1588–1629) in Isfahan. There, Mir 'Imad clashed with his rival, Riza-yi 'Abbasi, the head of the royal workshop and Shah 'Abbas's favored calligrapher. He was assassinated in 1615, possibly at the command of the shah. In Iran, Mir 'Imad's style was followed by several calligraphers well into the nineteenth century, notably by Mirza Ghulam Riza Isfahani, who is credited with perfecting Mir 'Imad's style and infusing it with his own innovative spirit. Mir 'Imad's influence proliferated widely beyond Iran, finding admirers as far east as Mughal India and as far west as Ottoman Turkey.

Revival *Naskh*

Revival *naskh* is a later variation of the *naskh* script known for its large proportions, elegance, and clarity. It was codified and perfected by Ahmad Nairizi (active 1682–1739) at the turn of the seventeenth century in Iran, in an effort to render *naskh* larger and, thus, more readable. The lines are well spaced, and the letters are bold and well formed and contain vocalization marks (fig. 26). The introduction of revival *naskh*, used primarily in Qur'ans, prayer books, and other holy texts, was part of a movement in Iran in the second half of the seventeenth century to make religious texts in Arabic more accessible to Persian speakers. For this reason, Qur'ans by Nairizi often included interlinear translations in Persian. Nairizi was a follower of the late Safavid-era calligrapher Muhammad Ibrahim Qummi, as indicated by the signature at the bottom of a few of his works, acknowledging the role of his master. The nineteenth-century poet-calligrapher Muhammad Shafi' Vesal-i Shirazi and his sons were faithful followers of Nairizi's style, ensuring its continuation into the nineteenth century (fig. 27).

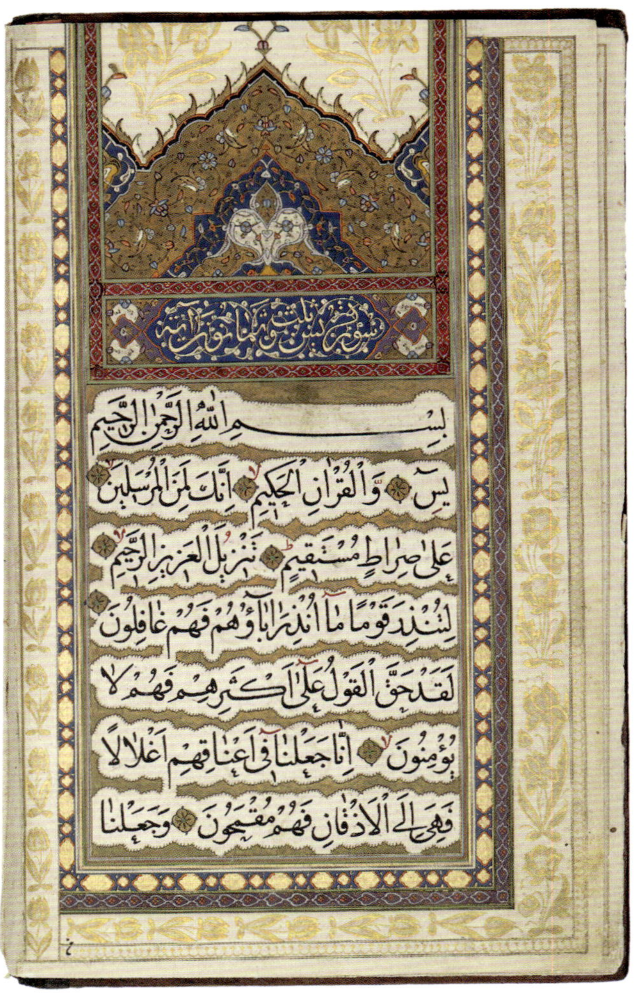

Fig. 26. Bifolium from a prayer book in revival *naskh*. Calligrapher: Ahmad Nairizi (active 1682–1739); illuminator: attributed to Muhammad Hadi (d. ca. 1771). Iran, probably Isfahan, dated A.H. 1132/A.D. 1719–20. Ink, opaque watercolor, and gold on paper; lacquer binding, 9¾ x 6⅛ in. (24.7 x 15.6 cm). Purchase, Friends of Islamic Art Gifts, 2003 (2003.239)

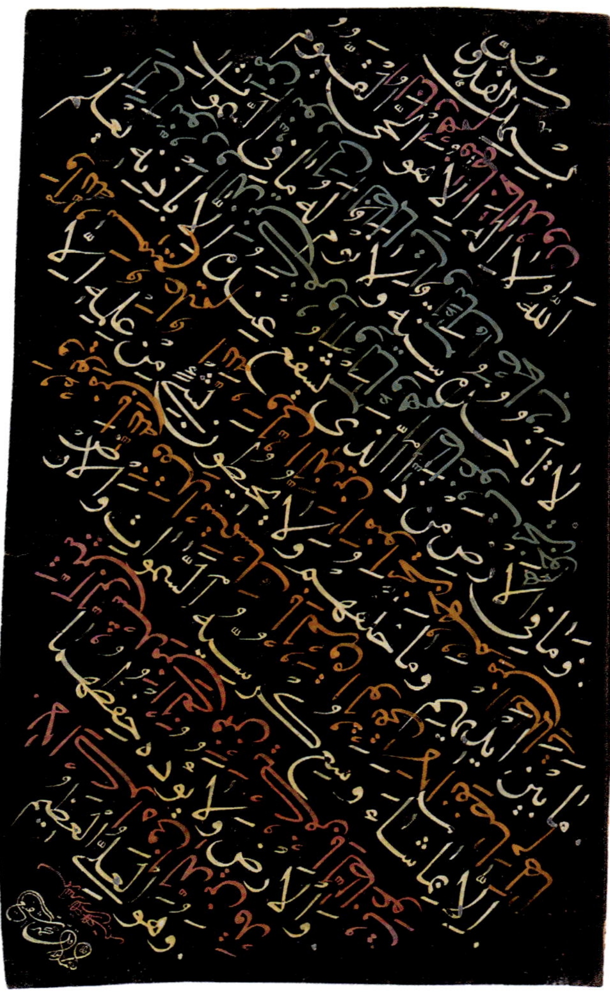

Fig. 27. Folio of calligraphy in revival *naskh*. Calligrapher: Muhammad Shafi' Vesal-i Shirazi (1779–1846). Iran, early–mid-19th century. Ink, opaque watercolor, and gold on paper, 9 x 5⅝ in. (22.9 x 14.3 cm). Gift of Charles K. Wilkinson, 1979 (1979.518.6)

1

GOLD COIN (*DINAR*)

Excavated in Iran, Nishapur, A.H. 164/A.D. 780
Gold, Diam. 11/16 in. (1.7 cm); Wt. 0.1 oz. (2.8 g)
Rogers Fund, 1939 (39.40.127.556)

Excavated at Nishapur, in northeastern Iran, this coin is a fine example of an epigraphic gold dinar of the early Abbasid period. In contrast to coins minted before A.D. 697, which in keeping with pre-Islamic traditions of the Byzantines and Sasanians included figures of rulers and other symbols, the ones minted after the caliph ʿAbd al-Malik's (r. 685–705) coinage reforms in the late seventh century were solely epigraphic and included Qur'anic verses and religious phrases.

Issued during the reign of the Abbasid caliph al-Mahdi (r. 775–85), this coin was minted in A.H. 164 (A.D. 780). The inscription resembles those on dinars issued about a century earlier, which are written in an early variation of *kufic*, a utilitarian script that emphasizes legibility and clarity. The text on its obverse proclaims the *tawhid*, the oneness of God, surrounded by a circular margin that quotes verse 33 of Qur'an *sura* 9 (*al-Tawba*, "Repentance"). On the reverse the central inscription names Muhammad as the Prophet of God, while the margin indicates the year of minting. No information is provided regarding the location of the royal mint.

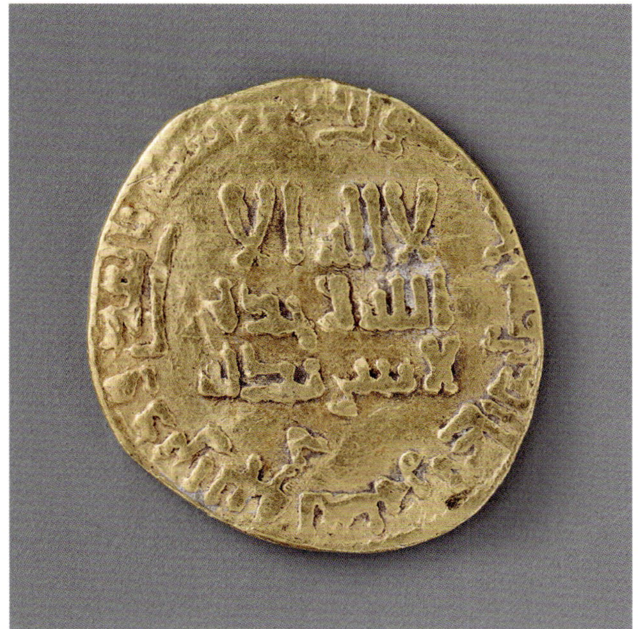

Obverse

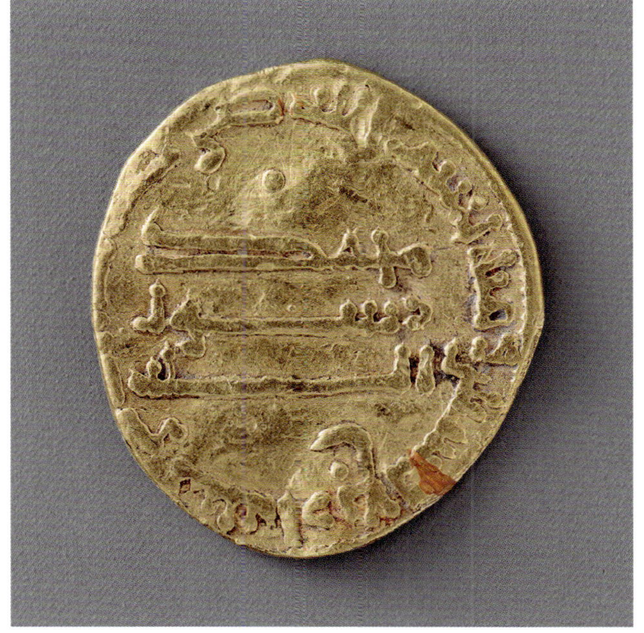

Reverse

BIFOLIUM FROM A QUR'AN IN *KUFIC* SCRIPT

Central Islamic Lands (possibly Syria), late 9th–10th century
Ink, opaque watercolor, and gold on parchment, overall 9⅛ x 25⁵⁄₁₆ in. (23.2 x 64.3 cm)
Purchase, Friends of Islamic Art Gifts, 2004 (2004.268)

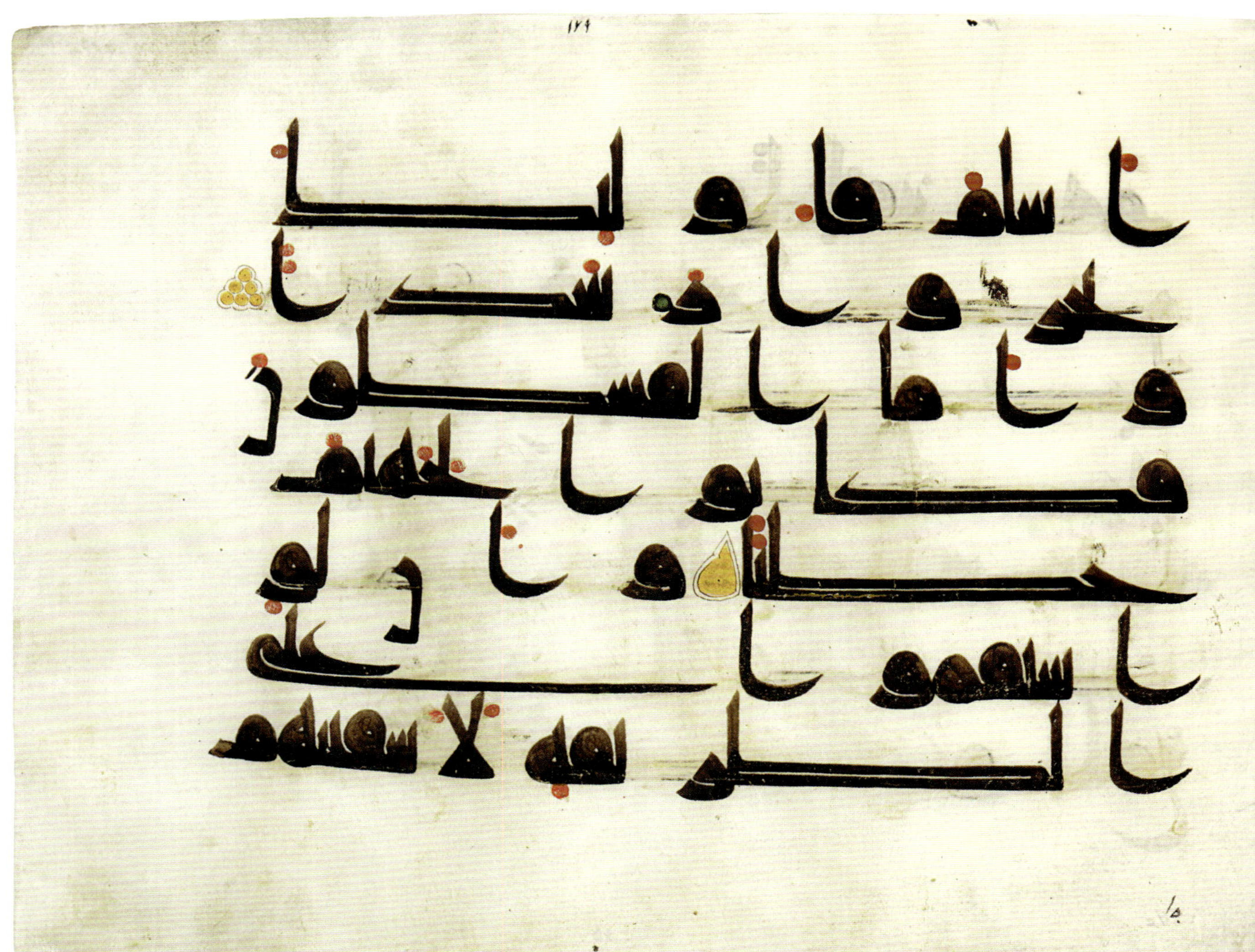

This bifolium once belonged to a multivolume Qur'an on parchment in an oblong format typical of those produced in the early Abbasid period. The text was executed in dark brown ink with a wide-nibbed reed pen. Each folio bears seven lines in thick, bold *kufic*, which follows the horizontal format of the manuscript. The double-page spread features the consecutive text of *sura* 72 (*al-Jinn*, "The Jinn"), verses 14–22, indicating that it once constituted the innermost section of a quire, which was typically composed of four double pages. The folios also bear gilded verse markers, represented by a triangular cluster of dots after each verse; the letter *ha* marking every five verses;

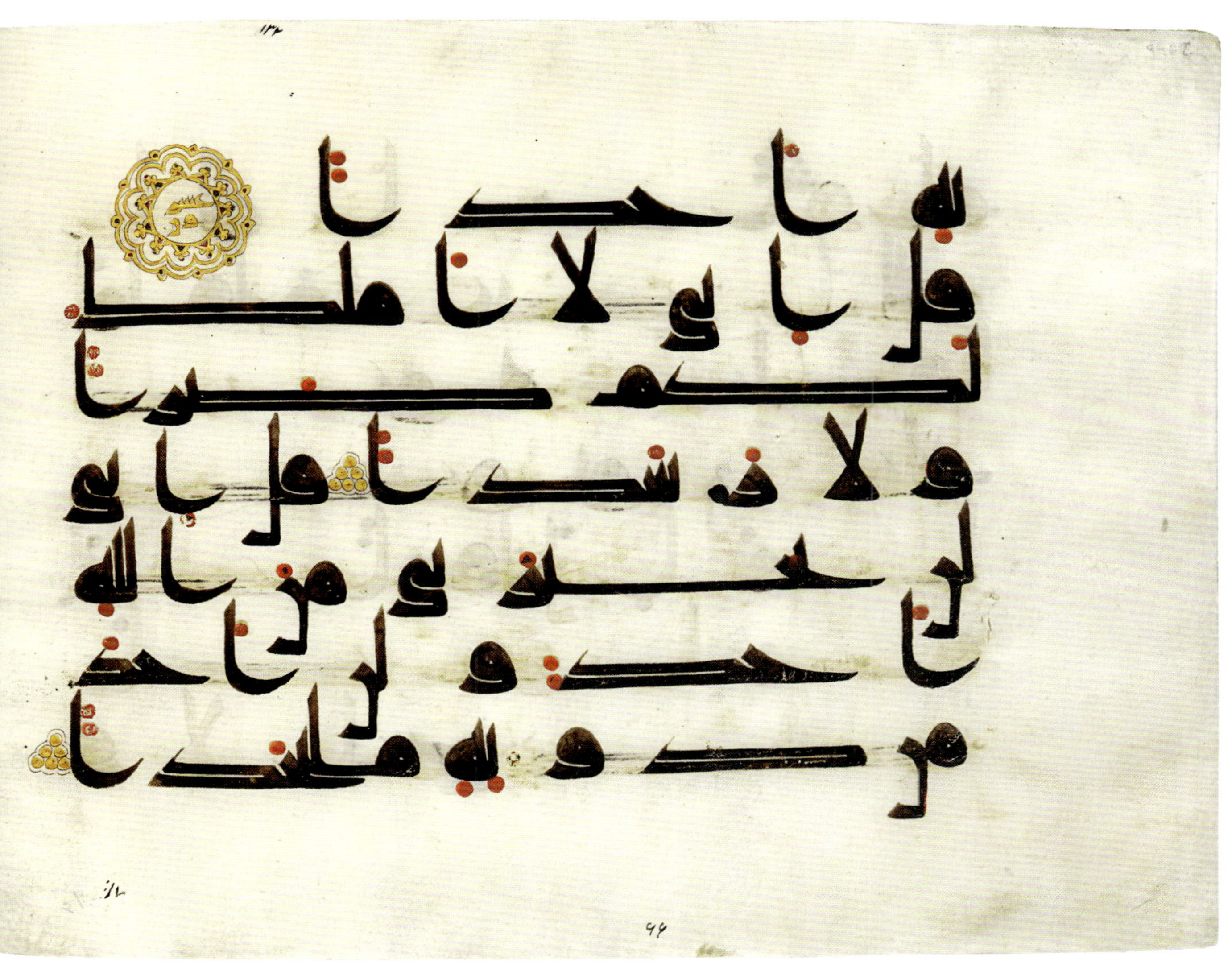

and a large lobed medallion marking every twenty verses, indicated by the Arabic word *'ashrun* (twenty) at the center. The horizontal elongation of the *kufic* letters across the page, a hallmark of oblong Qur'ans, not only creates a stunning visual effect but also may have served as a signal to the reciter to prolong or emphasize a letter or word. Vocalization is indicated by red or green dots, but consonant points, which phonetically distinguish letters of the same shape, are largely absent from the text.

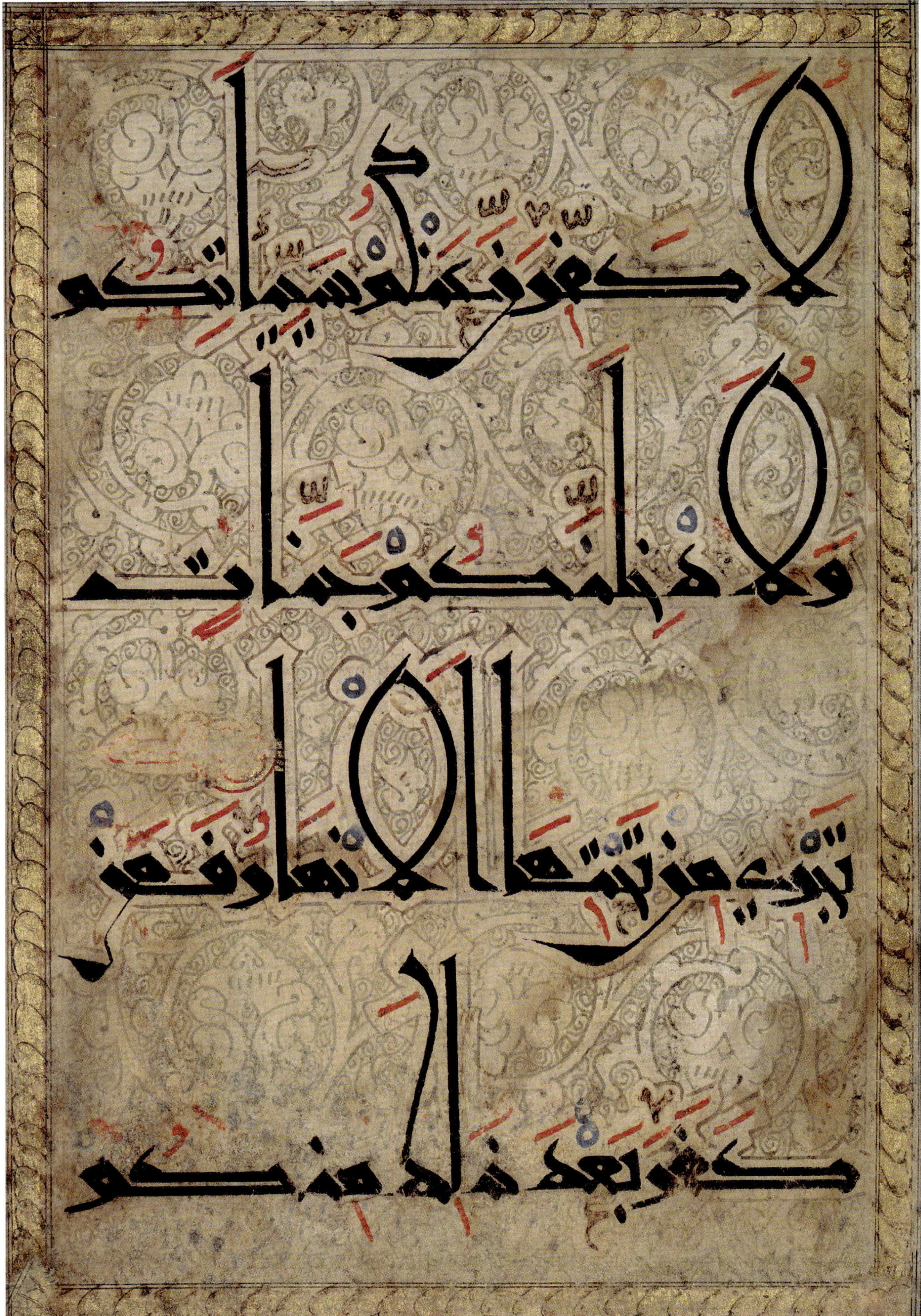
لاكفرن عنكم سيئاتكم
ولادخلنكم جنات
تجري من تحتها الانهار فمن
كفر بعد ذلك منكم

3

FOLIO FROM A QUR'AN IN NEW-STYLE SCRIPT

Eastern Iran or present-day Afghanistan, ca. 1180
Ink, opaque watercolor, and gold on paper, 11¾ x 8¾ in. (29.8 x 22.2 cm)
H. O. Havemeyer Collection, Gift of Horace Havemeyer, 1929 (29.160.24)

This folio belongs to a dispersed Qur'an that is said to have contained roughly 2,250 folios. It is considered to be the most lavish Qur'an manuscript ever produced in the new-style script. Each folio, bordered by a gold braid, contains four lines of text set against a dense background of dark and light brown stylized palmette scrolls. The composition alludes to an architectural surface, possibly a panel of carved stucco or marble, in which the calligraphy stands in relief against the dense pattern of vegetation. The writing is characterized by slender verticals that often tower above the baseline; a careful modulation of thick and thin strokes; and the combination of the letters *lam* and *alif* to form a perfect oval. Letters that extend below the baseline, such as *nun* and *waw*, are rendered as thin diagonal strokes that terminate in thicker bowl-shaped forms.

The sharp angles and tall shafts of the vertical letters recall scripts found on ceramic wares from Nishapur and Samarqand of the Samanid era. The writing on these bowls is elegant and legible, despite the absence of diacritical and vocalization marks (fig. 28). They feature palmette scrolls at the center that bear some resemblance to those of the Qur'an folio, but parallels with carved stucco or marble seem more convincing. Recent studies associate this specific vegetal form with those found in the Gunbad-i Alaviyan, a mid-twelfth-century mausoleum at Hamadan, in northwestern Iran. These connections suggest that both the vegetal motif and the new-style script were popular and in use from the late tenth through late twelfth centuries in Iran and the surrounding regions.

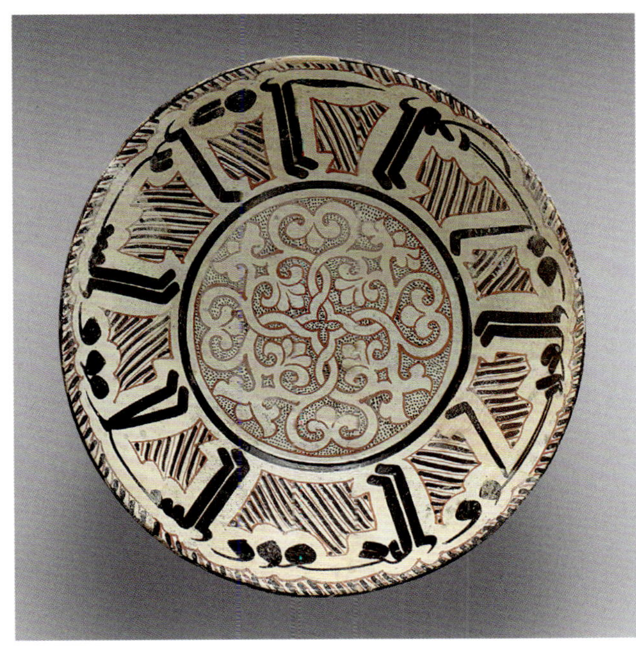

Fig. 28. Bowl with Arabic inscription in new-style script. Made in present-day Uzbekistan, probably Samarqand; excavated in Iran, Nishapur, late 10th–11th century. Earthenware; white slip with polychrome slip decoration under transparent glaze, H. 4¼ in. (10.8 cm); max. Diam. 14 in. (35.6 cm). Rogers Fund, 1940 (40.170.15)

4

BIFOLIUM FROM THE MUSHAF AL-HADINA ("NURSE'S QUR'AN")

Calligrapher: ʿAli ibn Ahmad al-Warraq
Probably Tunisia, Qairawan, ca. A.H. 410/A.D. 1019–21
Ink, opaque watercolor, and gold on parchment, 17½ x 23⅝ in. (44.5 x 60 cm)
Purchase, James and Diane Burke Gift, in honor of Dr. Marilyn Jenkins-Madina, 2007 (2007.191)

This bifolium featuring a passage from *sura* 6 (*al-Anʿam*, "The Cattle") comes from a monumental sixty-part Qur'an manuscript on parchment probably produced in Qairawan, Tunisia. Each side of each folio contains five lines of text in brown ink, executed in a variation of the new-style script associated with the western reaches of the Islamic world. Here, great attention has been devoted to the contrast between the thick, rounded forms and the thin strokes descending below the baseline. Vocalization marks are rendered in red, blue, and green.

The colophon of this dispersed Qur'an notes that the entire manuscript, including its binding, was vocalized, illuminated, and gilded by ʿAli ibn Ahmad al-Warraq ("the papermaker"), a renowned calligrapher and artist of the eleventh century who was supervised by Durra al-Katiba ("the lady scribe"). However, the writing is not completely consistent throughout the manuscript, indicating the possible involvement of more than one hand. Another annotation reveals that the manuscript was commissioned by Fatima, the nursemaid of a Zirid prince, before it was endowed to the Great Mosque of Qairawan during the month of Ramadan in A.H. 410 (A.D. 1019–20). The work is therefore known as the Mushaf al-Hadina, or "Nurse's Qur'an," and it remains the best-known extant manuscript commissioned by a North African female patron.

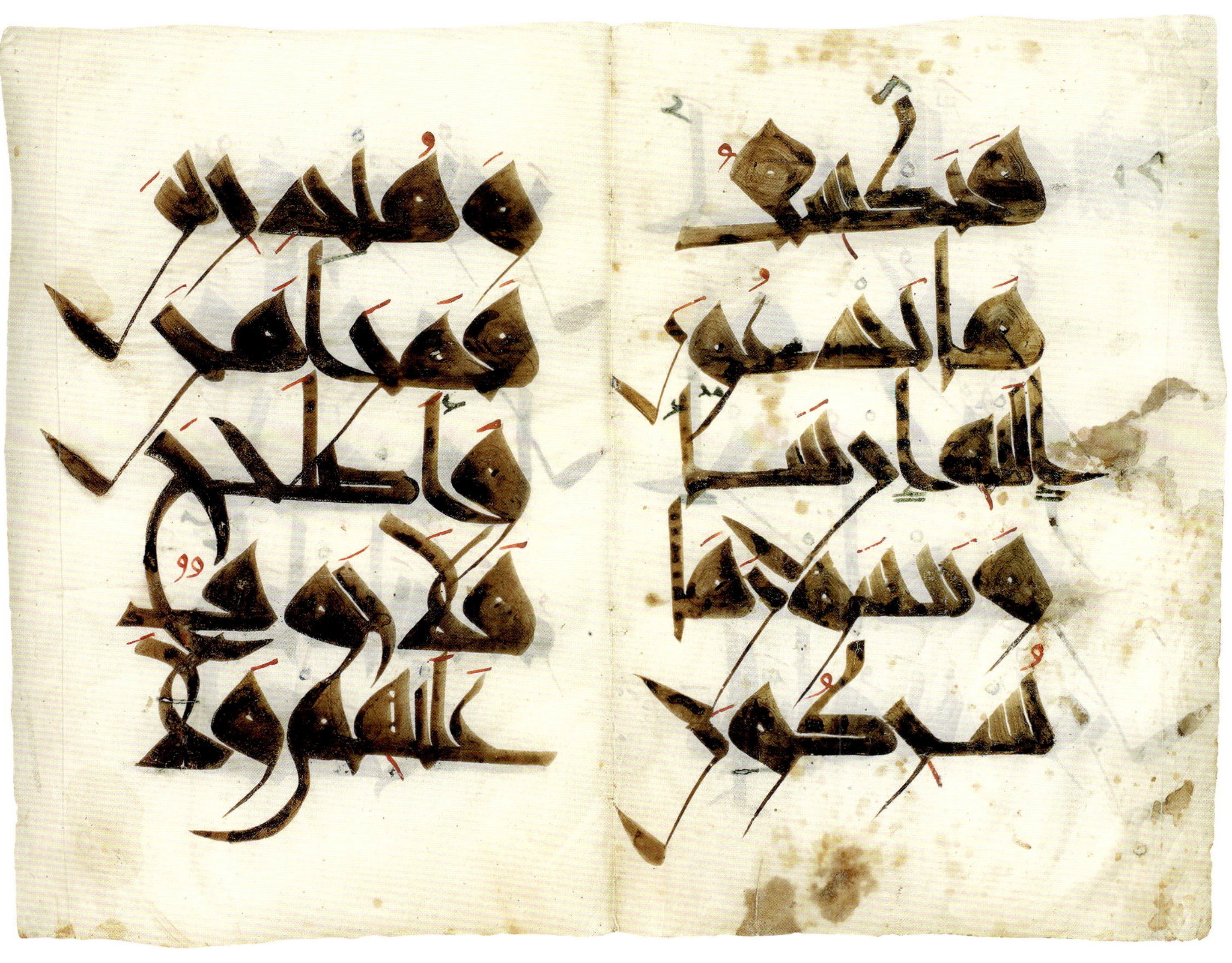

5

COLOPHON FROM THE "ANONYMOUS BAGHDAD QUR'AN" IN *MUHAQQAQ* SCRIPT

Calligrapher: Ahmad ibn al-Suhrawardi al-Bakri; illuminator: Muhammad ibn Aibak ibn ʻAbdullah
Iraq, Baghdad, dated A.H. 707/A.D. 1307–8
Ink, opaque watercolor, and gold on paper, 20¼ x 14½ in. (51.3 x 36.8 cm)
Rogers Fund, 1955 (55.44)

The calligrapher of this folio, Ahmad ibn al-Suhrawardi al-Bakri, was a pupil of the master Yaqut al-Mustaʻsimi (d. 1298). He was known to have penned numerous luxurious copies of the holy book and designed a number of architectural inscriptions for buildings in Baghdad. He is best known for his work on the so-called Anonymous Baghdad Qur'an, a large, thirty-part Qur'an manuscript produced at Baghdad, of which the present folio is the colophon. Given its production during the Ilkhanid period, the lavish Qur'an was possibly commissioned by the ruler or a statesman of the time, perhaps Sultan Ghazan Uljaitu or one of his viziers (possibly Rashid al-Din or Saʻd al-Din Savaji), as an endowment to a mosque or a tomb.

The three lines of text on the page give the name of the calligrapher and the date and place of production. Together, they epitomize the refinement, balance, and flow of the *muhaqqaq* script. The inscriptions in the gold-and-blue illuminated borders at top and bottom are rendered in a stately variation of the new-style script (detail); each band is accompanied by a teardrop-shaped pendant. The illuminator of these decorative embellishments, Muhammad ibn Aibak ibn ʻAbdullah, is named on a few of the other folios from the manuscript.

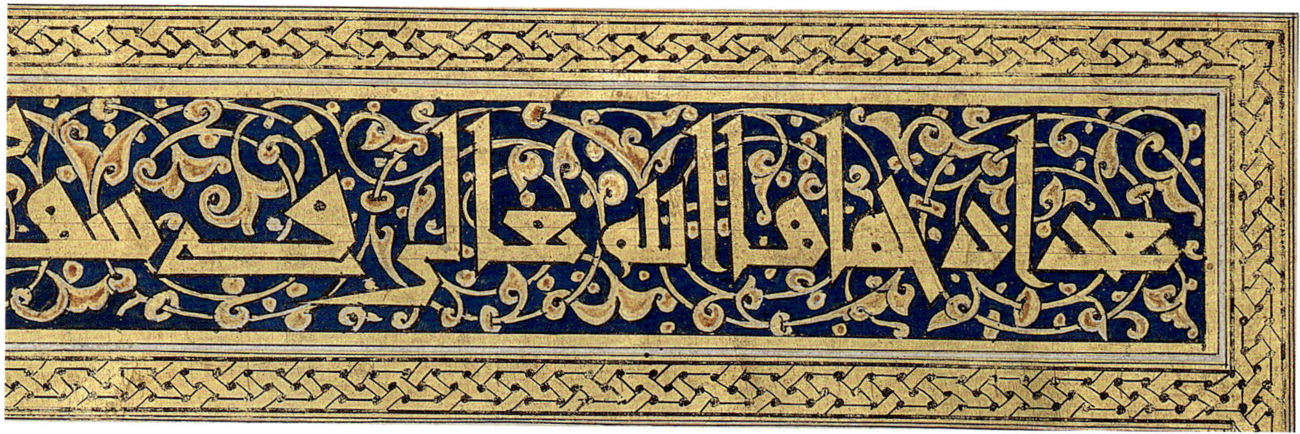

Detail of illuminated inscription

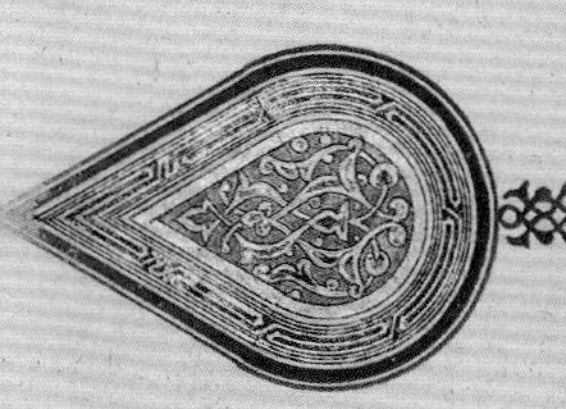

[illegible] الله تعالى في شهور

أحمد بن السهروردي البكري

حامداً لله ومصلياً على نبيه

محمد وآله وصحبه ومسلماً

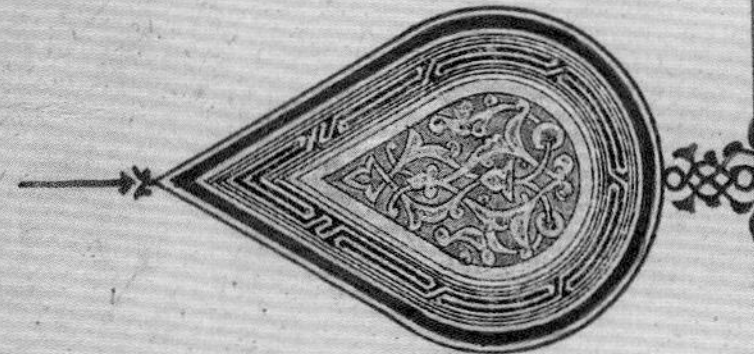

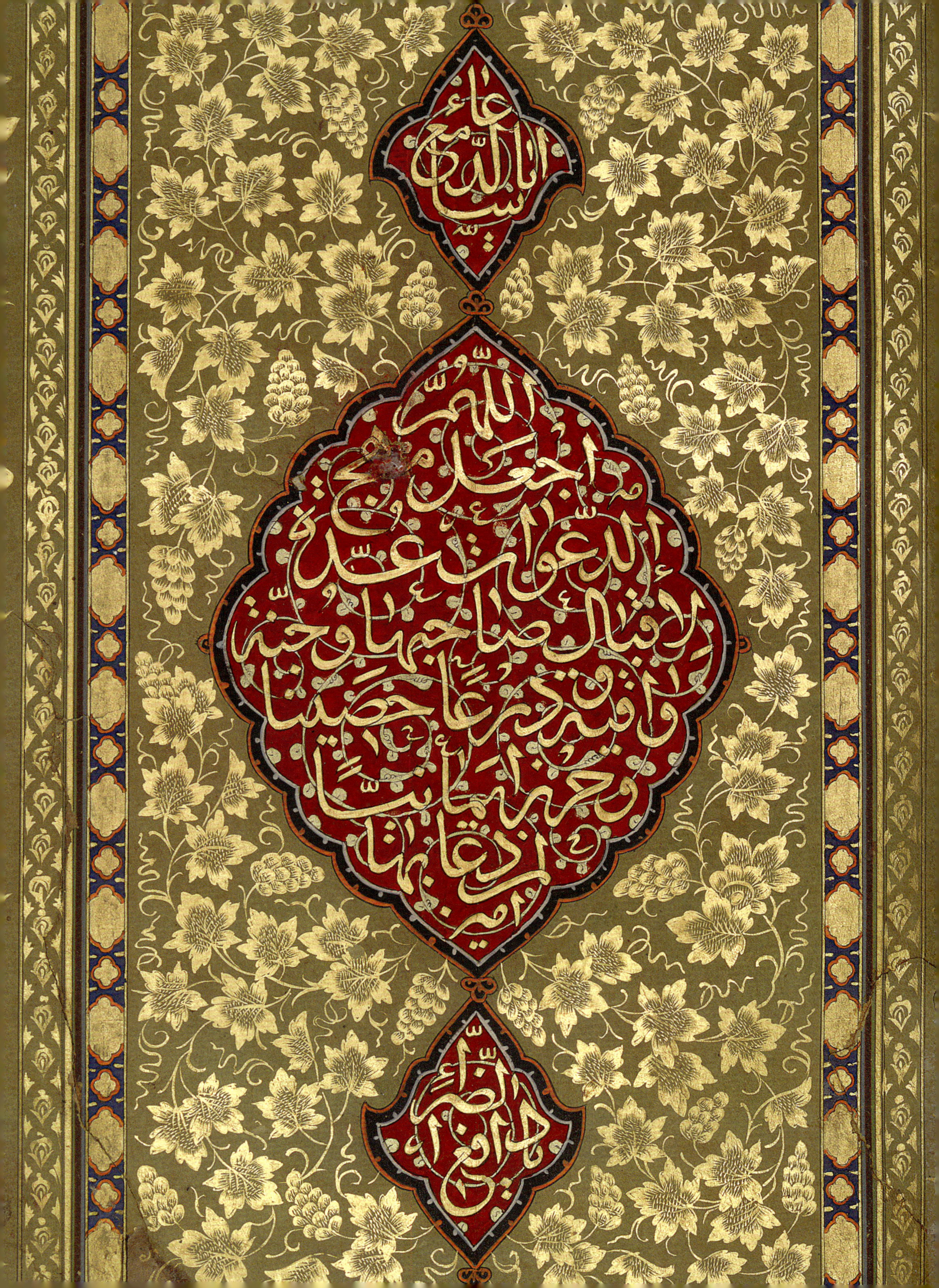

6

CARPET PAGES FROM A PRAYER BOOK WITH INSCRIPTIONS IN *RIQA'* SCRIPT

Calligrapher: Ahmad Nairizi (active 1682–1739); illuminator: attributed to Muhammad Hadi (d. ca. 1771)
Iran, probably Isfahan, dated A.H. 1132/A.D. 1719–20
Ink, opaque watercolor, and gold on paper; lacquer binding, 9¾ x 6⅛ in. (24.8 x 15.6 cm)
Purchase, Friends of Islamic Art Gifts, 2003 (2003.239)

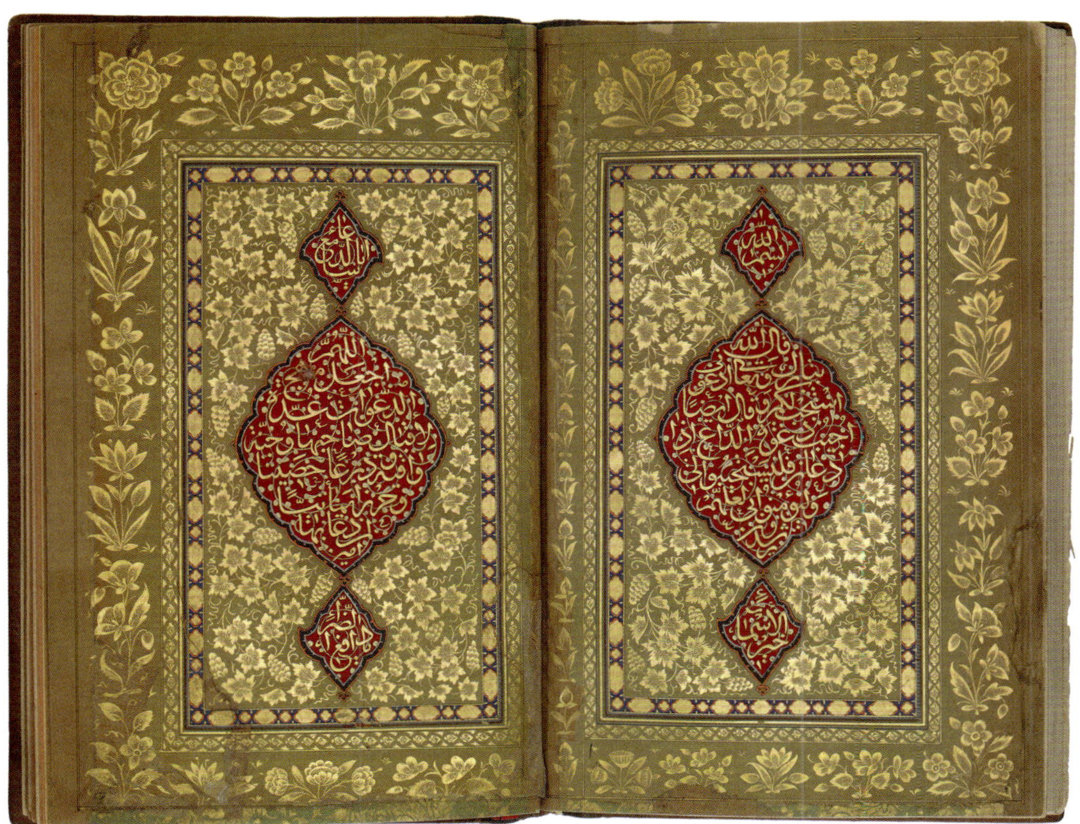

These carpet pages from a book of prayers show the collaboration of two great early eighteenth-century masters, the calligrapher Ahmad Nairizi and the illuminator Muhammad Hadi. Each page consists of a central medallion with two pendants, one above and one below, bearing prayers in Arabic in *riqa'* script, written in gold on a crimson ground. The medallion and pendants are surrounded by a dense pattern of grape-bearing vines and vegetal scrolls, in gold against a pistachio-green ground. Blooming, stemmed flowers in the Indo-Persian style of the time embellish the borders. These pages are two of four in the manuscript that demonstrate the decorative use of *riqa'* within the context of the illuminations, such as the unorthodox ligation of letters that ordinarily do not connect, including *alif* and *lam*, or *re* followed by another *re*.

7

ALBUM FOLIOS WITH PAIRING OF *THULUTH* AND *NASKH* SCRIPTS

Calligrapher: Hamdullah ibn Mustafa Dede (Shaikh Hamdullah; d. 1520)
Probably Turkey, Istanbul, ca. 1500
Ink, watercolor, and gold on plain and marbled paper; leather and gold binding, 12⅝ x 9⅜ in. (32.1 x 23.8 cm)
Purchase, Edwin Binney 3rd and Edward Ablat Gifts, 1982 (1982.120.3)

Album-making was a popular practice in the Ottoman empire. These folios from an album of religious poetry, prayers, and prophetic traditions (the Hadith) are mounted in a horizontal format with colorful marbled (Turkish: *ebru*) borders. Here, the paired, complementary scripts, a large *thuluth* (Turkish: *sulus*) at the top and a minute *naskh* (Turkish: *nesih*) below it (detail), create a balanced composition. The short vowels and diacritical marks are carefully rendered to facilitate readability.

The calligrapher, whose signature is found at the back of the album, is the renowned Hamdullah ibn Mustafa Dede (d. 1520), better known as Shaikh Hamdullah. A follower of Yaqut al-Musta'simi and royal scribe at the imperial atelier of Sultan Beyazid II (r. 1481–1512), he is credited with introducing reforms to certain scripts such as *naskh* that had an enduring impact on Ottoman calligraphy. The combination of the superb hand of Shaikh Hamdullah and the rich and varied marbled borders endows this album with an overall stunning visual effect.

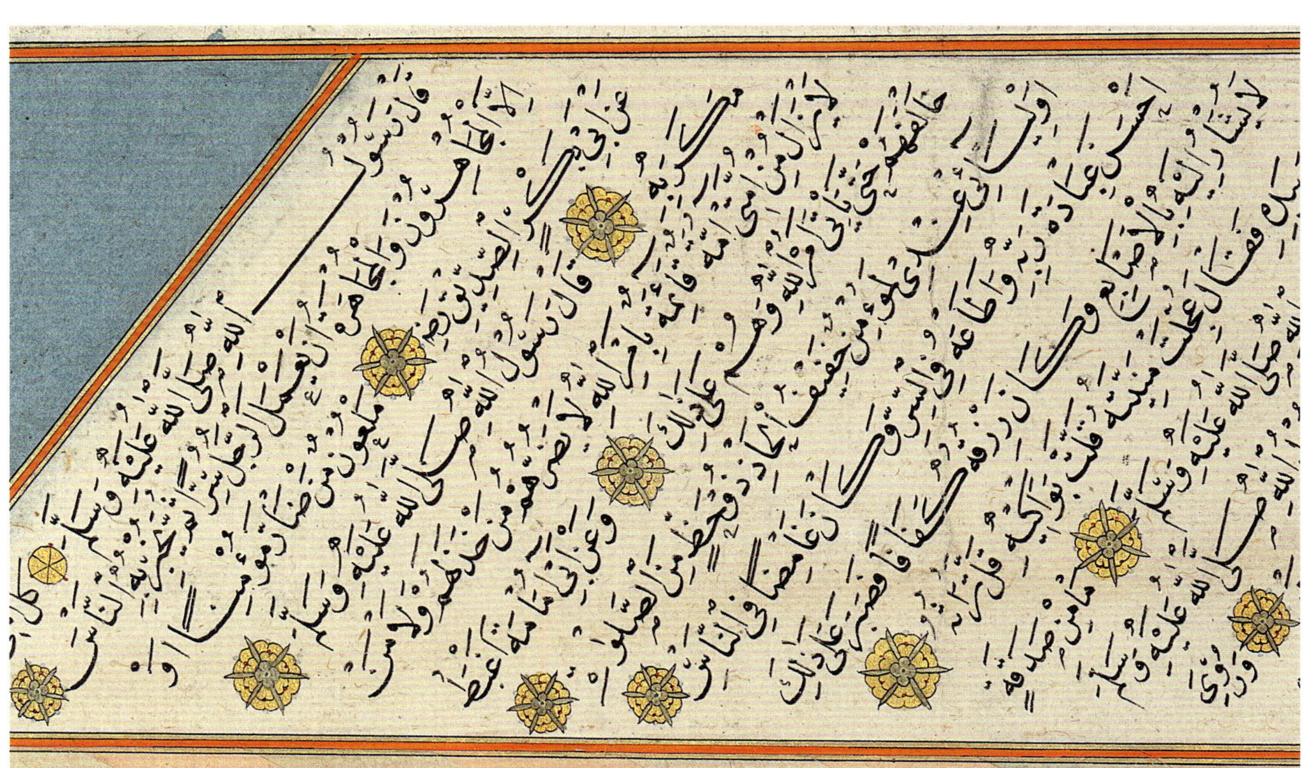

Detail of *naskh* script

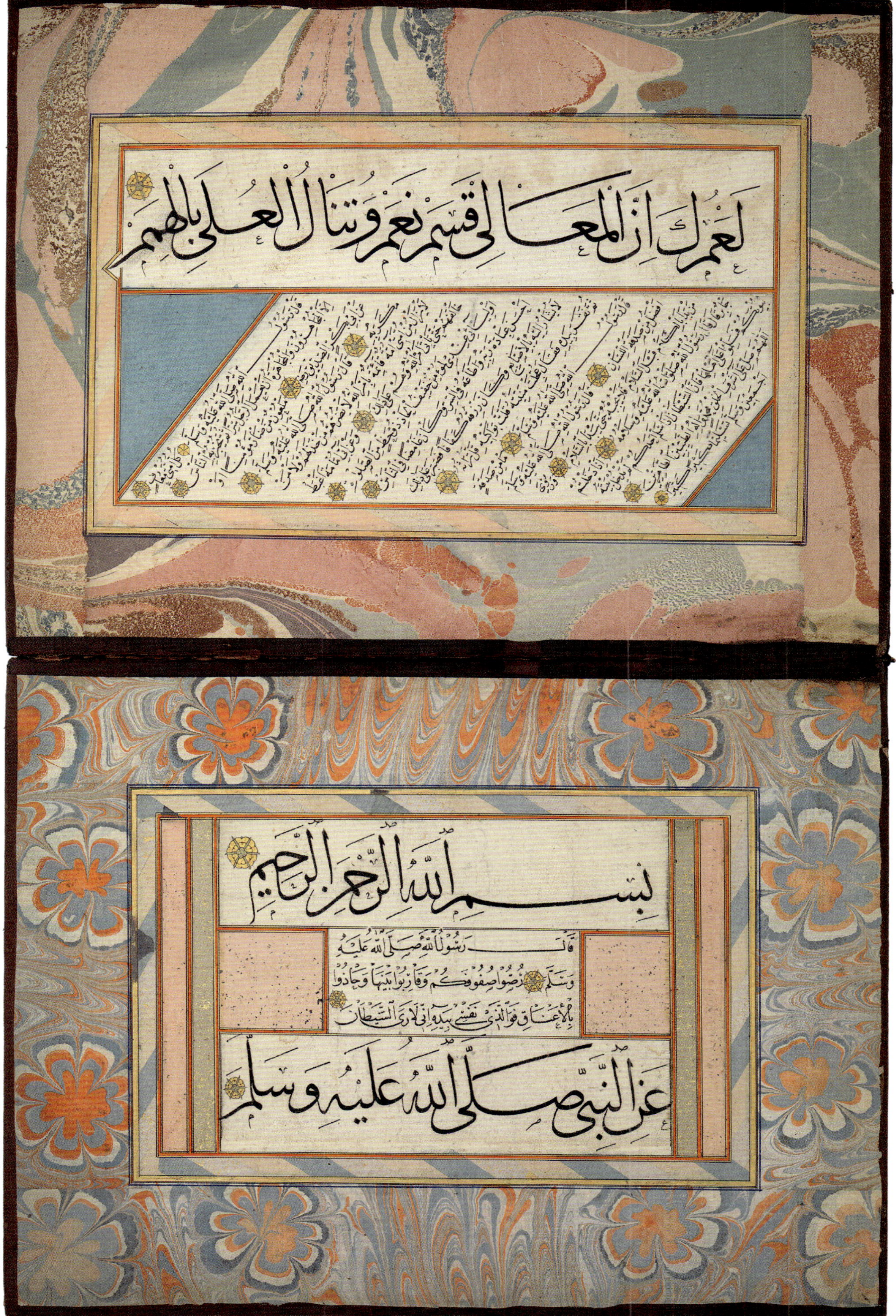

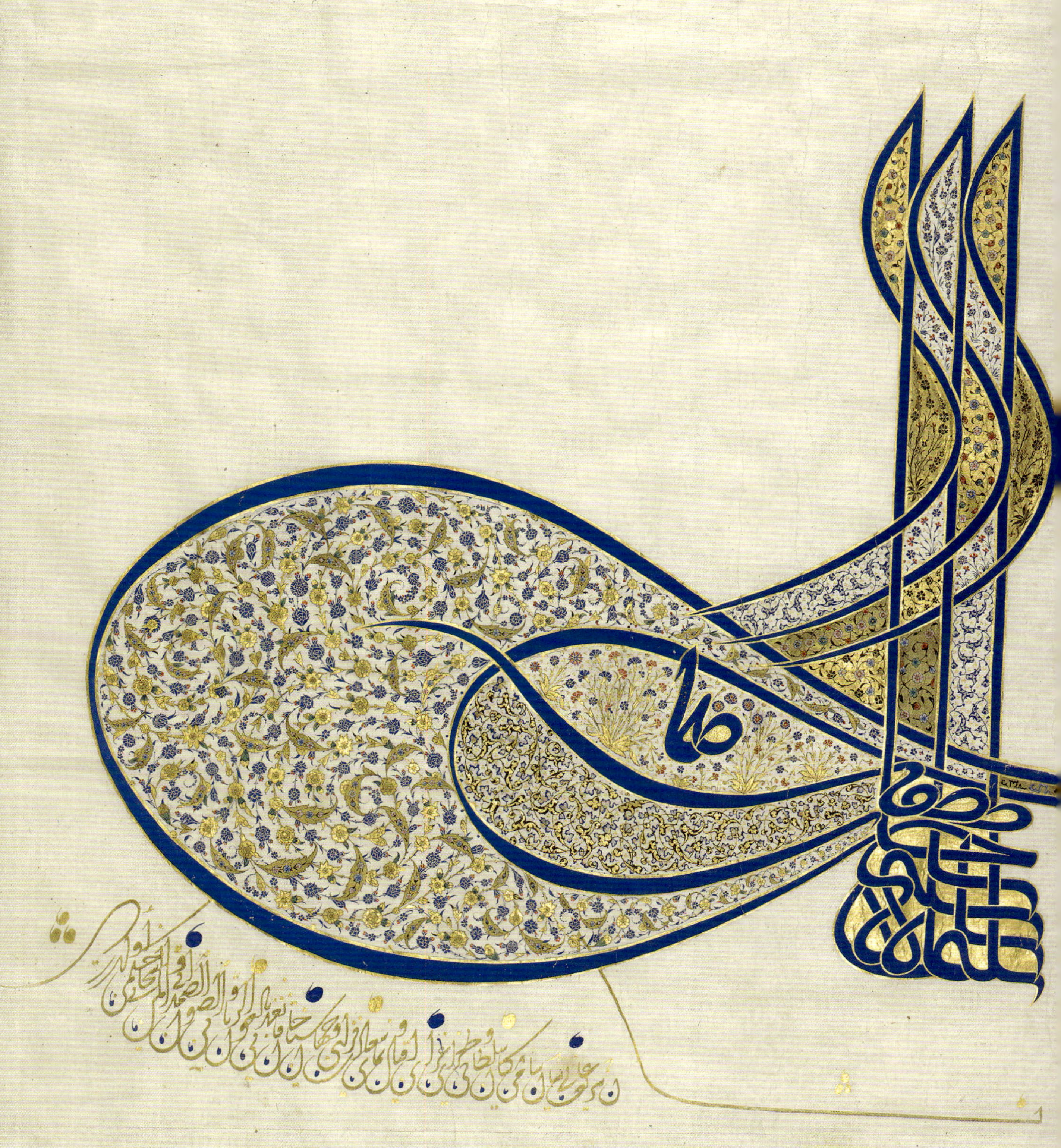

8

INSIGNIA (*TUGHRA*) OF SULTAN SÜLEYMAN THE MAGNIFICENT

Turkey, Istanbul, ca. 1555–60
Ink, opaque watercolor, and gold on paper, 20½ x 25⅜ in. (52.1 x 64.5 cm)
Rogers Fund, 1938 (38.149.1)

This *tughra*, or insignia, of the Ottoman sultan Süleyman I (r. 1520–66) follows a classic four-part format: three loops to the left; a plume of three ligatures at the top; two horizontal ligatures on the right that eventually merge; and, at the bottom, an intertwined inscription that usually includes the name of the sultan, that of his father, and the invocation "May his reign endure forever." Each Ottoman sultan after Orhan (1284–1359) had his own distinct *tughra* that consisted of these four elements. The goal of any document bearing a *tughra* was to communicate a message of authority.

Tughras were not easily read or copied. Therefore, designated court artists known as the *tughrakeş* worked with an illuminator to draw the *tughra* on important imperial documents and to embellish it with exquisite scrolling designs. These skilled artists worked in the Imperial Chancery (Divan), located in the Topkapi Palace in Istanbul, where they created, copied, and recorded all official government *firmans* (orders or decrees), treatises, and correspondence. Their main goal was to render documents aesthetically superb in order to reflect the power and magnificence of the ruling sultan. The script used in the body of *firmans*, known as *divani*—literally, "of the [imperial] council"—was intricate, compact, and very difficult to read; the letters and words intertwine in a slightly upward-sloping manner, reminiscent of the bow of a ship.

This *tughra* reads, "Süleyman, son of Selim Khan, eternal victorious." The text written in gold *divani* script below it is the first line of a long scroll, now truncated. It reads, "This is the noble, exalted, brilliant sign-manual, the world-illuminating and adoring cipher of the *khaqan* [may it be made efficient by the aid of the Lord and the protection the Eternal]. His order is that [. . .]."

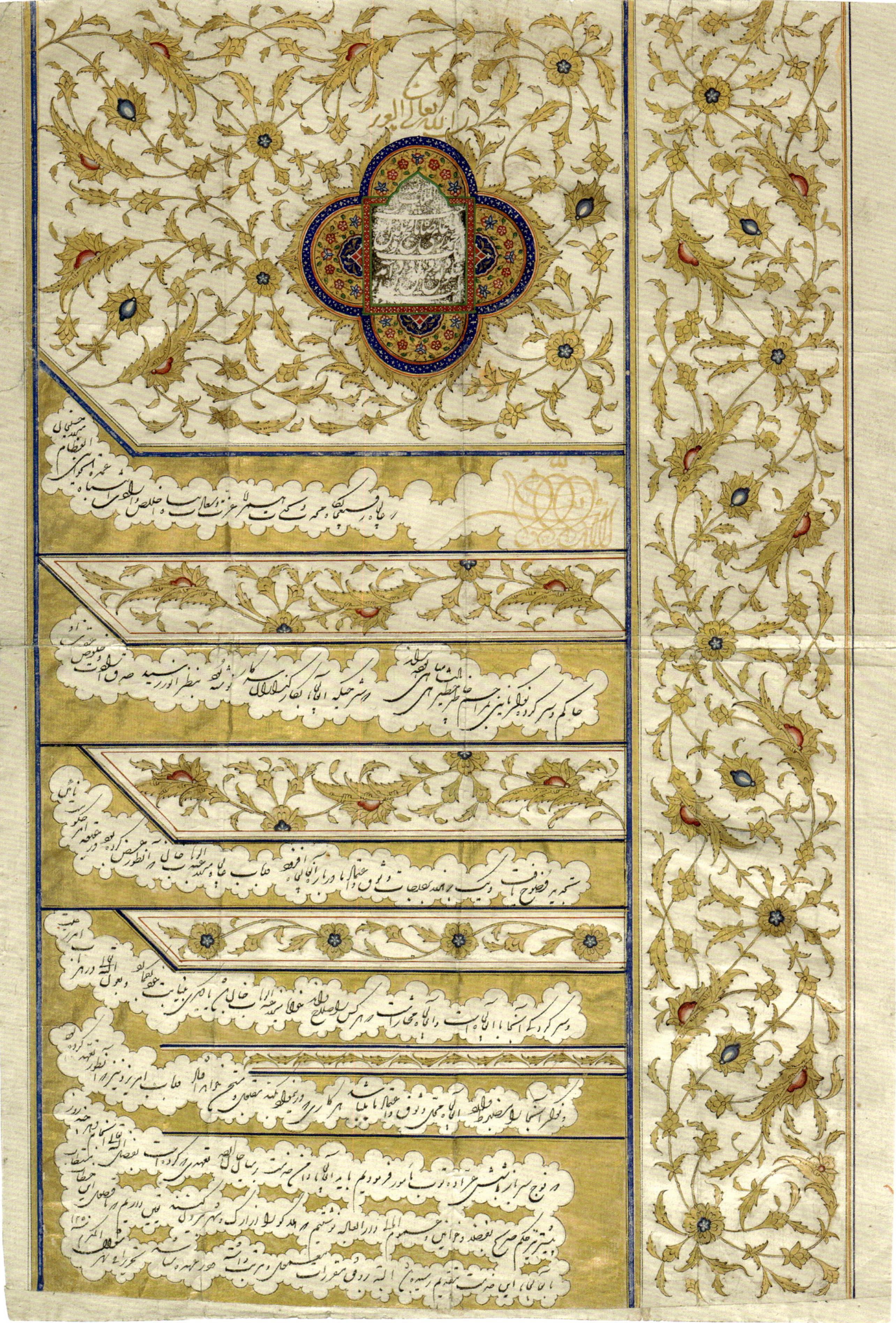

9

EDICT (*FIRMAN*) OF MUHAMMAD SHAH QAJAR IN *SHIKASTA-NASTA'LIQ* SCRIPT

Iran, dated A.H. 1250/A.D. 1835
Ink, opaque watercolor, and gold on paper, 16½ x 11¼ in. (41.9 x 28.6 cm)
Gift of Layla S. Diba, in memory of Mahmood T. Diba, 2013 (2013.243)

Firmans, or royal edicts, are both important historic documents and impressive works of art in their own right. This edict contains eight lines of text; it is a response to a letter addressed to Mirza Husain Khan, the governor of the Na'in region, in central Iran. It is crowned by the seal of Muhammad Shah Qajar (r. 1834–48), third ruler of the Qajar dynasty, enclosed in a polylobed medallion and set against an elaborate web of gold vegetal scrolls.

The text is written in fine *shikasta-nasta'liq*, a script used exclusively for *firmans* and letters. Each line is enclosed in a cloud-shaped cartouche and set against a background of gold leaf (detail). An illuminated panel of serrated vegetal scrolls in gold and other colors appears between each line. In a manner similar to that of *divani* script (see cat. 8), the words at the end of each line are stacked and slope upward. Although this may be attributed to a lack of space, it was more likely an aesthetic choice on the part of the calligrapher, whose name is not mentioned, a feature shared by many royal edicts. The overall effect is one of authority, refinement, and luxury.

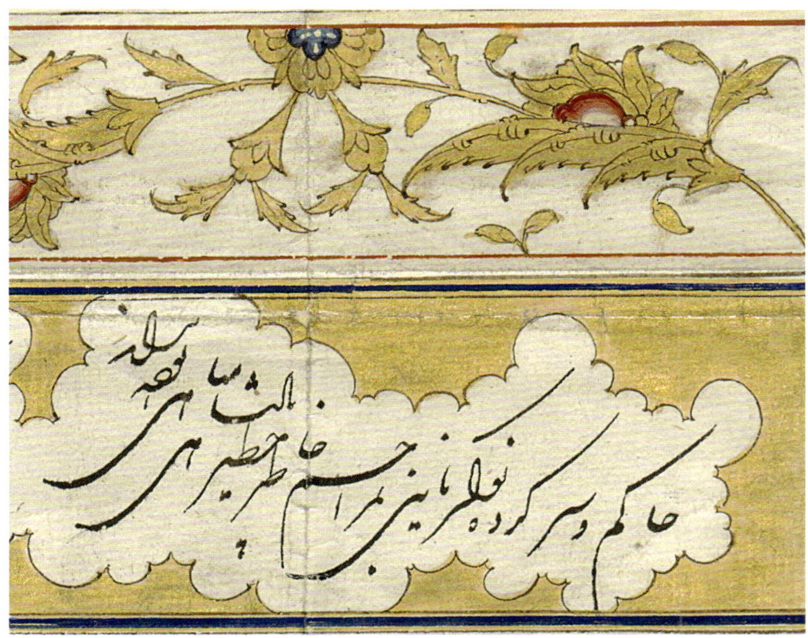

Detail of *shikasta-nasta'liq* script and illuminated flowers

LETTER IN *TA'LIQ* (HANGING) SCRIPT

Calligrapher: Darvish 'Abdullah Munshi (active early 16th century)
Iran, A.H. 911/A.D. 1505–6
Ink, opaque watercolor, and gold on paper, 10¼ x 7⅛ in. (26 x 18 cm)
Purchase, Friends of Islamic Art Gifts, 2015 (2015.139)

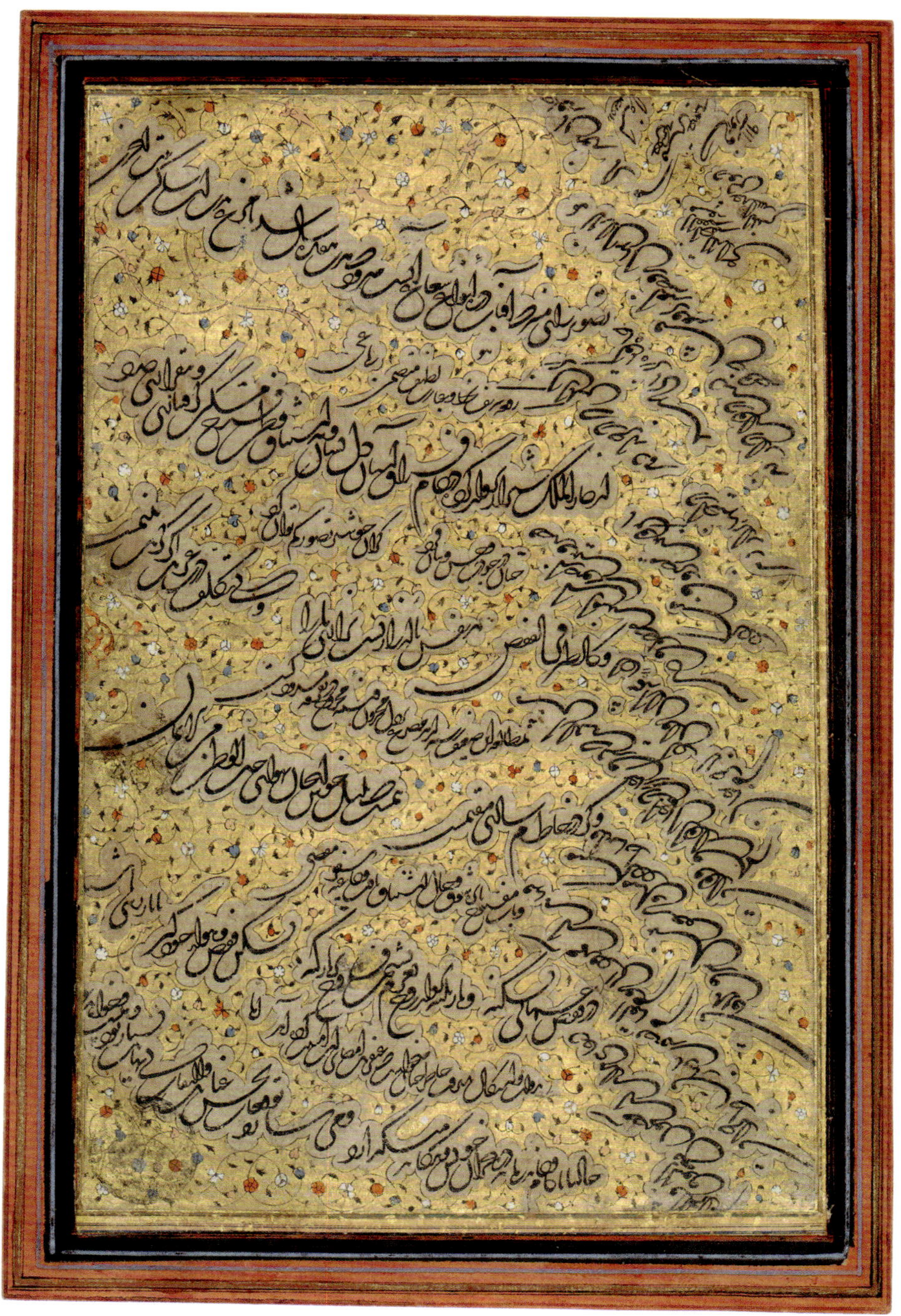

10b

LETTER IN *SHIKASTA* (BROKEN) SCRIPT

Calligrapher: ʿAbd al-Majid Taliqani (1737–71)
Iran, dated A.H. 1176/A.D. 1763
Ink, opaque watercolor, and gold on paper, 9½ x 4½ in. (24.1 x 11.4 cm)
Rogers Fund, 1946 (46.126.4)

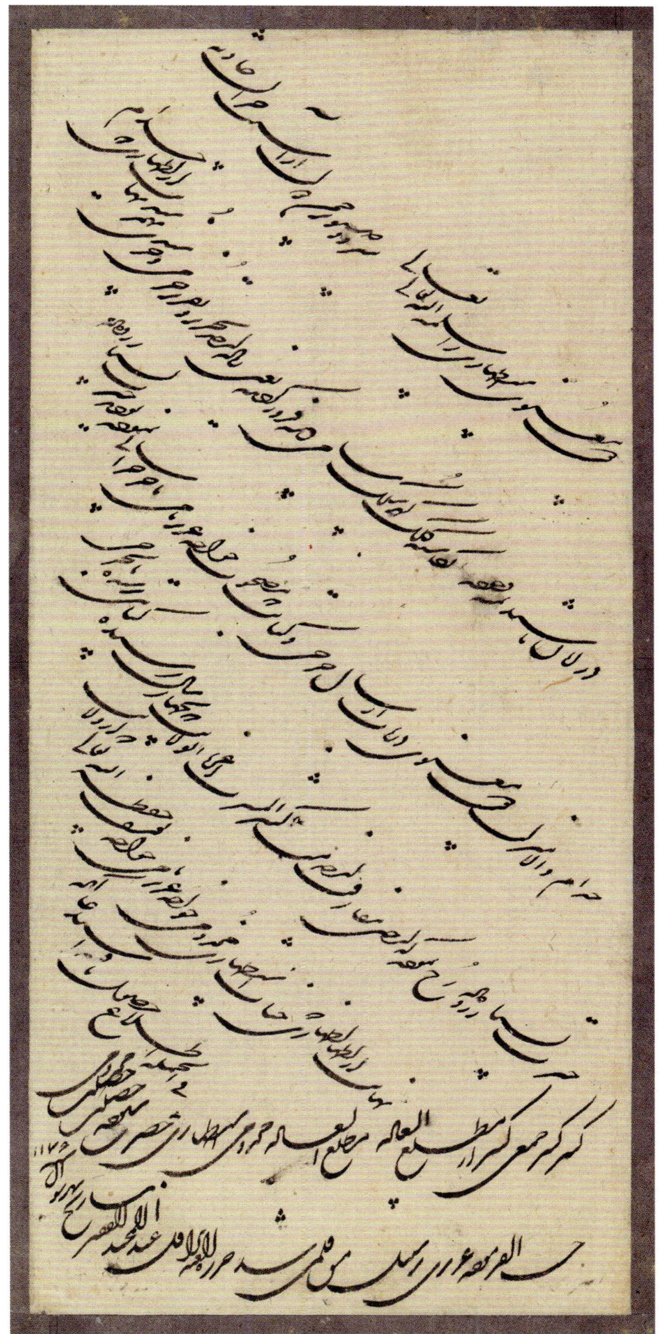

The first letter presented here (cat. 10a) is written in *taʿliq* (hanging) script, which is notable for its emphasis on the descending elements of letters. The sheet is signed by Darvish ʿAbdullah Munshi, a well-known *munshi*, or secretary, of the early Safavid period. In it, the sender/author expresses homesickness for his hometown, Shiraz, which he left some seventeen years before. These sentiments are interspersed with prayers and a quatrain of poetry in Persian. Toward the end, Darvish ʿAbdullah includes a brief personal commentary, saying that it would be hard to imagine a more eloquent and moving text, which leads us to believe that the letter was likely intended by its patron as a gift for a friend, and that Darvish ʿAbdullah was commissioned to copy and embellish it. Such letters were often dictated to a scribe, who penned and decorated them for his patron. Here, irregularity and whimsy are prized, and attention is lavished on the compositional and decorative aspects of the work. In fact, to read the letter, the recipient would have had to rotate the page several times.

The second letter (cat. 10b) is signed by one of the great masters of the *shikasta* (broken) script, ʿAbd al-Majid Taliqani. It consists of eight lines of text, six of which are written diagonally, while the two at the bottom are written horizontally. With its unusual composition and the upward sloping and stacking of words at the end of each line, the letter exhibits the characteristic features of the *shikasta* script. The sweeping quality of the descending letters and the airy flow of the text on the page enhance its compositional dimension.

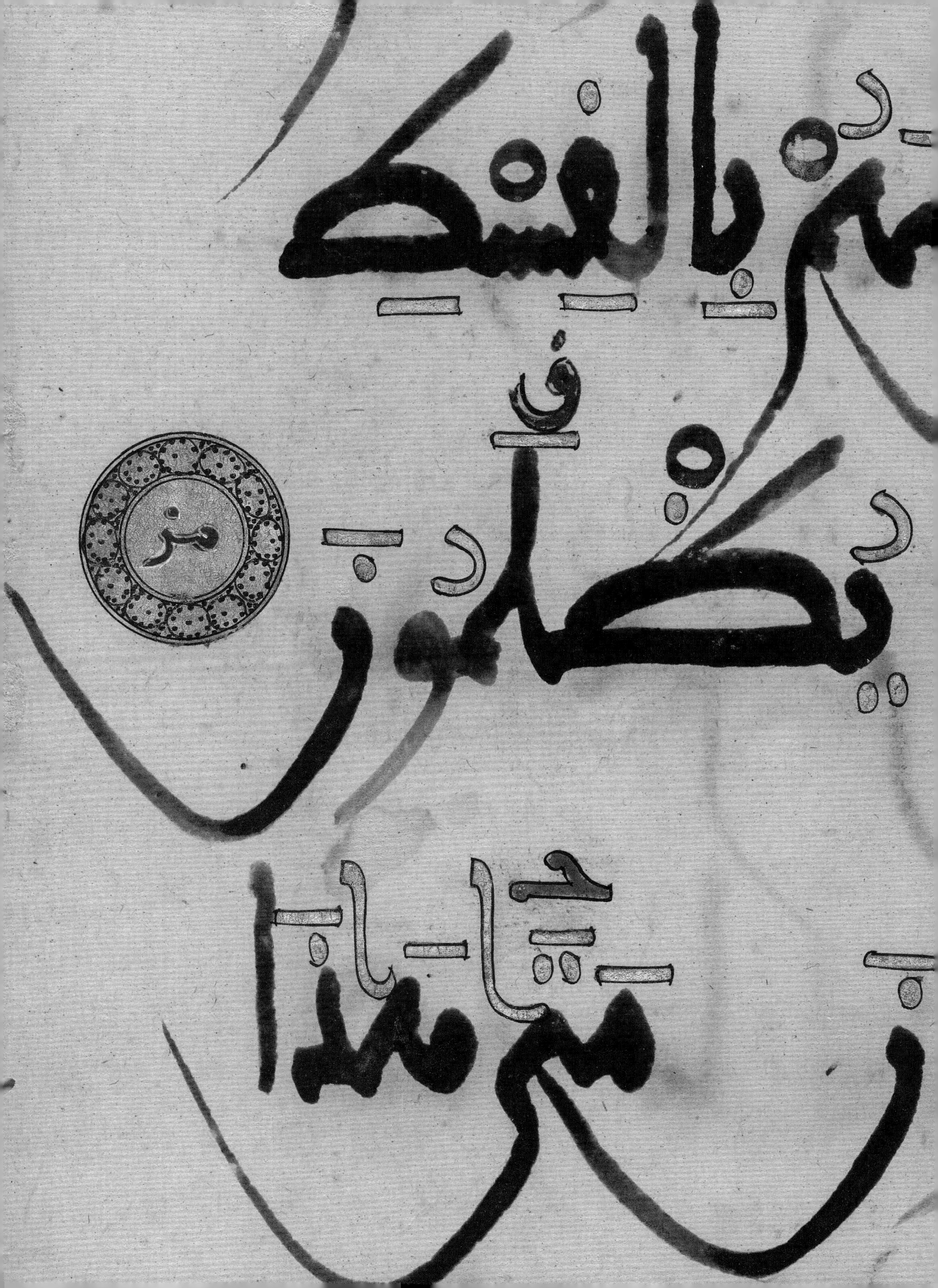

BIFOLIUM FROM THE ANDALUSIAN "PINK QUR'AN" IN *MAGHRIBI* SCRIPT

Spain, ca. 13th century
Ink, gold, silver, and opaque watercolor on paper, 12½ x 19¾ in. (31.8 x 50 cm)
Purchase, Friends of Islamic Art Gifts, 2017 (2017.232)

Qur'ans from the Islamic West, including North Africa and Spain, diverged at an early date from the mainstream of developments farther east. They were nearly always written on parchment in the *maghribi* script, a form of writing exclusive to the region. Although its origins have not been confirmed, *maghribi*, according to some scholars, was the only script to derive from *kufic*. Unlike *kufic*, however, *maghribi* was written freehand and did not adhere to a particular set of proportions. It was limited to manuscripts and rarely appeared on architectural surfaces or objects.

The bifolium belongs to a manuscript attributed to early thirteenth-century Spain known as the "Pink Qur'an," so named for the pinkish hue of the paper. Each folio consists of five lines of verse from *sura* 7 (*al-A'raf*, "The Heights") in a bold *maghribi* script. The text is rendered in dark brown ink, with gold diacritical and vocalization marks outlined in brown, blue, and green. Blue verse numbers, outlined in white, appear within gold disks, and the prostration mark is a teardrop-shaped element in gold. The verse numbers take the form of *abjad* letters, a centuries-old coded system whereby the letters of the Arabic alphabet are assigned numerical values. In addition, the folio contains the word *hubus*, or "pious foundation," which is pricked with a needle at the top left and right corners. The fine and consistent calligraphy, extensive use of gold, and elaborate illumination suggest that this manuscript was probably made for a royal or noble patron in Granada or Valencia, in southern Spain.

The bifolium is rare in that it is rectangular rather than square, the latter being the more traditional format for Qur'ans of the period from Spain and North Africa. Moreover, since the use of parchment for Qur'ans continued well into the fourteenth century in the region, the paper support is also an unusual departure from convention. The paper is believed to have come from the town of Jativa, thirty-five miles southwest of Valencia, and for this reason is referred to in Arabic as al-Warraq al-Shatibi—literally, "Jativa paper." The town was reportedly the site of the earliest paper mill in Spain.

الذي نعدهم أو
نتوفينك فإلينا مر
جعهم ثم الله شهيد
على ما يفعلون
ولكل أمة رسول

يستاخرون ساعة ولا
يستقدمون ○ قل ارا
يتم ان اتكم عذابه
بياتا او نهارا ماذا
يستعجل منه المجرمون

FOLIO FROM THE SHAH JAHAN ALBUM IN *NASTAʿLIQ* SCRIPT

Calligrapher: Sultan ʿAli Mashhadi (active late 15th–early 16th century);
illuminator: Manohar (active ca. 1582–1624)
India, Mughal, recto: late 16th century; verso: ca. 1500
Ink, gold, and colors on paper, 15⁵⁄₁₆ x 10¼ in. (38.9 x 26 cm)
Purchase, Rogers Fund and The Kevorkian Foundation Gift, 1955 (55.121.10.32)

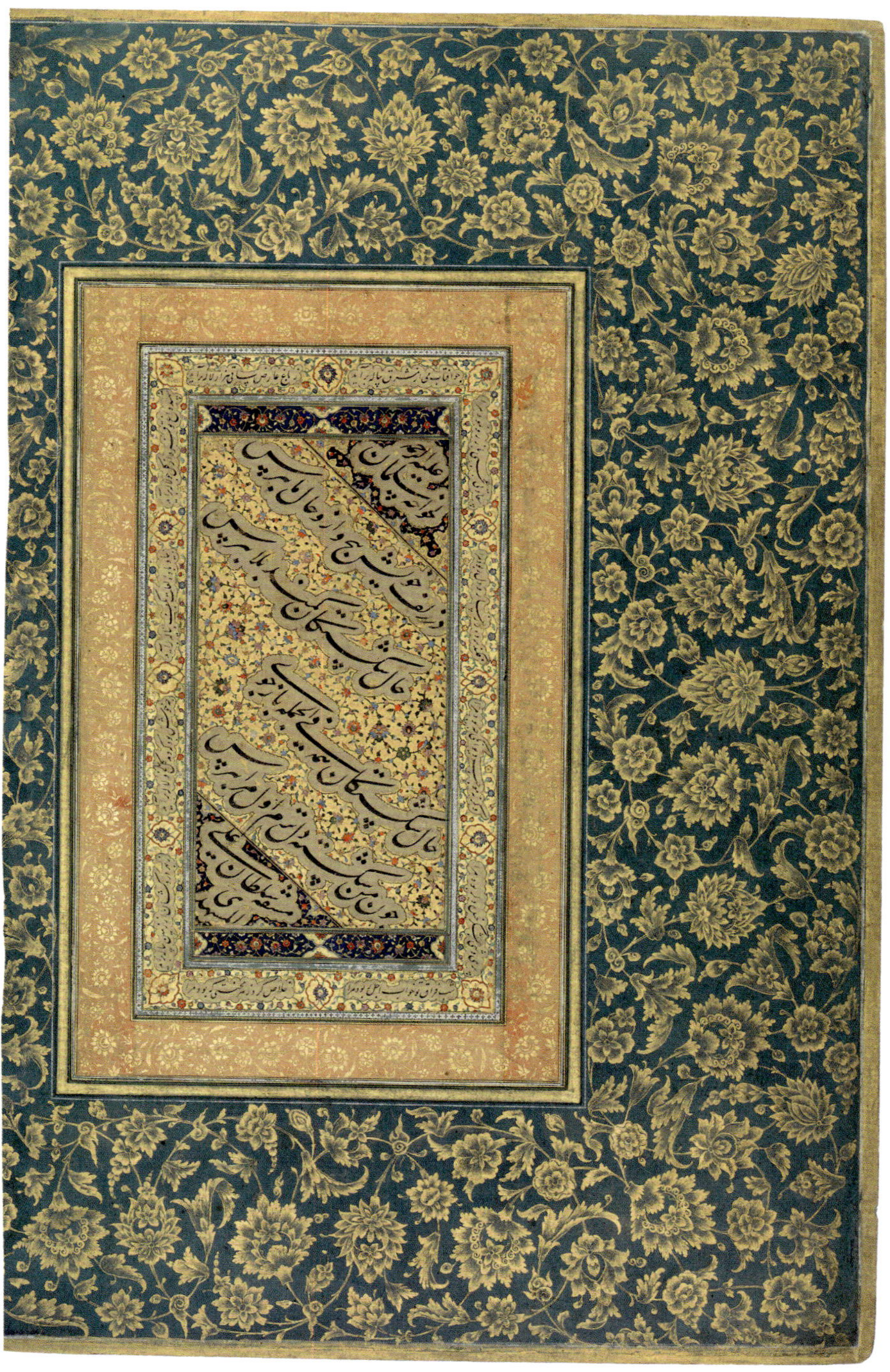

12b

FOLIO FROM THE SHAH JAHAN ALBUM IN *NASTA'LIQ* SCRIPT

Calligrapher: Mir 'Ali Haravi (1476–1544); illuminator: Nanha (active 17th century)
India, recto: ca. 1535–45; verso: ca. 1610–15
Ink, opaque watercolor, and gold on paper, $15\frac{1}{16}$ x $10\frac{5}{16}$ in. (38.3 x 26.2 cm)
Purchase, Rogers Fund and The Kevorkian Foundation Gift, 1955 (55.121.10.4)

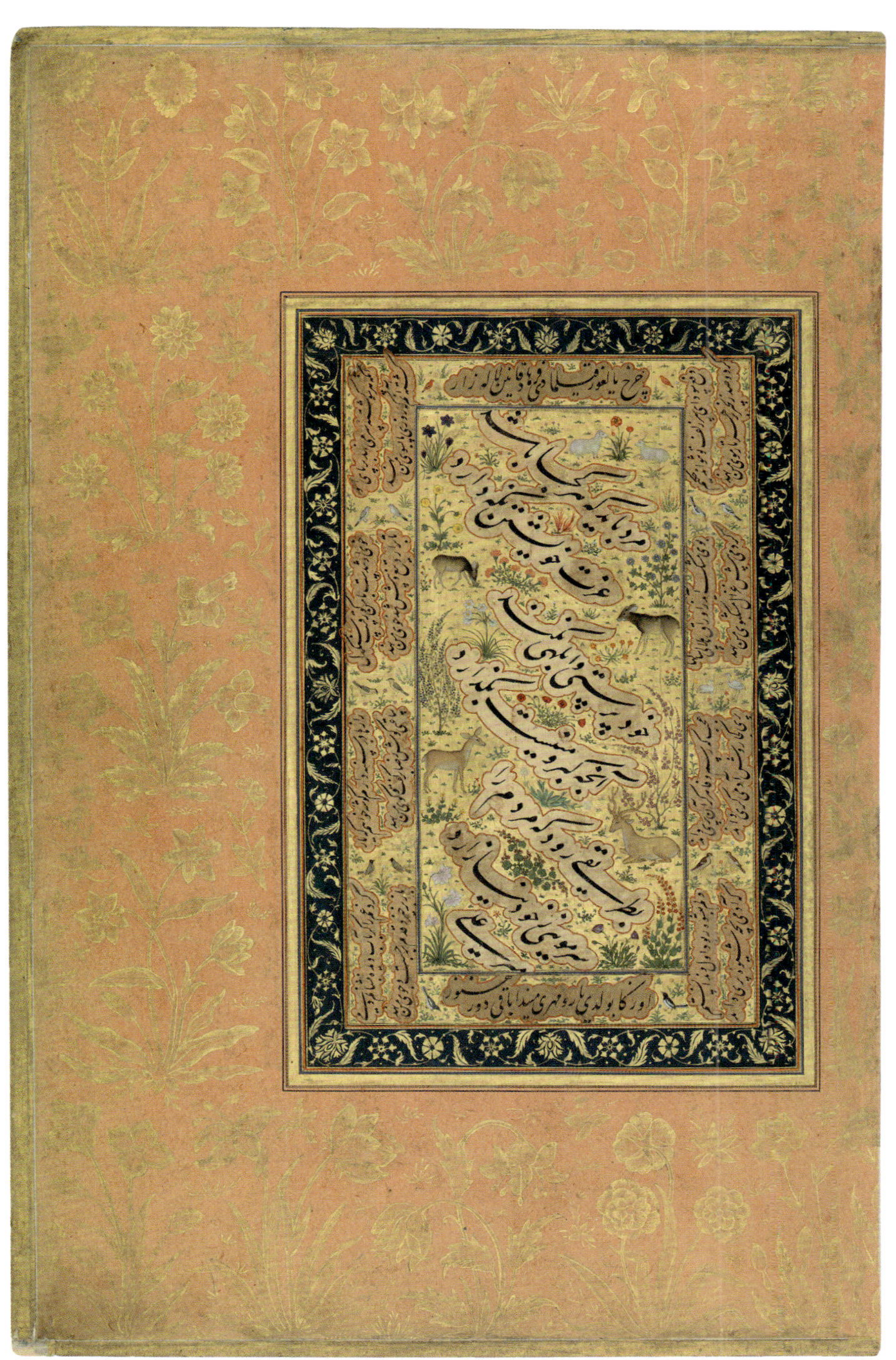

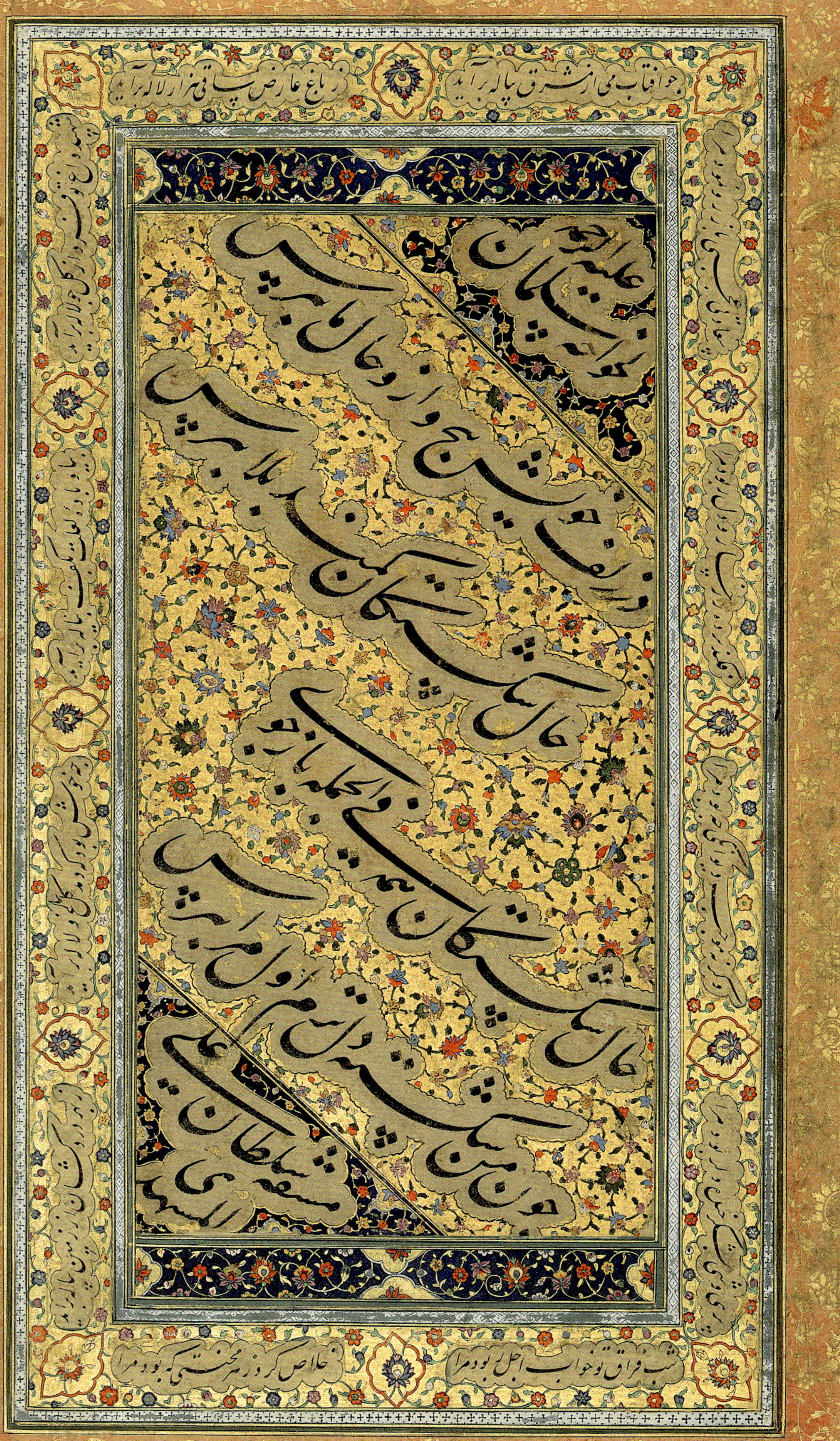

Both of these folios come from the Shah Jahan Album, an album of calligraphies, portraits, and animal studies initiated by the Mughal emperor Jahangir (r. 1605–27) and continued by his son Shah Jahan (r. 1628–58). The first folio (cat. 12a), by Sultan ʻAli Mashhadi, features a quatrain, or series of couplets, of love poetry characterized by mystical allusions and Sufi metaphors, written in diagonal lines of *nastaʻliq*. The main poem, composed by the fourteenth-century poet Khwaja Salman al-Savuji, equates the tresses of the beloved with the snares entangling the hearts of lovers. The surrounding couplets were probably written by Sultan ʻAli. The border illumination of gold floral scrolls and serrated leaves against a background of teal green is as delicate and lyrical as the calligraphy. The main poem reads:

> Coil up in your own tress / And then ask how I am,
> How are those whom the snare / Of your affliction broke:
> You want to know how all / Those broken lovers fare—
> Then ask me first, for I / Am the most broken one.

The second folio (cat. 12b) features a quatrain in Persian by the late fourteenth-century Persian poet Ibn Yaqmin. It is written in fine *nastaʻliq* and signed by the Timurid calligrapher Mir ʻAli Haravi of Herat. Calligraphies by Mir ʻAli were admired and collected by both Jahangir and Shah Jahan, who had them reset within contemporary seventeenth-century illuminated margins and, as here, included in albums along with finely painted portraits of rulers, princes, and courtiers, as well as animal studies, by an array of Mughal masters.

The flowering plants and grazing animals surrounding the verses on this folio are presented in pairs and painted with extraordinary sensitivity and accuracy (detail). They have been identified as egrets, magpies, robins, and nightingales on the outer borders, and animals including sambars, goats, and *nilgai* (blue bulls native to India) on the central panel. The seventeenth-century Mughal court painter Nanha probably painted them from direct observation. The poem on the central panel reads:

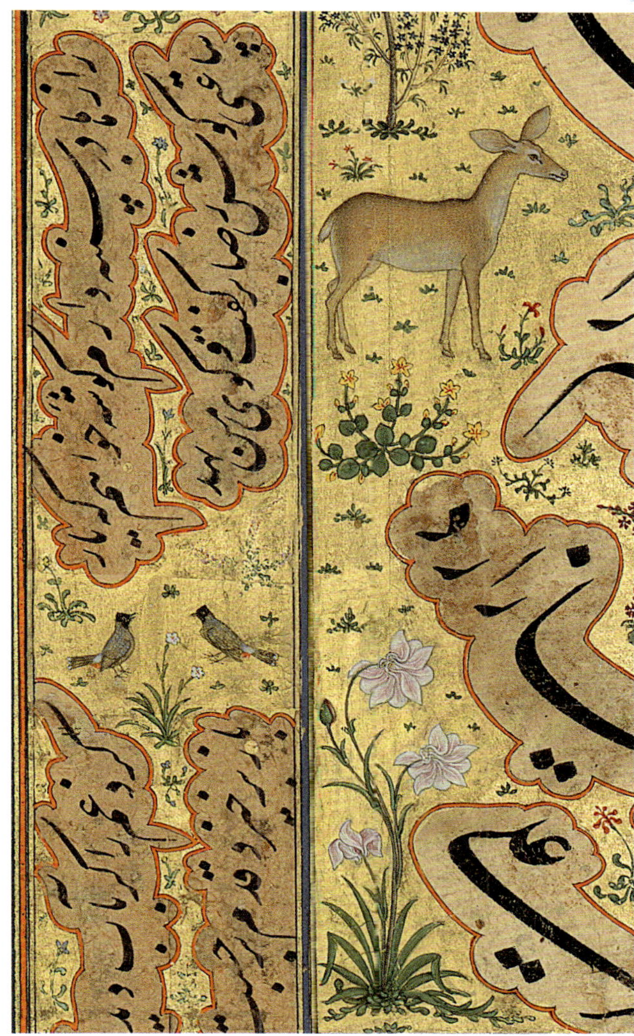

Detail of illuminated flora and fauna in cat. 12b

> A true man should, wherever he is / Preserve his honor
> well;
> Show no conceit or foolishness / Or selfish pride in life
> And act so that nobody's hair / Is touched or hurt by him

13

PRAYER BOOK IN PRAISE OF IMAM ʿALI IN LARGE *NASTAʿLIQ* SCRIPT

Calligrapher: Hasan ʿAli (d. 1594/95)
Iran, dated A.H. 970/A.D. 1562
Ink, opaque watercolor, and gold on paper; leather and gold binding, 11½ x 7½ in. (29.2 x 19.1 cm)
Purchase, Friends of Islamic Art Gifts, 2017 (2017.95)

With only seven lines to a page on a background of gold floral scrolls, the folios of this prayer book in praise of Imam ʿAli are notable for the unusually large size of their *nastaʿliq* script and spacious layout. The opening page features a delicately illuminated heading, or *sarlawh*, and the last page contains a colophon with the name of the calligrapher, Hasan ʿAli, and the date of production, A.H. 970 (A.D. 1562).

Hasan ʿAli is one of a group of documented calligraphers during Shah Tahmasp's reign (1524–76). He is cited in a sixteenth-century treatise on calligraphers and painters as one of two pupils of Mir ʿAli Haravi from Herat. Other sources refer to him as a talented practitioner of *nastaʿliq* who was particularly adept at writing at a large scale. The prayer book represents a particular moment in Tahmasp's reign when the shah is said to have given preference to and rewarded poets who wrote eulogies of Imam ʿAli and the other Shiʿi Imams, rather than those who composed verses praising him. Given the date and content of the manuscript, this prayer book could very well be one of these eulogies documenting this important development in Tahmasp's patronage.

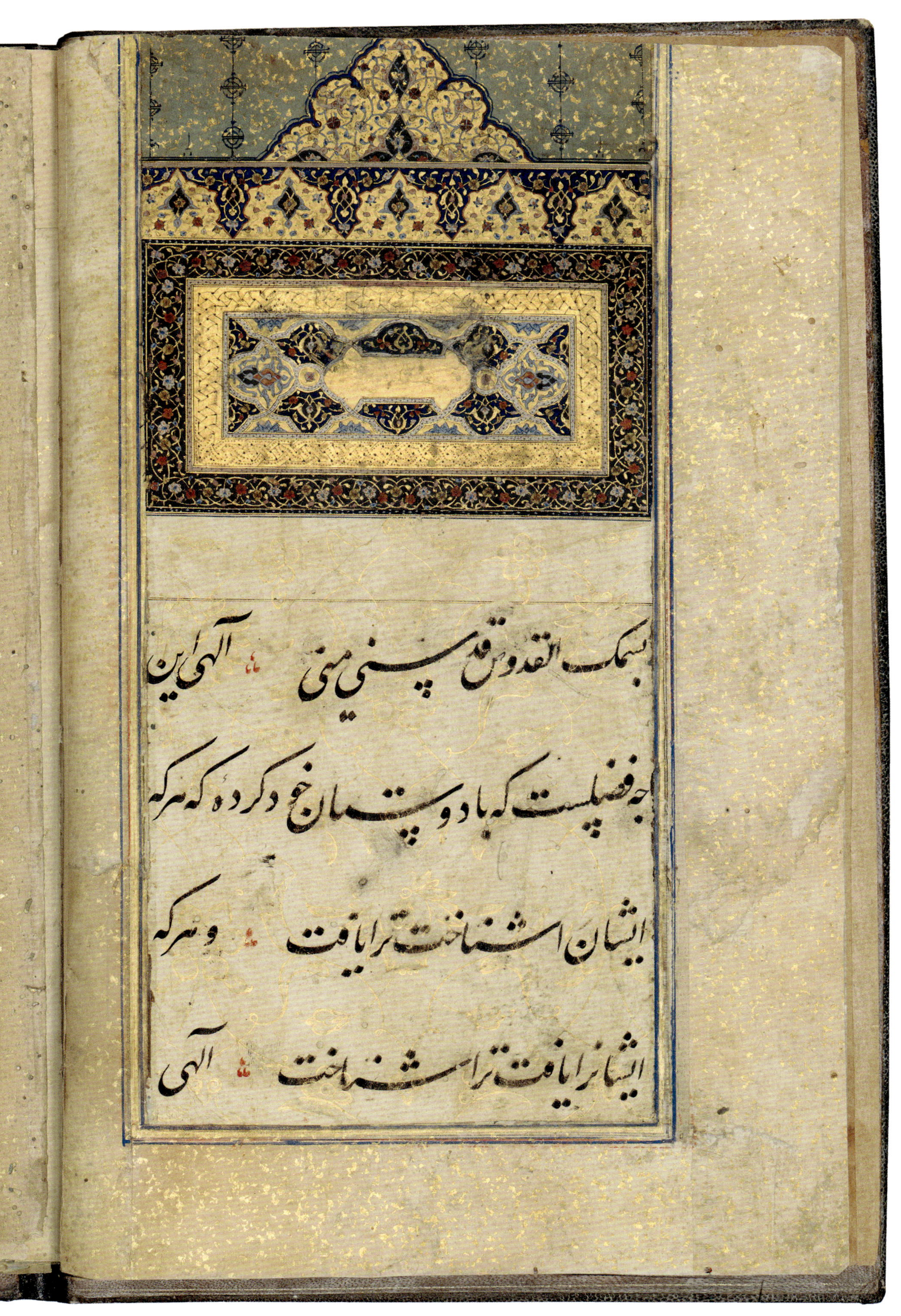

بسمك القدوس قدسني مني ۞ الهی این
چه فضلیست که با دوستان خود کرده که هر که
ایشانرا شناخت ترا یافت ۞ و هر که
ایشانرا یافت ترا شناخت ۞ الهی

همه را از آن حرف بسوخت

نقل از خط شریف حضرت استادی مخدومی

امیر سید احمد الحسینی

مشقه العبد الفقیر الحقیر المذنب حسن علی

غفر الله ذنوبه

و ستر عیوبه

۹۷

اول با توبه آخر ٭ اگر هنر از فهم داری

فرا آب ده ٭ خاک قدم مردان را

آب ده ٭ حرفی که از قلم خیزد

پیداست کز آن چه خیزد ٭ حرف آنست

که الله بر دل بنده ریزد ٭ یکی هفتاد سال

علم آموخت چراغی نیفروخت ٭

یکی در همه عمر یک حرف شنید

14

BRUSH REST WITH INSCRIPTION IN PERSIAN

China, Ming dynasty (1368–1644), Zhengde period (1506–21)
Porcelain painted with cobalt blue under transparent glaze (Jingdezhen ware), L. 8¾ in. (22.2 cm)
Rogers Fund, 1918 (18.56.14)

This Chinese blue-and-white porcelain brush rest takes the shape of a mountain with five peaks, representing the five great mountains of Taoism. Its unusual shape is perfectly suited to its function: the rounded grooves are ideal for holding a calligrapher's brush. Each side bears a Persian inscription at its center. When combined, the words read *khama-dan*—literally, "pen-holder"—which discloses the purpose of the object.

The work belongs to a group of blue-and-white wares, including bowls, platters, pen boxes, containers, and vases, that were produced in China during the Zhengde period and are characterized by the use of Arabic and Persian inscriptions. Many retain their regnal marks; the one on this example appears on the underside. This particular shape was apparently new within this category of wares, and many such objects, including the present example, were intended as accessories for a scholar's writing table. They were likely made for high-ranking Muslim officials, particularly the Central Asian eunuchs who had been captured or purchased by the

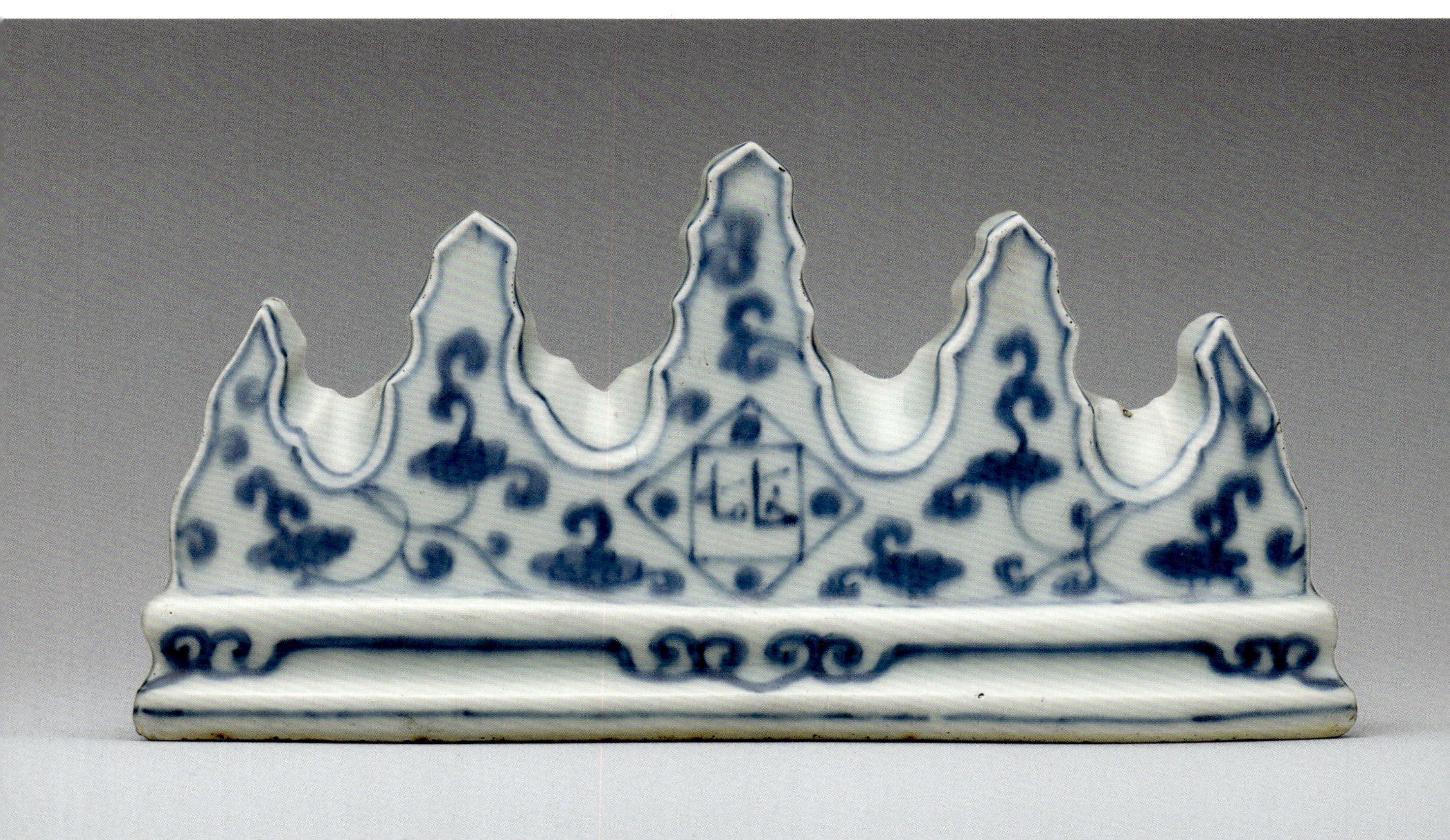

Front

Ming court. These individuals exercised great power at the court of the Zhengde emperors and were often tasked with overseeing the operation of the royal Jingdezhen kilns. According to historical sources, Muslim communities thrived in sixteenth-century southern China, and many Muslims held prominent positions. Furthermore, the Ming dynasty was an active trade partner of the great Muslim empires of the time—the Ottomans, Safavids, and Mughals—as well as the kingdoms of Southeast Asia. While this brush rest may well have been made for a Muslim at the Ming court, it may just as likely have been intended as a fine export item.

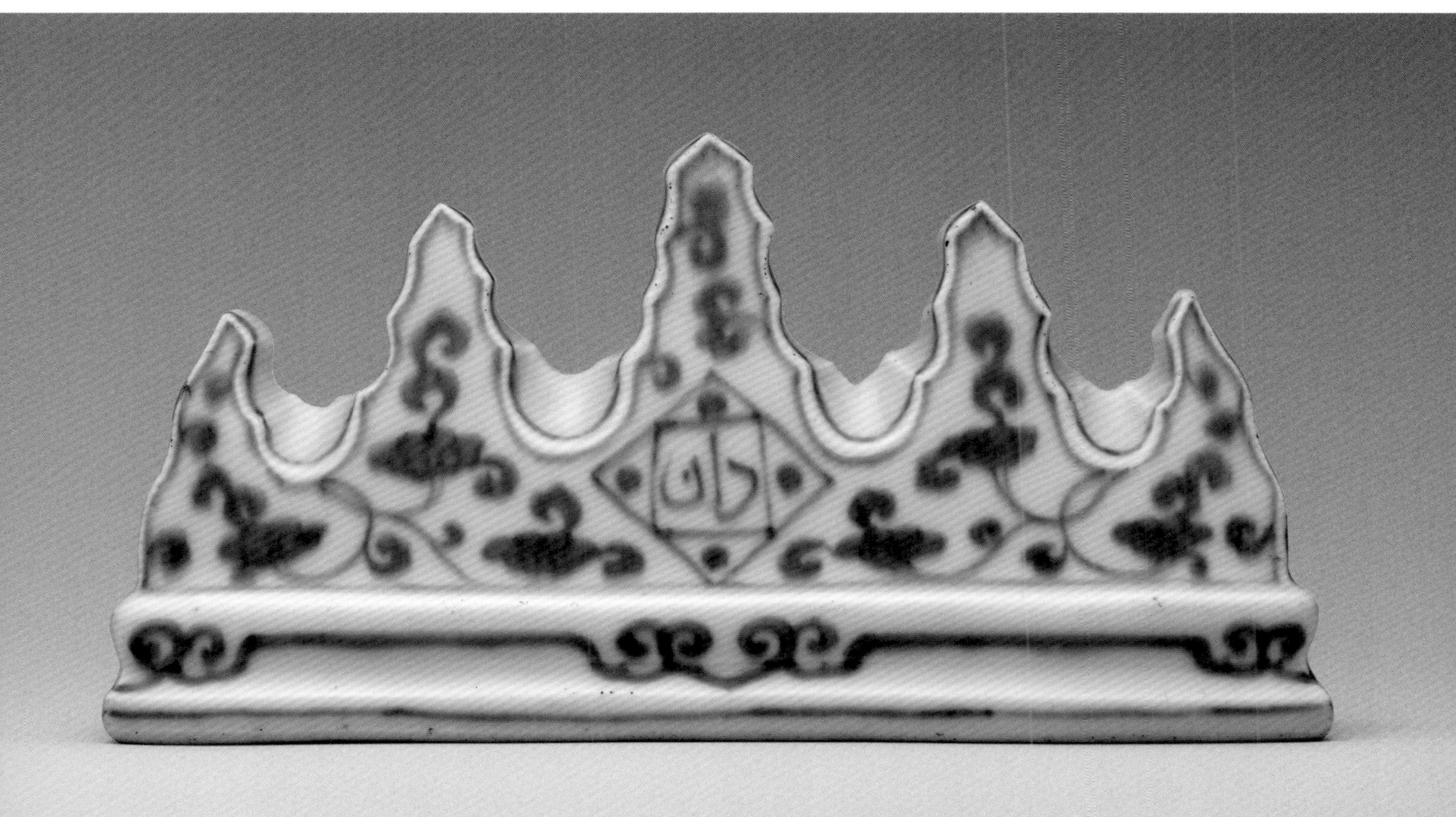

Back

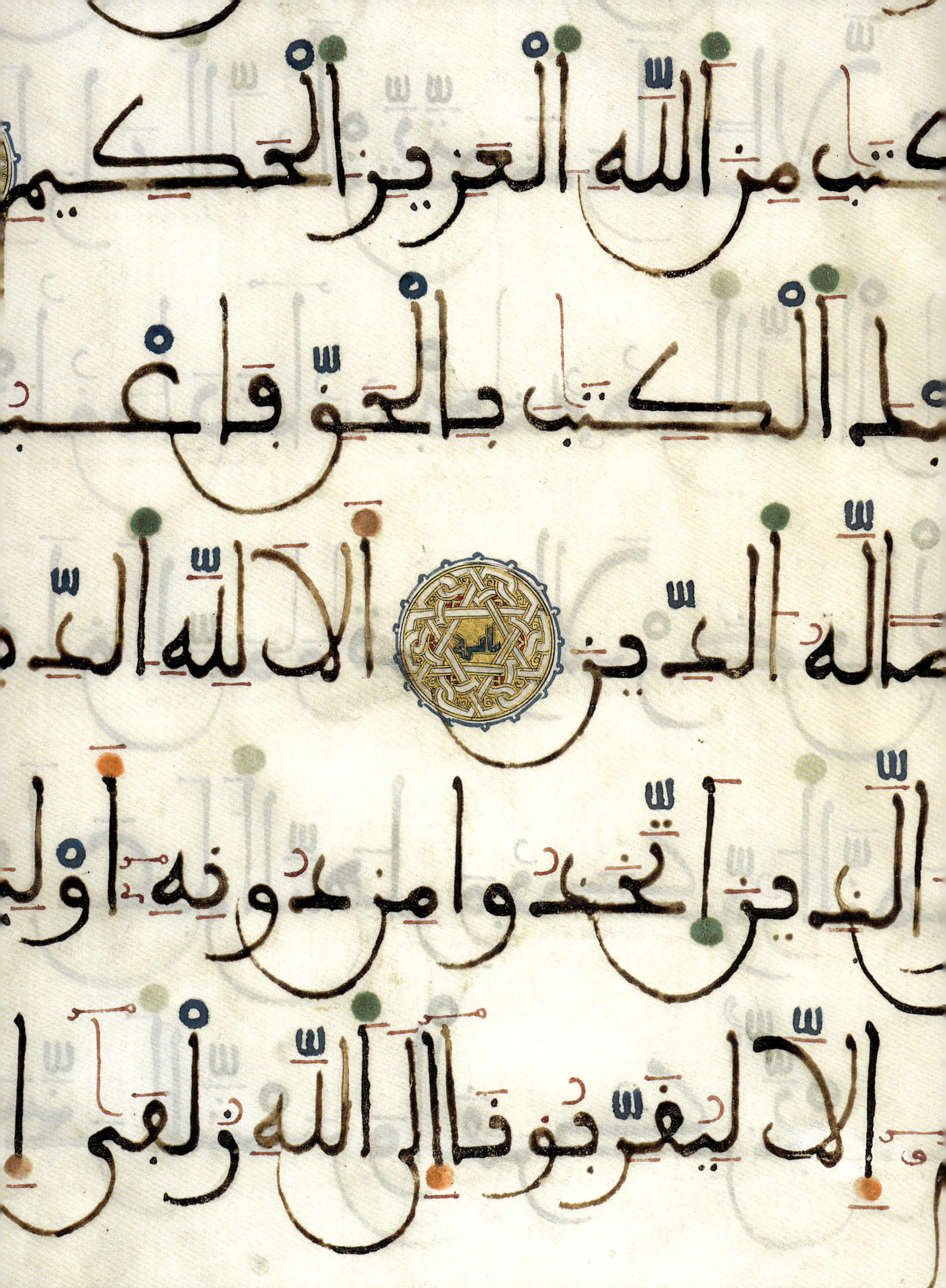

ـب من الله العزيز الحكيم

ـك الكتب بالحق فاعبـ

ـصا له الدين ۝ ألا لله الد

الذين اتخذوا من دونه أولـ

إلا ليقربونا إلى الله زلفى إ

EMBELLISHING THE WORD OF GOD

ARABIC AND THE ART OF THE QUR'AN

The unparalleled prominence of the written word in Islamic culture is innately connected to the Muslim holy book, the Qur'an, which Muslims believe was conveyed to the Prophet Muhammad by the Archangel Gabriel during what is known as the Divine Revelation. Muslims therefore regard the Qur'an as a physical manifestation of God's message—that is, the literal word of God—and copying the holy book as an act of devotion. The organic link between the Qur'an and Arabic, the language in which Gabriel spoke the Revelation, rendered Arabic the primary language of Islam and helped establish the artistic supremacy of calligraphy throughout the Islamic world.

Muhammad began having visions when he was forty years old. Searching for an understanding of their significance, he would sometimes meditate at Mount Hira, near his hometown of Mecca, on the Arabian Peninsula. On one of these occasions, the Archangel Gabriel (Jibra'il in Arabic) appeared to him and instructed him to repeat "in the name of [your] Lord who created; created man from an embryo; recite, for your Lord is most beneficent, who taught by the pen, taught man what he did not know" (Qur'an 96:1–5). It was the first of many revelations that became the basis of the Qur'an (fig. 29). This *aya* (verse) also contains two key terms that served to forever elevate the status of the written word in Islamic culture: first, that the Prophet was asked to "recite" the word of God, and second, that he was "taught by the pen."

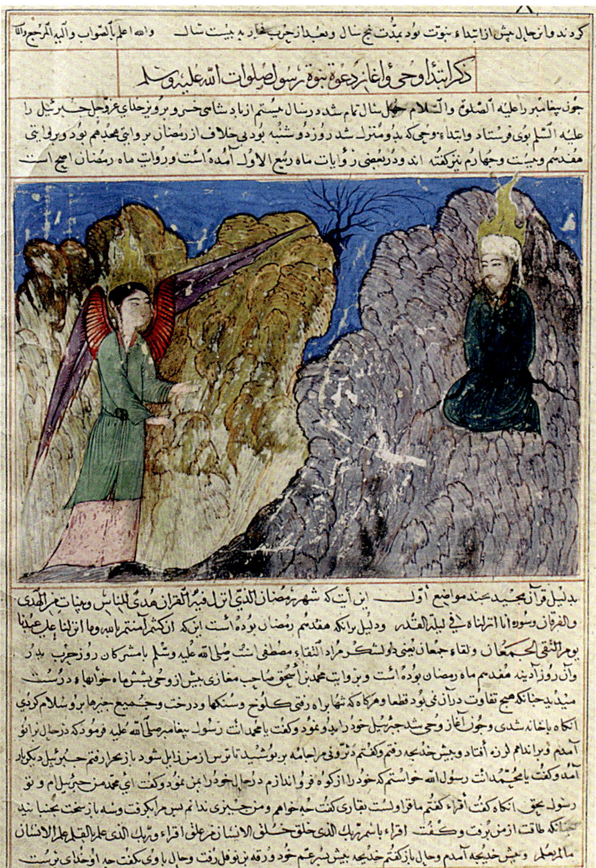

Fig. 29. "Muhammad's Call to Prophecy and the First Revelation," folio from a *Majma' al-Tavarikh* (Compendium of Histories). Present-day Afghanistan, Herat, ca. 1425. Opaque watercolor, silver, and gold on paper, 16⅞ x 13¼ in. (42.8 x 33.7 cm). Cora Timken Burnett Collection of Persian Miniatures and Other Persian Art Objects, Bequest of Cora Timken Burnett, 1956 (57.51.37.3)

The Prophet continued to receive divine messages over the course of the next twenty years. They stressed the existence of a single God, contradicting the polytheistic beliefs of the pre-Islamic Arabian Peninsula. Initially, Muhammad's strong monotheistic message angered many of the Meccan merchants, who were afraid that trade, which they believed was protected by the pagan gods, would suffer. As the situation in Mecca became increasingly dire, Muhammad was ostracized and, in 622, fled to Medina, where his message was embraced. The Prophet's flight from Mecca to Medina is referred to as the *hijra*, which means "flight" in Arabic and marks the first year of the *hijri* calendar (denoted as "A.H.").

Muhammad recorded the revelations as they occurred, transcribing Gabriel's words onto stones, palm leaves, bone, and any other material at hand, and he repeated them orally to his circle of companions. Toward the end of his life, he began to create a comprehensive record of these revelations but was unable to complete the project before his death, in 632. In the following years, for fear of losing parts of the scriptures, his most trusted companions undertook the task of collecting and compiling these texts, beginning with Abu Bakr (r. 632–34), the first of the four Rightly Guided Caliphs. (According to Sunni Muslims, the Rightly Guided Caliphs, or *khulafa-yi rashidun*, are the legitimate successors of the Prophet and leaders of the Islamic community.) The final codified, consonantal form of the Qur'an is thought to have been produced during the reign of 'Uthman (r. 644–56), the third Rightly Guided Caliph, and its text has remained almost unaltered to the present day. 'Uthman sent copies of the holy book to the chief centers of the caliphate—Damascus, Kufa, Basra, and Mecca—together with a reciter, who instructed each community on the text's correct recitation. Later, to preserve the authentic vocalization of the Qur'an, a system of written diacritical marks, indicating short vowels, was developed to complement the consonantal structure.

'Uthman's actions underscore the extent to which both the oral and written dimensions of the divine message are critical to a full understanding of the Qur'an, which according to the scholar Marmaduke Pickthall is an "aural-oral phenomenon." In other words, one cannot fully appreciate the text if one has never heard it, for as Pickthall explains, "it is an inimitable symphony, the very sounds of which move men to tears and ecstasy." And indeed, the Qur'an is meant to be heard as much as read or seen. Hearing its verses is considered the most immediate encounter with the divine. It is chanted in mosques and from the minarets of cities, and recited at weddings, births, and burials. The "art of recitation" (*tajwid*)—perfecting the correct pronunciation, rhythm, timbre, and structure of the text—remains a key discipline into the present day.

Transcribing the Earliest Qur'ans

Traditionally, verses from the Qur'an were rarely written on papyrus; instead, parchment, a generic term referring to the skins of animals such as sheep, goats, and calves,

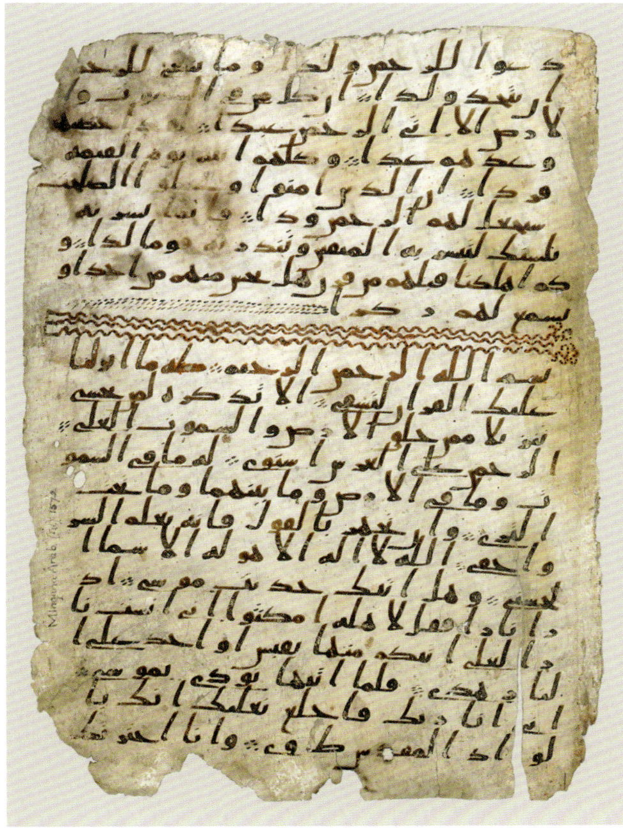

Fig. 30. Folio from an early Qur'an manuscript in *hijazi* script. Hijaz Province, Arabian Peninsula, probably mid-7th century. Ink on parchment. Cadbury Research Library, University of Birmingham (Mingana 1572a)

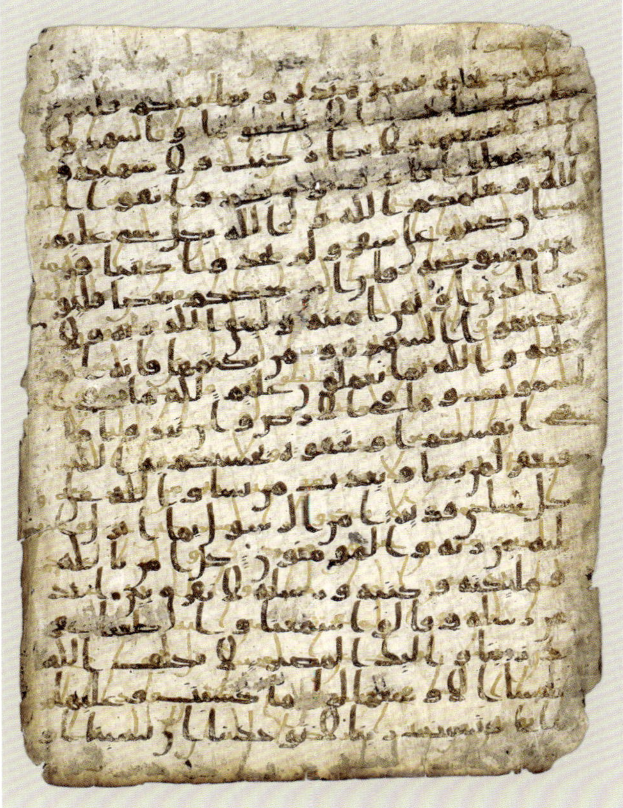

Fig. 31. Qur'anic palimpsest. Syria or Hijaz Province, Arabian Peninsula, second half of 7th century. Ink on parchment, 14⅜ x 11⅛ in. (36.6 x 28.2 cm). David Collection, Copenhagen (86/2003)

was deemed the ideal support for carrying the divine message. Qur'an manuscripts on parchment are referred to as *al-masahif* in Arabic. The fragmentary nature of surviving copies on parchment before the ninth century and the absence of colophons, dates, names of calligraphers, and other identifiers complicate their precise dating, attribution, and classification. Thus, scholars have had to rely on other types of documentation, such as notices of pious endowments, or *waqfiyyahs*, and scientific methods like carbon-14 dating.

The earliest Qur'an folios are vertical in format and executed in *hijazi*, an unofficial script named after a province in northwest Arabia where the holy cities of Mecca and Medina are located. (It is, however, unlikely that these texts were made in that region.) *Hijazi* is characterized by the rightward slanting of the letter shafts and the distinct shape of the final *ya*, which turns backward to underline the letter that precedes it (fig. 30). These early Qur'ans were largely devoid of consonant points (*i'jam*) that phonetically distinguish letters of similar shape, and of short vowel marks that aid pronunciation. As the text of the Qur'an was often memorized and not read word for word, early copies were designed as an aide-mémoire for oral recitation. Another distinguishing feature of these early Qur'ans is the single column of text, which differed from the multicolumn codices of other cultures within the region, such as the Hebrew Bible and the Greek New Testament, which were originally in vertical scroll format and mimicked the multicolumn layout of their manuscript pages.

A few early Qur'an fragments are palimpsests in which the original text was scraped off to make way for a new text on the same surface. Since parchment was expensive, this practice allowed for a more economical use of available resources. With the passage of time, traces of the original text might reveal themselves (fig. 31). Scientific methods such as the use of ultraviolet light have enabled scholars to read the different strata of texts,

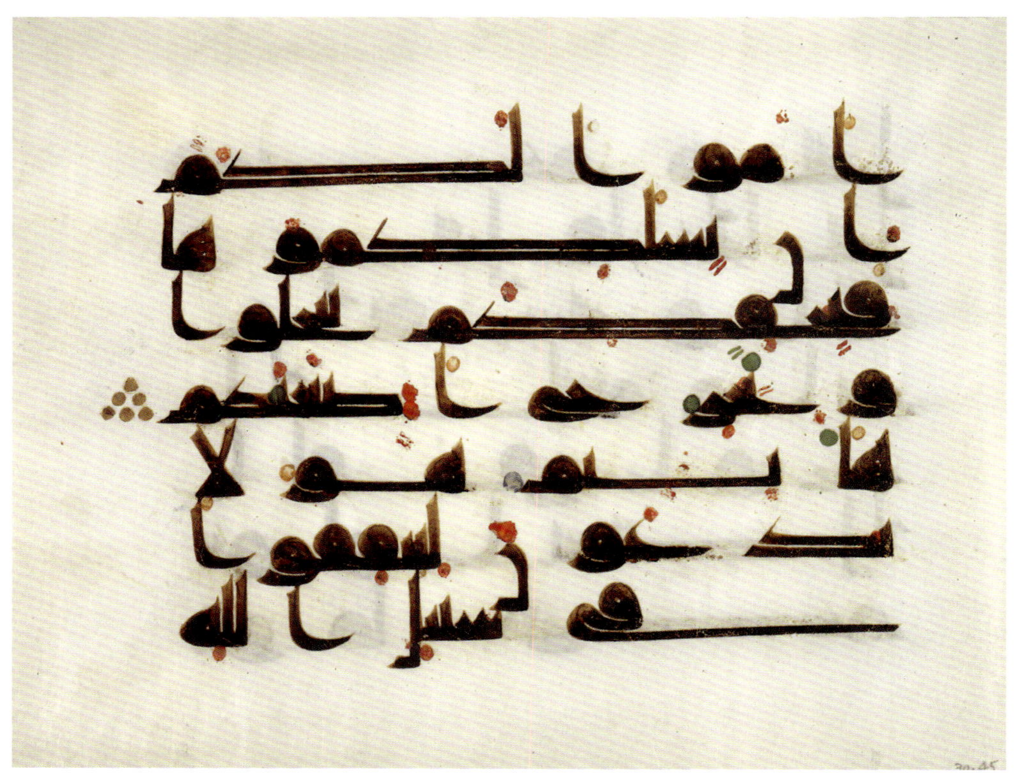

Fig. 32. Folio from a Qur'an manuscript. Probably Syria, Abbasid, late 9th–early 10th century. Ink and gold on parchment, 13⅛ x 9⅜ in. (33.3 x 23.8 cm). Gift of Rudolf M. Riefstahl, 1930 (30.45)

sometimes yielding fascinating results. In one case, a text written in Syriac was found under the present Arabic one, and in another the original text was a passage from a Qur'an that may have been written before 'Uthman's codification of the text.

Structure and Embellishment

The divine origin of the Qur'an makes it a model of beauty and perfection while also imbuing it with authority and prestige. It is thus considered by Muslims to be the "mother of all books," or *'umm al-kitab*, and not only does it play a vital role in the daily lives of believers, but its impact on the arts of the book in the Islamic world has been indelible. Due to its elevated status, copying the Qur'an was considered a pious act, and the structure, divisions, and phonetic requirements of the text offered calligraphers, illuminators, and bookbinders endless

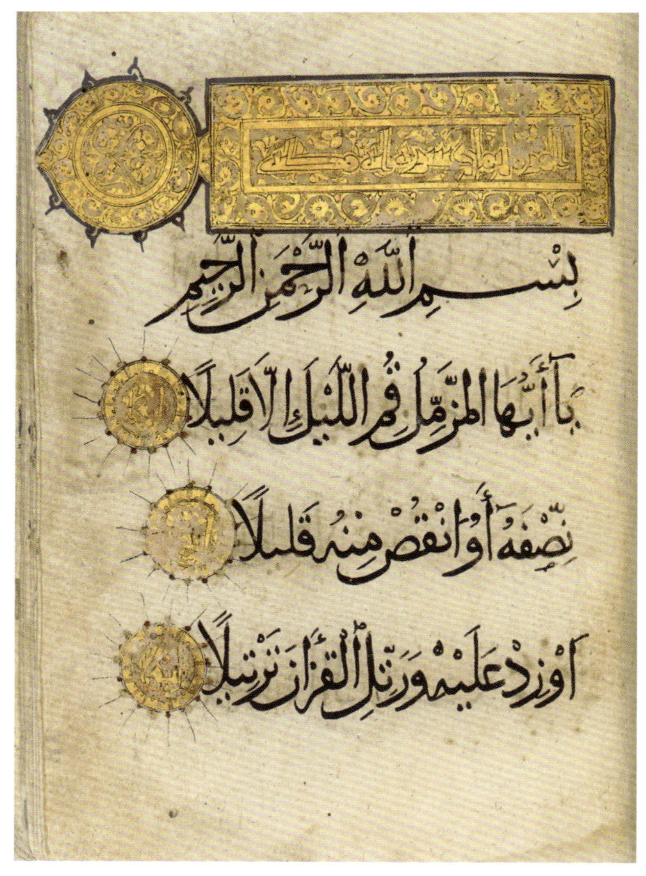

Fig. 33. Folio from an illuminated Qur'an. Iraq, Baghdad, A.H. 588/A.D. 1192–93. Ink, gold, and opaque watercolor on paper, 8³⁄₁₆ x 5¹¹⁄₁₆ in. (20.8 x 14.5 cm). Purchase, Harris Brisbane Dick Fund, funds from various donors, and Dodge Fund, 2004 (2004.89)

opportunities for demonstrating their talent and inventiveness while carrying out this act of religious devotion. Some copies are sparsely ornamented (fig. 32), while others are lavishly illuminated using gold and vibrant pigments (fig. 33). Manuscripts of the Qur'an were gifted as endowments to mosques, shrines, and other religious establishments and exchanged by rulers as diplomatic gifts. Luxurious copies came to symbolize both political might and legitimacy and religious sanctity.

The Qur'an is structured in a sequence of 114 *suras* (chapters or units), which, save for one exception, are arranged inversely according to length—that is, the first *sura* is the longest and the last is the shortest. The order of *ayas* within each *sura* follows the same rubric. For convenience of use, the Qur'an can be further divided into thirty parts, called *juz'* or *ajza'*; sixty parts, referred to as *hizb*; and other, less common divisions, such as seven parts (*manzil*) for the seven days of the week. Ornamental devices (figs. 34, 35) are used to highlight the headings of *suras*, vocalize the text, and provide cues to the reciter about when to pause, perform a prostration (*sajada*), or keep count of verses, usually marking every fifth (*khams*), tenth (*'ashr*), and twentieth (*'ashrun*) verse, sometimes denoted in *abjad* letters.

In some copies, full-page illuminated folios are placed at the opening and the conclusion of a volume. Referred to, respectively, as a frontispiece and a finispiece, or alternatively as carpet pages, these folios typically do not contain any text; instead, the entire surface is richly patterned (fig. 36). They offered an illuminator the opportunity to display his artistry but also prepared the reader mentally and spiritually to read its contents. Scholar Colin Baker compares opening a Qur'an to entering a sacred building, with the frontispiece as the gateway or portal to the holy text and the finispiece serving to balance the frontispiece both functionally and decoratively. Sometimes the pages immediately following the frontispiece are also embellished, in which case they are referred

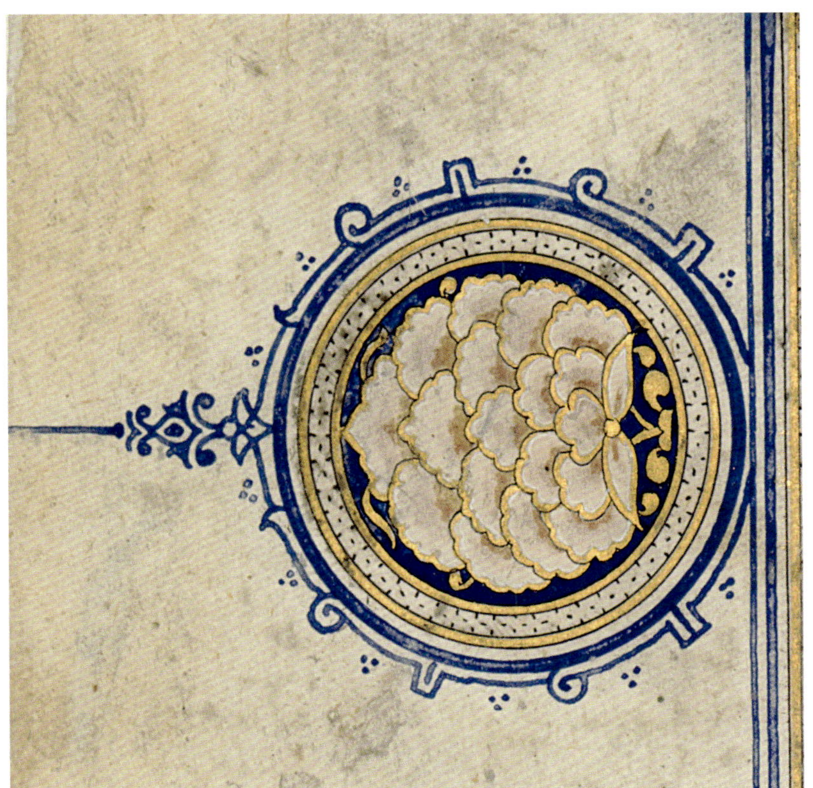

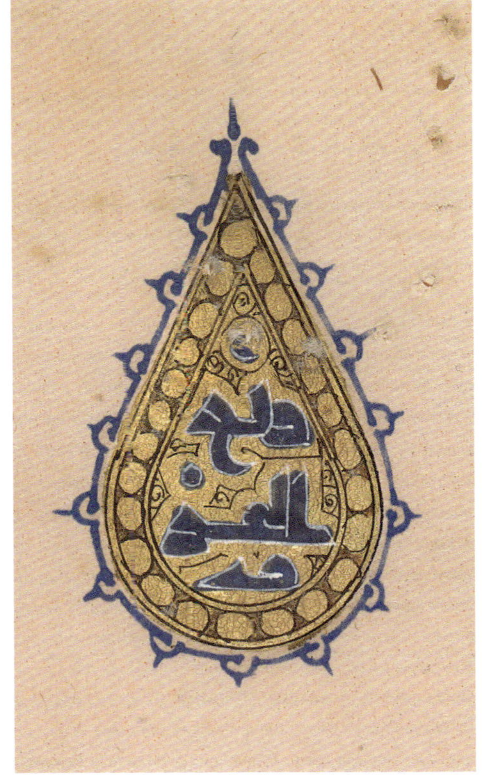

Above left: Fig. 34. An illuminated medallion in the margin of an early 14th-century Qur'an (cat. 17a). Above right: Fig. 35. An illuminated teardrop medallion from a 13th-century Qur'an (cat. 11).

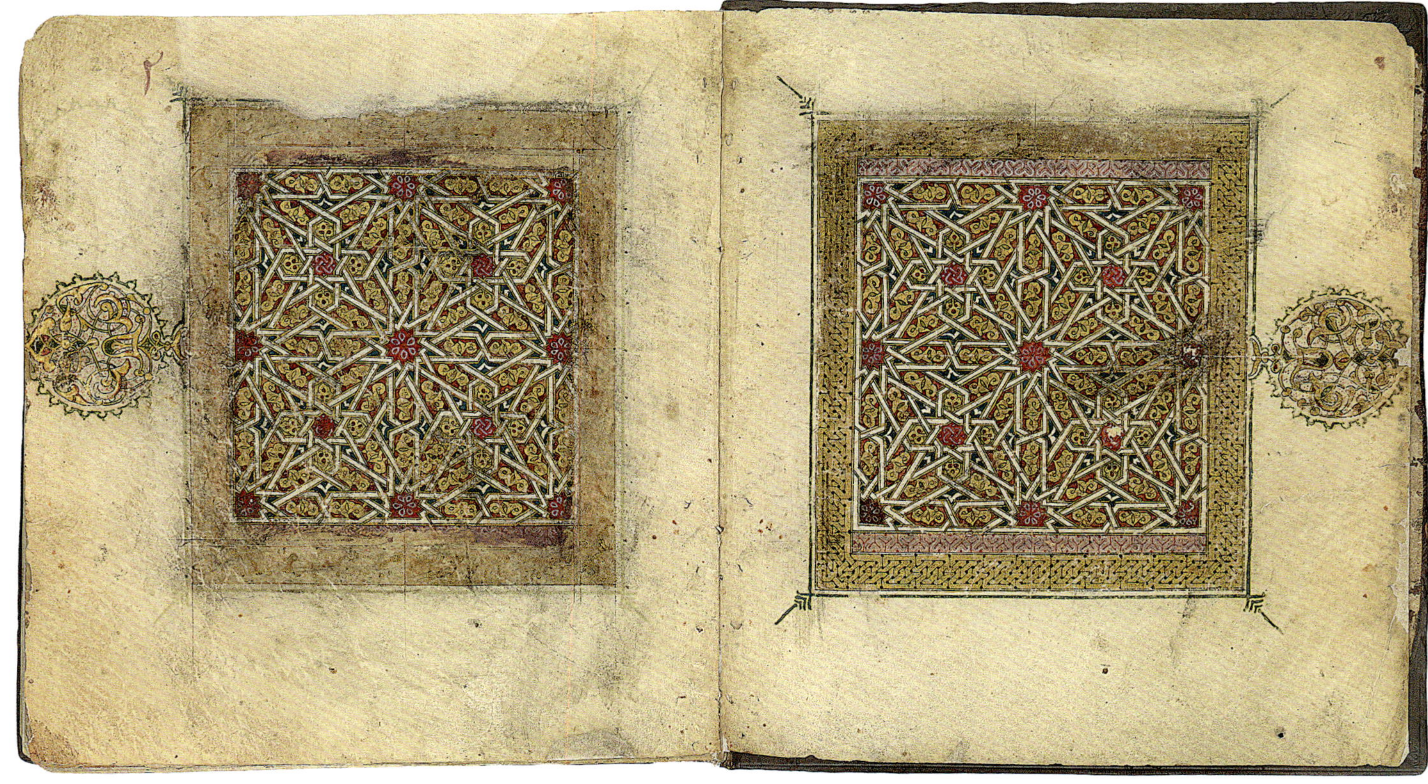

Fig. 36. Frontispiece to a Qur'an manuscript. Morocco or southern Spain, ca. 1300. Ink, gold, and opaque watercolor on parchment, each page 7 15/16 x 7 9/16 in. (20.2 x 19.2 cm). Purchase, Lila Acheson Wallace Gift, 2004 (2004.90)

to as incipit pages. Of course, not all Qur'an manuscripts contain carpet pages, and in many instances a decorative heading (*sarlawh*) at the top of the first verse functions as a substitute.

As early as the eighth century, Qur'ans penned in *hijazi* script contained decorative *sura* headings, and after the tenth century, illuminated medallions were added to the margins. Marginal devices marked larger divisions of the Qur'an, such as the thirty *juz'* or *ajza'* that allowed for the entire text to be read in a month, especially during the holy month of Ramadan. Sometimes each of the thirty sections was bound into a separate volume. Alternatively, larger Qur'ans might be physically separated into two or three volumes, depending on size. The bindings of Qur'an manuscripts were often as elaborate as the illumination. They were usually made of fine leather that was tooled or stamped, gilded, painted, and, occasionally, inset with precious stones (fig. 37). The doublures, or inner surfaces, of the bindings were also sometimes decorated.

Ubiquity and Perpetuity

In Arabic, the word for "writing" or "calligraphy" is *khatt*, which can also mean "trace" or "line." As an embodiment of God's word, the Qur'an brings the faithful into intimate contact with the divine. As such, manuscripts of the Qur'an were preserved at all cost. Even when damaged, they were considered too sacred to be discarded or destroyed when retired from use. Instead, they were preserved in chambers in mosques and other religious buildings, which has resulted in some spectacular discoveries, including that of a horde of detached parchment folios in the Great Mosque of Sana'a, in Yemen, and of fragments in the Great Mosque of Damascus, in Syria. These

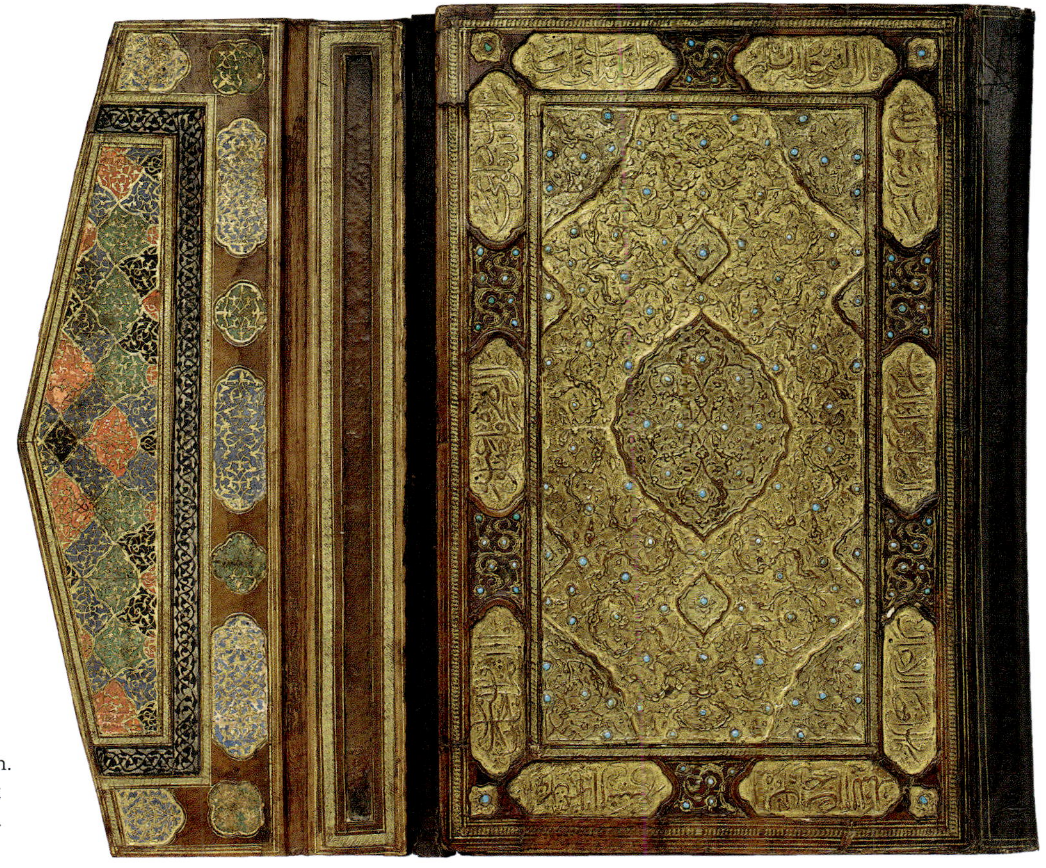

Fig. 37. Qur'an binding inset with turquoise. Iran, 16th century. Leather; stamped, painted, gilded, and inset with turquoise, closed: 14 x 10 x 1½ in. (35.6 x 25.4 x 3.8 cm); open: 14 x 27 x 1½ in. (35.6 x 68.6 x 3.8 cm). Rogers Fund, 1956 (56.222)

invaluable historical relics, several of which have now been assigned to the seventh century, have transformed our understanding of the earliest phases of Qur'an production. The same respect held true for pieces of paper and other materials bearing Arabic writing; they were handled with care for fear of damaging or soiling what could potentially be a holy inscription or a religious text. In the same way, a believer would not tread on a carpet with woven letters for fear of stepping on divine words.

The sanctity of God's word as preserved in the Qur'an permeated all aspects of life in the Islamic world. And beyond the pages of the holy book, Qur'anic inscriptions are ubiquitous on objects of all media, among them the enamel-painted glass mosque lamps, wood book stands (*rahla*), ceramic tiles, bronze lampstands, and the range of items that furnish and embellish mosques, madrasas, Sufi lodges, and other places of religious observance (see cats. 22–24). Muslims from all walks of life—from the masses to the ruling elite—believed (and still believe) that reading and touching objects bearing Qur'anic verses, prayers, and pious phrases had the power to ward off danger, misfortune, and sickness. Such beliefs extended to the word *Allah*, or "God," and all ninety-nine of his "beautiful names." Although orthodox Islam has traditionally discouraged the reliance on amulets and other magio-religious devices, these objects remained a vital aspect of popular culture throughout the Islamic world for centuries. They reflect the human need to influence various aspects of life over which an individual has little tangible control. Used in times of uncertainty and peril, such as war, natural disaster, and illness, among others, these talismans also served as conduits of intercession between the worshipper and the holy figures as a means of seeking protection and empowerment.

15a

FOLIO FROM THE MONUMENTAL "TASHKENT QUR'AN"

Syria, Yemen, or North Africa, ca. 775–85
Ink on parchment, 21⅝ x 27⁹⁄₁₆ in. (55 x 70 cm)
Purchase, Lila Acheson Wallace Gift, 2004 (2004.87)

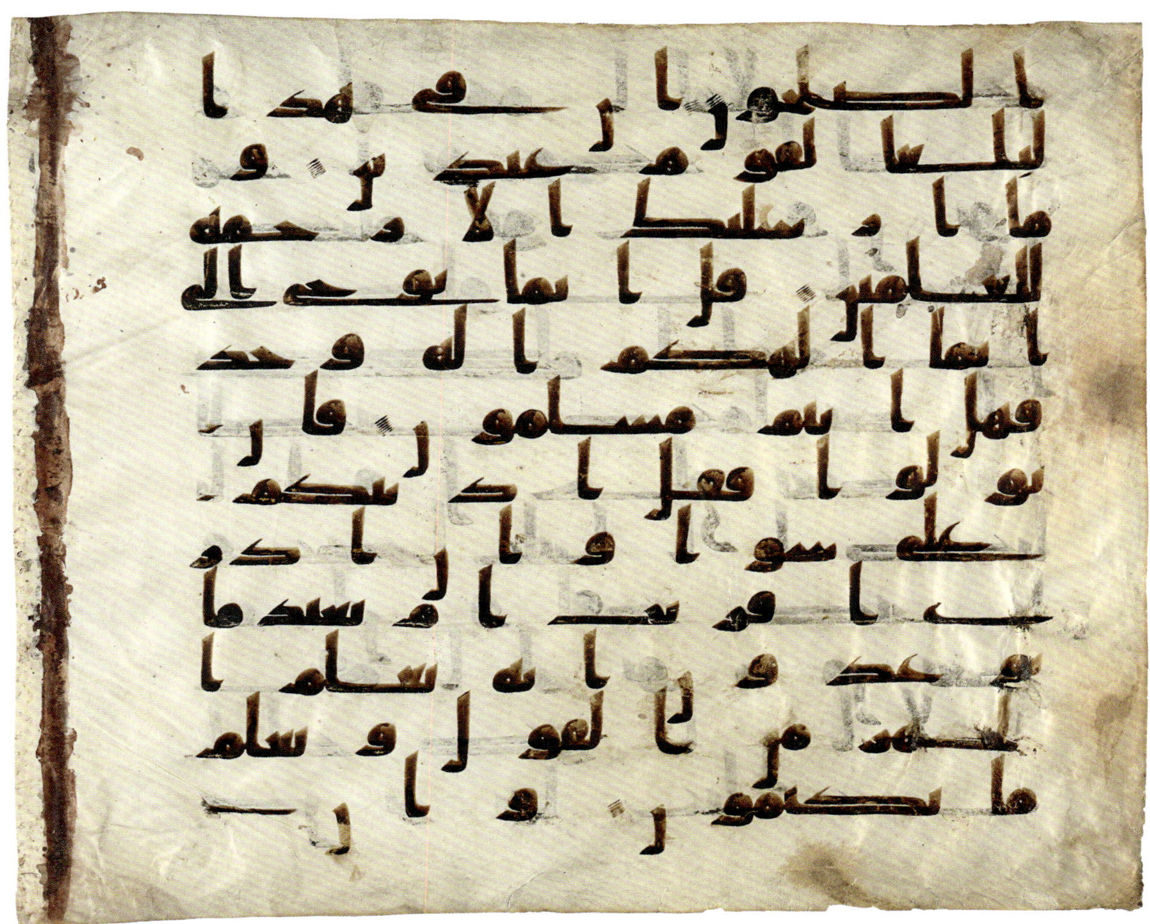

Both of these folios were transcribed at a time when *kufic* was just beginning to establish itself as a dominant script in the Near East. The first, majestic folio (cat. 15a) comes from the largest known Qur'an on parchment. Its unusual size and quality of calligraphy suggest that it was a major commission. Only two illuminated folios from the manuscript are known; the remaining folios, including this one, do not contain illumination or diacritical marks. Orthographic studies and carbon-14 analysis date the folio to the end of the eighth and the beginning of the ninth century. However, a recent study of folios from the same Qur'an in the collection of the Museum of Islamic Art in Doha, Qatar, proposes a more specific date, during the reign of al-Mahdi (r. 775–85), the third Abbasid caliph.

Written in an early variation of *kufic*, the text is from *sura* 21 (*al-Anbiya*, "The Prophets"), verses 103–11. The margins are almost perfectly justified at left and right, and the text is evenly spaced. Further distinguishing the calligraphy are the thick, bold strokes with horizontally extended ligatures on or above the baseline. Also unique are the words broken at the end of a line in the manner of a hyphenation, a tendency rarely seen in later copies.

15b

FOLIO FROM AN EARLY QUR'AN

Central Islamic Lands, late 8th–early 9th century
Ink, opaque watercolor, and gold on parchment, 11⅛ x 9½ in. (28.3 x 24.1 cm)
Gift of Adrienne Minassian, in memory of Dr. Richard Ettinghausen, 1979 (1979.201)

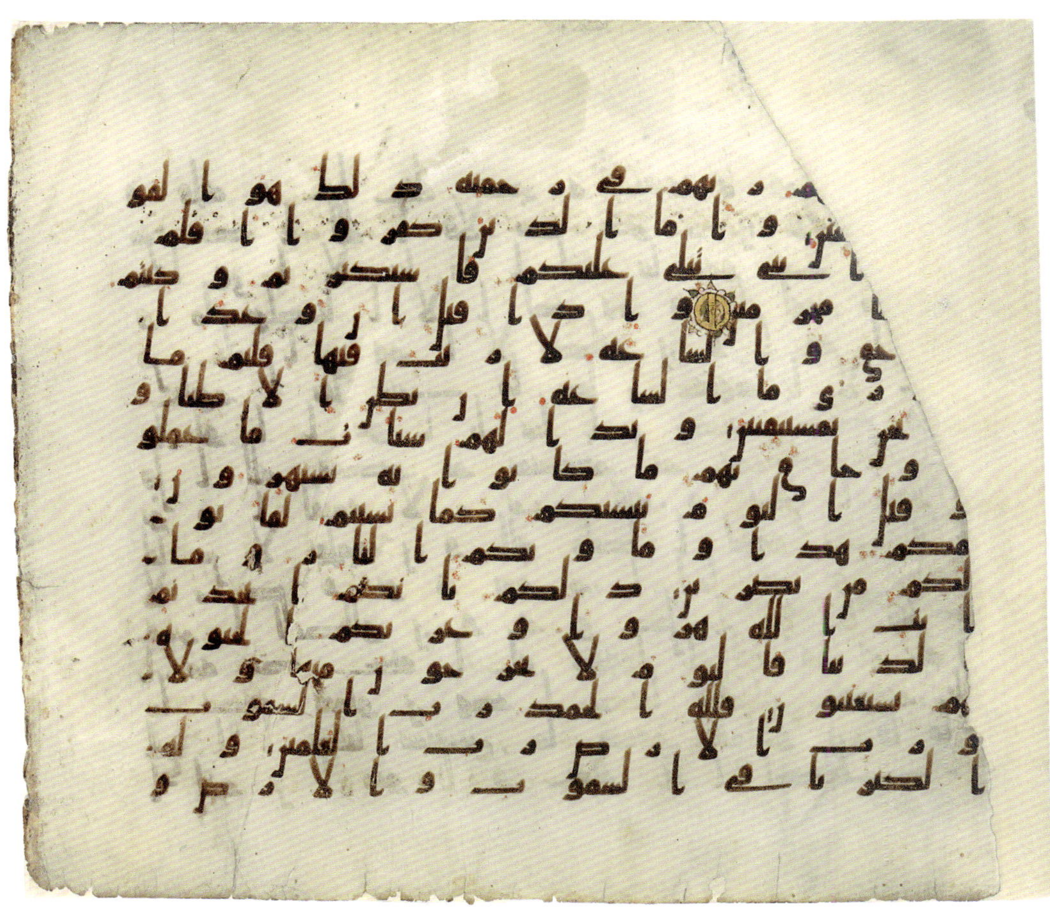

According to legend, the stains along the inner edges of the folios (in this case, at left) are from the blood of the third Rightly Guided Caliph, 'Uthman, assassinated in a mosque while reciting from this Qur'an in A.D. 656. The largest portion of the manuscript is presently kept in a madrasa library attached to the Tellya-Shaikh Mosque in Tashkent, Uzbekistan. How it made its way there is not entirely clear, but most likely it was carried along the Silk Road from the Near East or North Africa to Samarqand.

Although also assigned to the eighth or ninth century, the second folio (cat. 15b) is penned in a variation of *kufic* that exhibits traces of the earlier *hijazi* script. The writing is characterized by thin, compact letters with a rightward slant of the shafts of the *alif* and by the extension of the *ya* in the terminal position, which turns backward to underline the letters that precede it. Here, the format of the page is rectangular, with sixteen lines of text. Consonant points or dots (*i'jam*) are omitted, making it difficult for the reader to phonetically distinguish between letters with similar forms. However, red dots indicate short vowels, and gilded medallions act as verse markers.

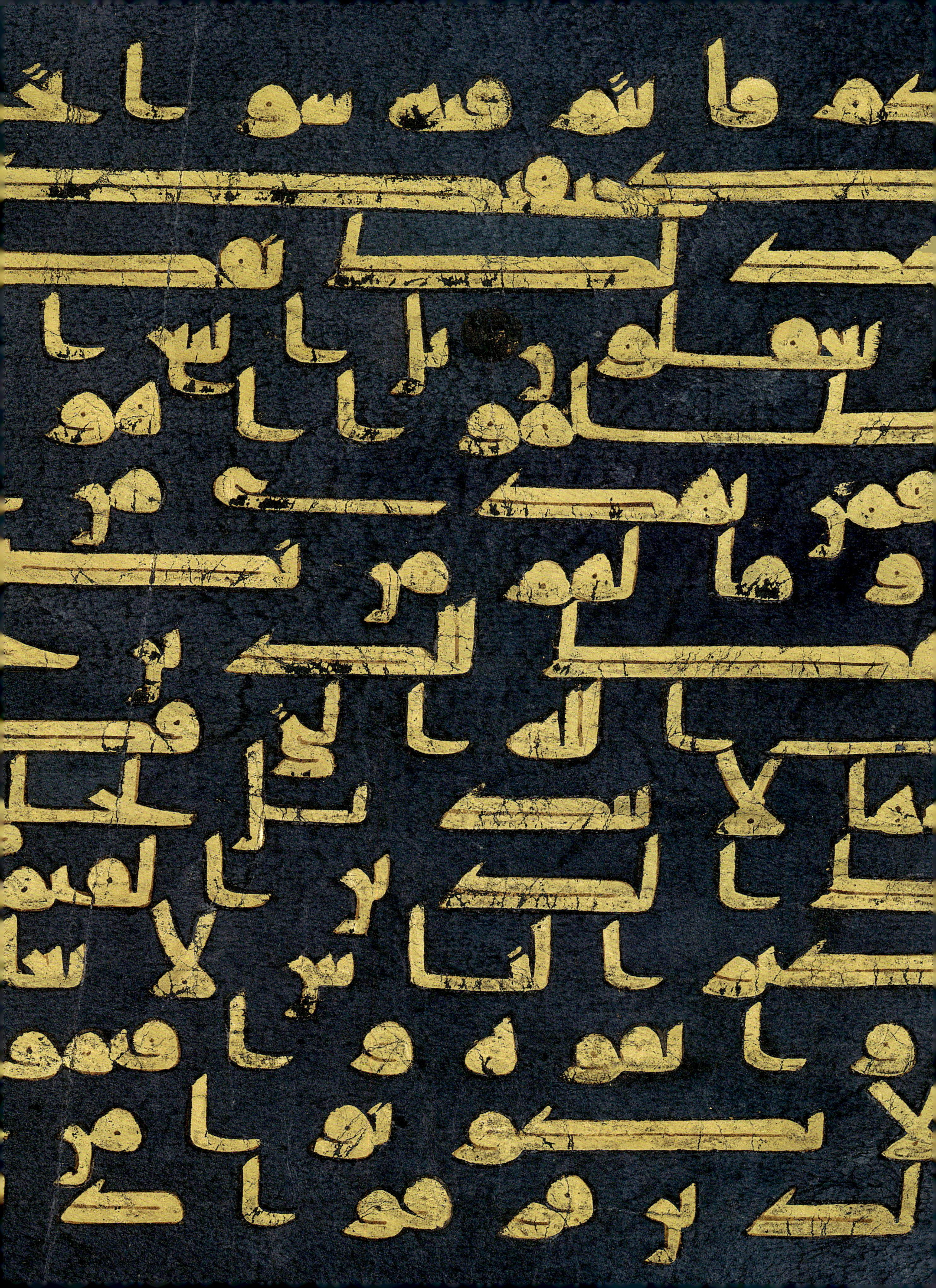

16

FOLIO FROM THE "BLUE QUR'AN"

Probably Qairawan, Tunisia, second half 9th–mid-10th century
Gold and silver on indigo-dyed parchment, $11\frac{15}{16}$ x $15\frac{13}{16}$ in. (30.4 x 40.2 cm)
Purchase, Lila Acheson Wallace Gift, 2004 (2004.88)

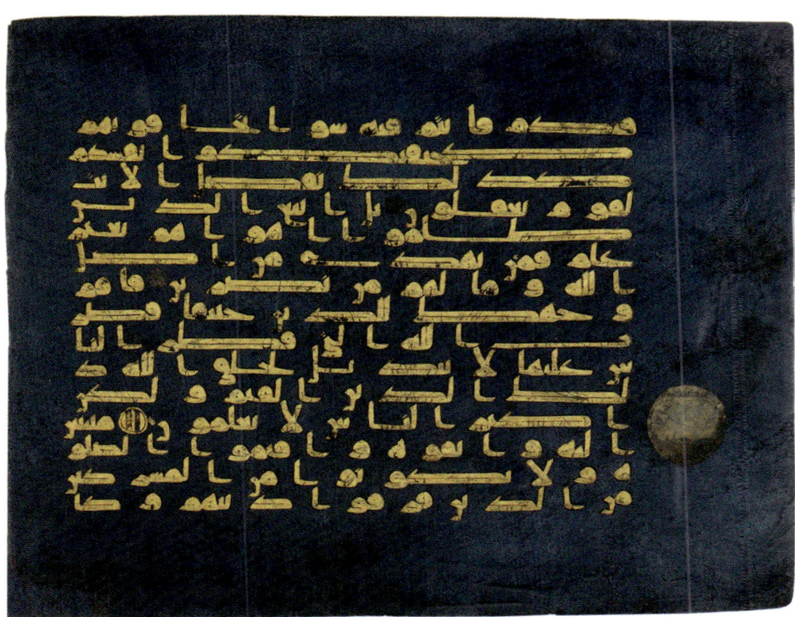

Looking at this folio, one is immediately struck by the contrast between the gold ink lettering and the indigo-dyed ground. It comes from a luxurious, multivolume Qur'an with fifteen lines of text per page, in gold *kufic* script outlined in black ink. Like that of most Qur'ans from the eighth through tenth centuries, its text is characterized by letters that stretch horizontally across the baseline; the absence of vowels and diacritical marks; and the minimal use of ornamentation. The only decorative devices seen here are the circular silver verse markers, now almost entirely faded to black (over time, when silver is exposed to oxygen, it tarnishes and blackens).

The text on the two sides comprises verses 24 to 32 of *sura* 30 (*al-Rum*, "The Byzantine Empire"). Although firm evidence is lacking regarding the origin, date, and patronage of the manuscript, all thirty-seven of the extant pages, now scattered among museums and private collections throughout the world, probably once formed a large portion of the Qur'an preserved at the Institut National d'Archéologie et d'Art in Tunis. Scholars have suggested a range of dates for the Blue Qur'an, from the ninth to the mid-tenth century, and have variably attributed its production to Qairawan, in present-day Tunisia, to Cordoba, in Umayyad Spain, as well as to Abbasid Baghdad. An inventory dated A.H. 693 (A.D. 1293) in the Great Mosque of Qairawan describes a manuscript with the same specifications, which suggests that, at the end of the thirteenth century, the Blue Qur'an was still in the city in which it was most likely produced.

Very few Qur'ans on colored parchment survive. The practice of writing in gold or silver ink on blue or purple parchment was most likely borrowed from the Christian Byzantine empire, where official documents and manuscripts were executed in these materials. The use of gold lettering makes this manuscript especially rare and sumptuous, suggesting that it could have been commissioned by a wealthy, pious patron such as a governor, if not by the caliph himself.

17a (opposite)

FOLIO FROM A QUR'AN WITH DECORATIVE PAUSE MARKS

Iran, early 14th century
Ink, opaque watercolor, and gold on paper, 14½ x 10⅞ in. (36.8 x 27.6 cm)
Gift of Richard Ettinghausen, 1975 (1975.192.7)

17b (following pages)

BIFOLIUM FROM A QUR'AN WITH STAR-SHAPED PROSTRATION MARK

Egypt or Syria, Mamluk, 13th century
Ink, opaque watercolor, and gold on paper, 20 x 13¼ in. (50.8 x 33.7 cm)
Fletcher Fund, 1924 (24.146.1)

Penned in *naskh* script, the single folio (cat. 17a), from Iran, is richly illuminated. It consists of five lines of text with vowels and diacritical marks in black and red ink, enclosed within cloudlike forms. The pause marks—cues prompting the worshipper to pause in recitation—take the form of gold disks and teardrops. The text is framed within a border of gold interlacing strapwork with two wide, richly illuminated gold, blue, and green panels above and below. The panels contain the following inscriptions, in new-style script: the *sura* heading (*al-Nas*, "Of Mankind"); the number of *aya*s featured (six); and a Qur'anic phrase ("And the word of your Lord has been fulfilled in truth and in justice. None can alter His words, and He is the Hearing, the Knowing"). The inscriptions are enclosed within extended polygonal cartouches joined at each end to partial stellated octagons with floral designs (detail). Two medallions outside the frame contain delicately rendered peonies. The style of illumination, copious use of gold, and types of flowers depicted reflect the prominence of Chinese-derived motifs that characterizes the luxurious book illumination of the Ilkhanid period.

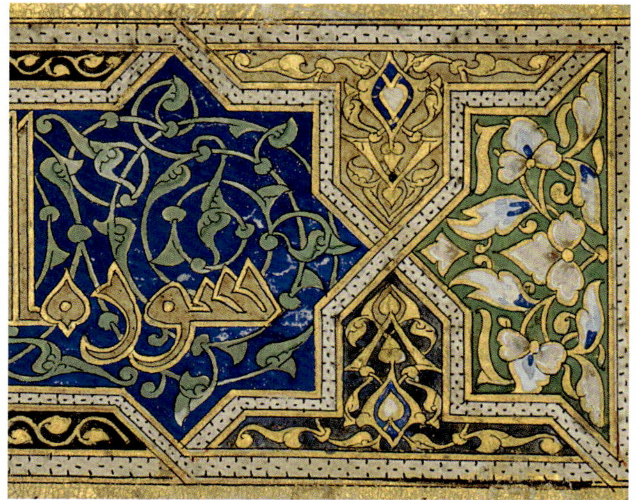

Detail of geometric interlacing in the illuminated *sura* heading in cat. 17a

The bifolium (cat. 17b), from Egypt or Syria, belongs to the second volume of a luxurious Qur'an manuscript in which all 274 folios are extensively illuminated. The text, written in a variation of *thuluth* in gold ink outlined in black, generally appears in eleven lines per page, with diacritical and other phonetic signs marked in gold, red, and blue. Illuminated disks inscribed with the word *aya* (verse) indicate verse endings, and marginal disks or teardrop shapes surrounded with colorful petal-like borders highlight the fifth and tenth verses, as well as other denominations. Marks instructing the worshipper to perform prostration take the form of medallions or large gold six-pointed stars enclosing the word *sajad*, or "prostrate."

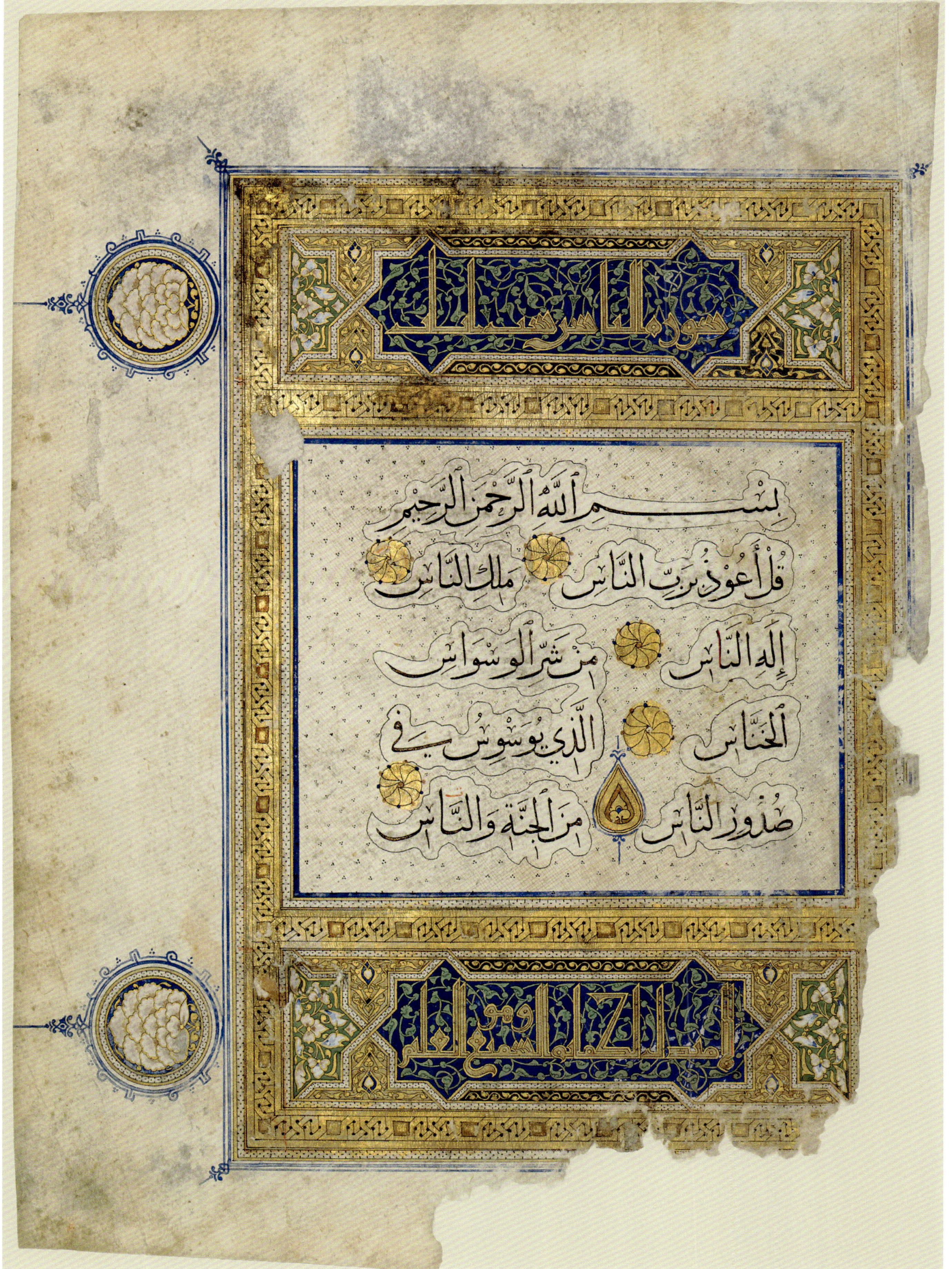
بسم الله الرحمن الرحيم
قل أعوذ برب الناس ملك الناس
إله الناس من شر الوسواس
الخناس الذي يوسوس في
صدور الناس من الجنة والناس

هطعين إلى الداع يقول الكافرون هذا

وم عسر ○ كذبت قبلهم قوم نوح فكذبوا

عبدنا وقالوا مجنون وازدجر ○ فدعا ربه

ني مغلوب فانتصر ○ ففتحنا أبواب السما

ء منهمر ○ وفجرنا الأرض عيونا فالتقى

الماء على أمر قد قدر ○ وحملناه على

ذات ألواح ودسر ○ تجري بأعيننا جزا

ء لمن كان كفر ○ ولقد تركناها آية فهل

من مدكر ○ فكيف كان عذابي ونذر ○

إنا أرسلنا عليهم ريحا صرصرا في يوم نحس

مستمر ○ تنزع الناس كأنهم أعجاز نخل

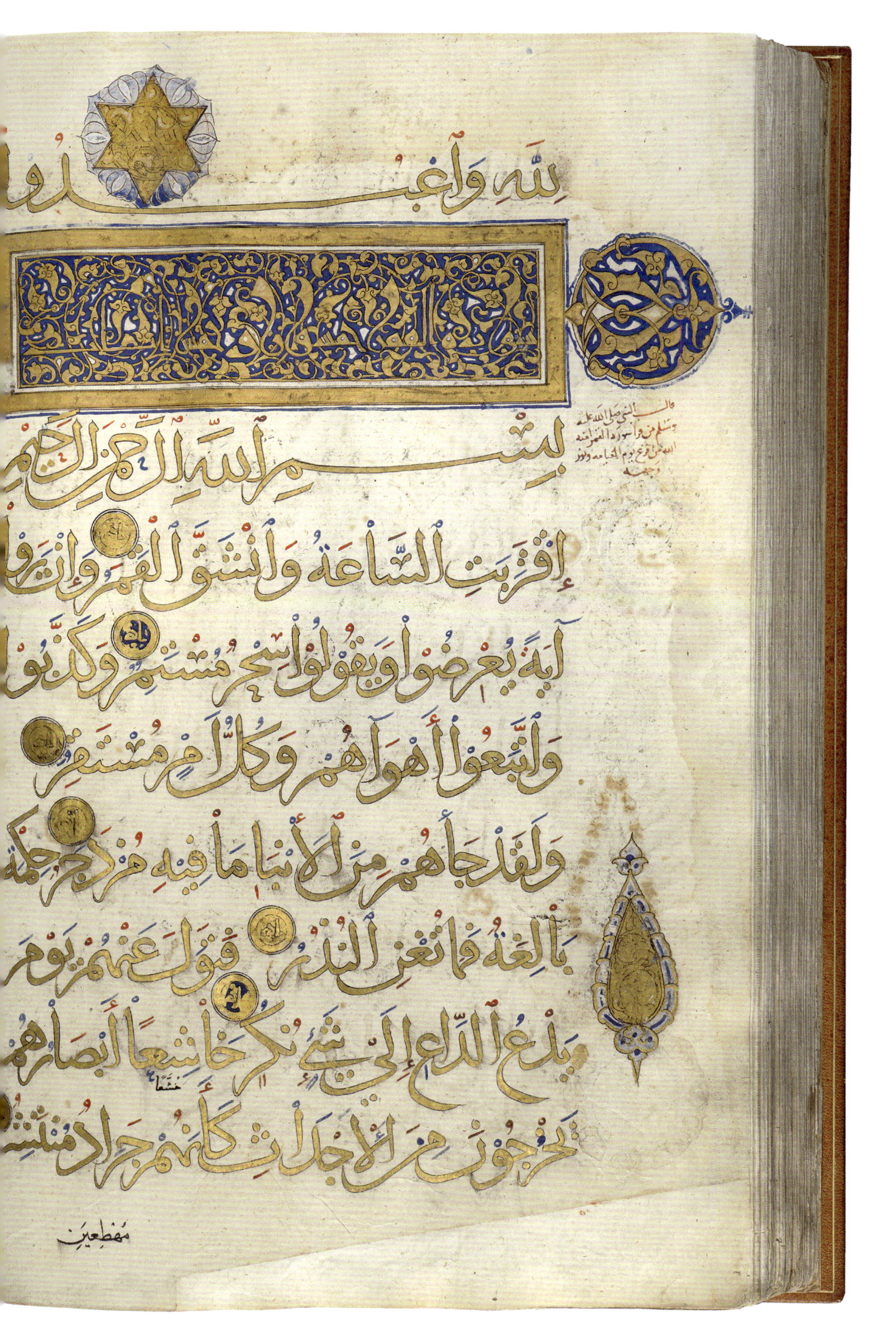

لله واعبدوا

بسم الله الرحمن الرحيم

اقتربت الساعة وانشق القمر وان يروا

آية يعرضوا ويقولوا سحر مستمر وكذبوا

واتبعوا اهواهم وكل امر مستقر

ولقد جاهم من الانبا ما فيه مزدجر حكمة

بالغة فما تغن النذر فتول عنهم يوم

يدع الداع الى شي نكر خاشعا ابصارهم

خشعا

يخرجون من الاجداث كانهم جراد منتشر

مهطعين

18

FOLIO FROM THE LIFE-SIZE QUR'AN OF 'UMAR AQTA'

Uzbekistan, Samarqand, late 14th–early 15th century (before 1405)
Ink, opaque watercolor, and gold on paper, 19½ x 43⅝ in. (49.5 x 110.8 cm); 28⅞ x 42¼ in. (73.3 x 107.3 cm); 19½ x 43 in. (49.5 x 109.2 cm)
Gift of Samuel T. Peters, 1918; Rogers Fund, 1921 (18.17.1, .2; 21.26.2)

Distinguished by their monumental size and refined calligraphy, these fragments once belonged to a Qur'an that was reportedly seven feet tall, weighed half a ton, and contained roughly 1,500 pages—possibly the largest copy ever produced. The folio's seven generously spaced lines of text were brushed in elegant and balanced *muhaqqaq*, using a wide-nibbed pen for the letters and a finer pen for the phonetic and vocalization marks.

The manuscript is attributed to the left-handed calligrapher 'Umar Aqta' and was made for Timur (Tamerlane, d. 1405), founder of the Timurid dynasty. In his treatise on calligraphers and painters, the late sixteenth-century writer Qadi Ahmad tells the story of its production and mentions that the master 'Umar Aqta' "wrote a copy [of the Qur'an] in *ghubar* (dustlike) writing that was so tiny that it could fit under the socket of a signet ring and presented it to the Lord of the Time, [Amir Timur Gurkan]. Much to 'Umar's dismay, [Timur] was not pleased, so he wrote another copy, extremely large, each of its lines being a *dhira'* (cubit) in length, and even longer. Having finished, decorated and bound [the manuscript,] he tied it on a wheelbarrow and took it to Timur's palace. . . . The sultan came out to meet him . . . and rewarded 'Umar Aqta' with great honors." Qadi Ahmad's description seems to match the dispersed manuscript, which survives in extremely fragmentary condition in many institutions around the world.

Many extant folios from this monumental Qur'an are composed of strips that have been pasted together. It is not clear, however, whether they were originally produced in this way or cut into panels later. A colossal stone book stand in the courtyard of the Bibi Khanum Mosque in Samarqand is believed to have been added by Timur's grandson Ulugh Beg (d. 1449) in order to support the manuscript and enable the reader to turn its pages during the Friday prayer (fig. 38).

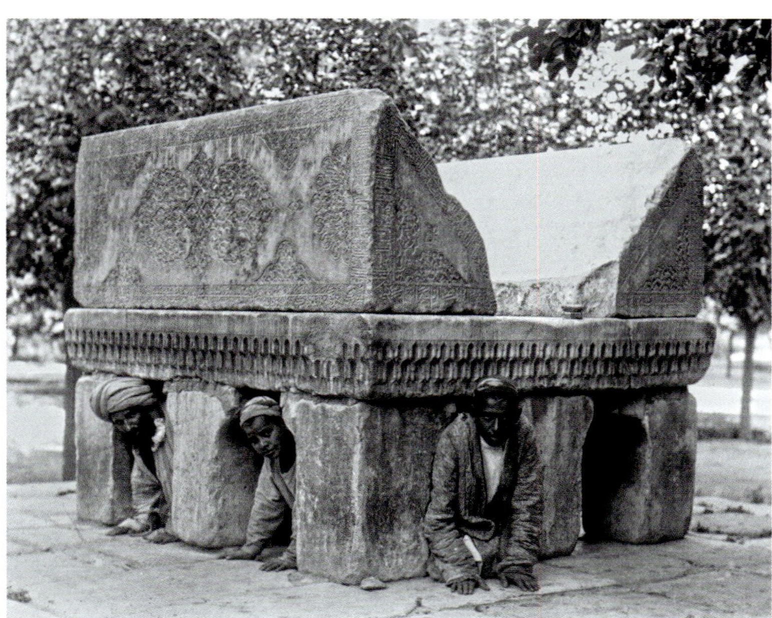

Fig. 38. Stone Qur'an stand in front of Bibi Khanum Mosque, Samarqand, Uzbekistan, 15th century

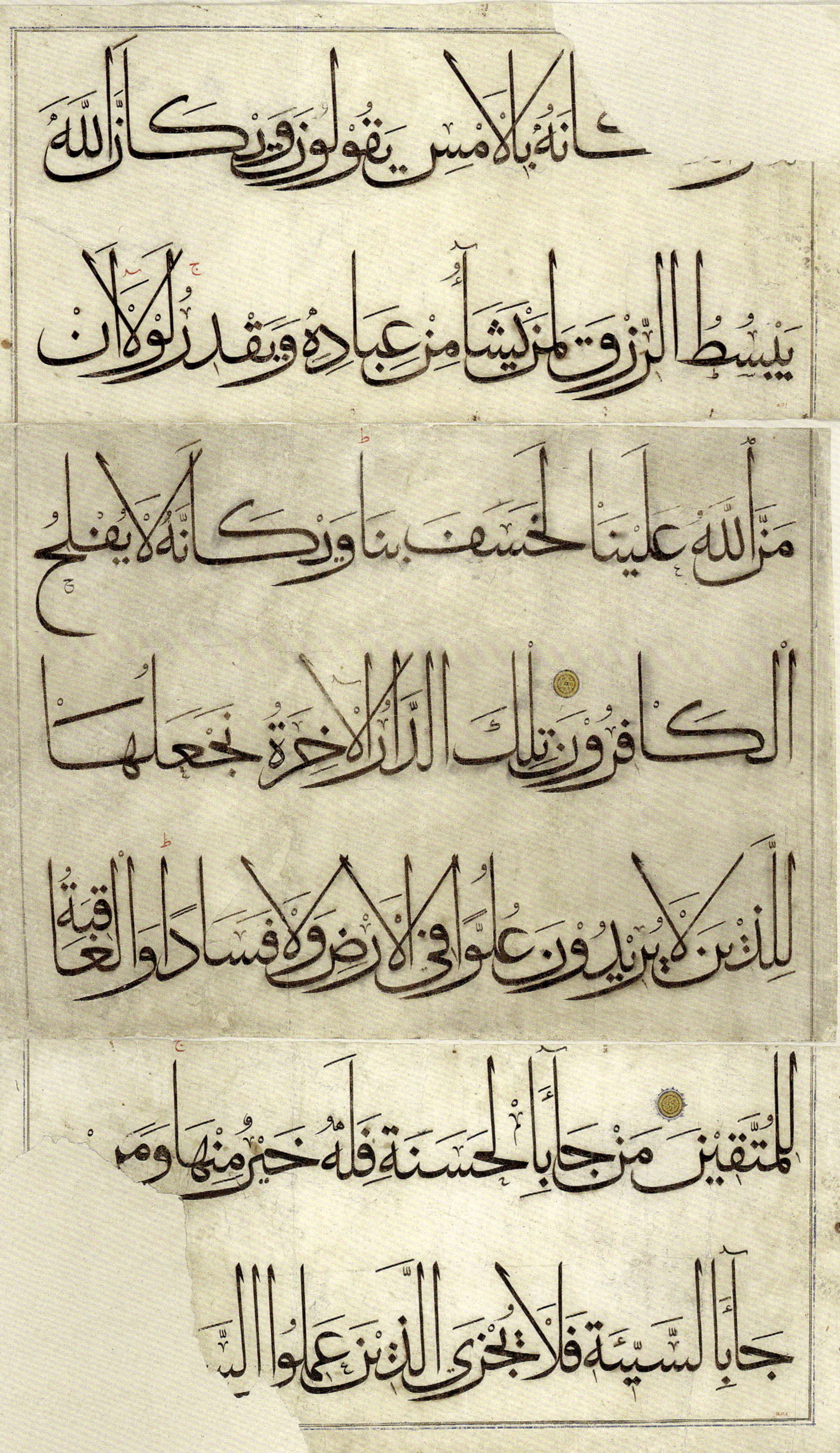

...كأنه بالأمس يقولون ويكأن الله
يبسط الرزق لمن يشاء من عباده ويقدر لولا أن
من الله علينا لخسف بنا ويكأنه لا يفلح
الكافرون تلك الدار الآخرة نجعلها
للذين لا يريدون علوا في الأرض ولا فسادا والعاقبة
للمتقين من جاء بالحسنة فله خير منها وم...
...جاء بالسيئة فلا يجزى الذين عملوا الس...

19

BIFOLIUM FROM A KASHMIRI QUR'AN

India, Kashmir, Mughal, late 18th–early 19th century
Ink, gold, and lapis on paper; leather binding, 6¾ x 4⅝ in. (17.1 x 11.7 cm)
Louis E. and Theresa S. Seley Purchase Fund for Islamic Art, 2009 (2009.294)

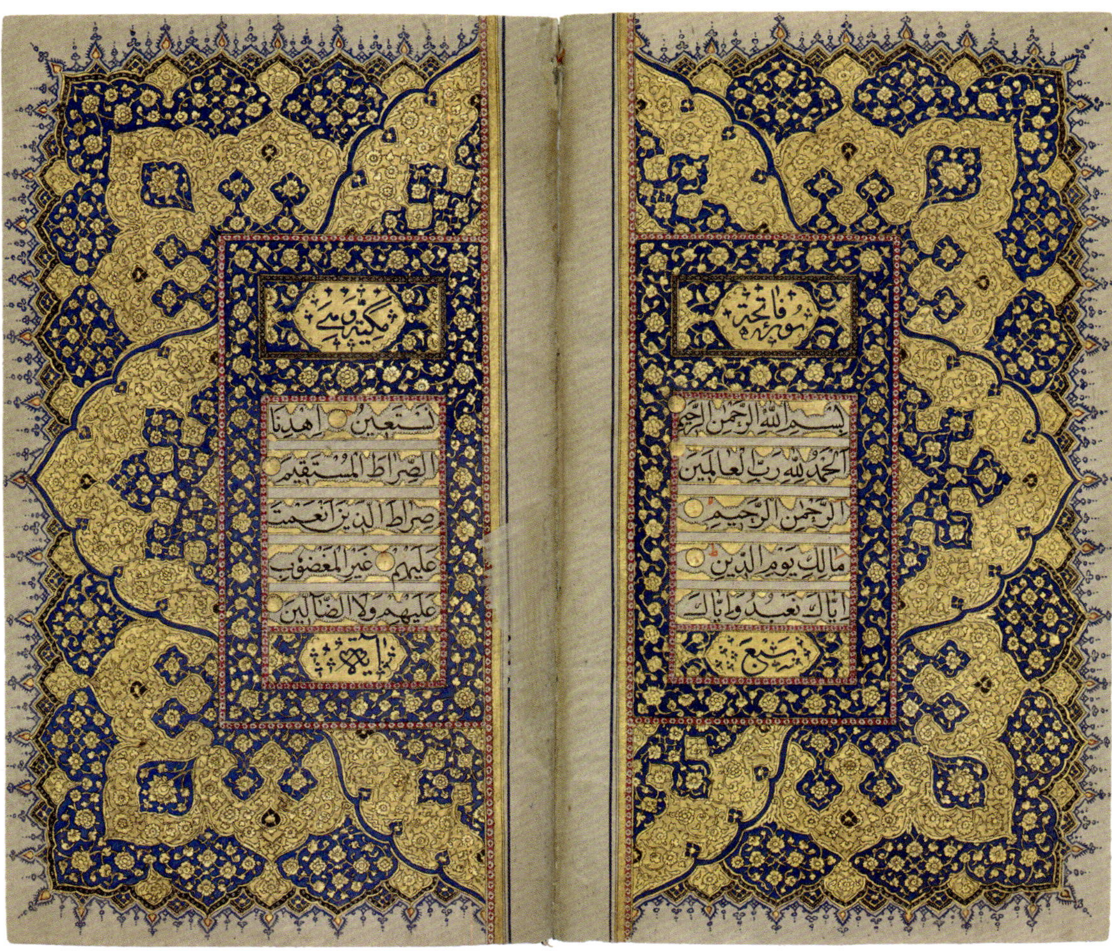

In the eighteenth century, Kashmir, a predominantly Muslim province in northern India, reemerged as a major art center on the Indian subcontinent after a period of artistic decline. Kashmiri artists of this period produced fine Qur'ans, illustrated manuscripts, textiles, and an array of decorative objects for patrons and the commercial market, including for export to other regions of the subcontinent and beyond.

This luxurious Qur'an bears the typical Kashmiri-style gold-and-blue illumination within a broad frame overlaid by lobed archlike interlacings (the hasp motif), which extend into the margins of the page. The Qur'an is divided into seven parts and has eight lavishly illuminated double pages inserted at the beginning of eight *suras*. It is written in fine *naskh* script, which is consistent in quality and evenness throughout the manuscript. Many Kashmiri Qur'ans, supposedly those intended for the local market, are crudely executed, but The Met's example is notable for its refined illumination and calligraphy.

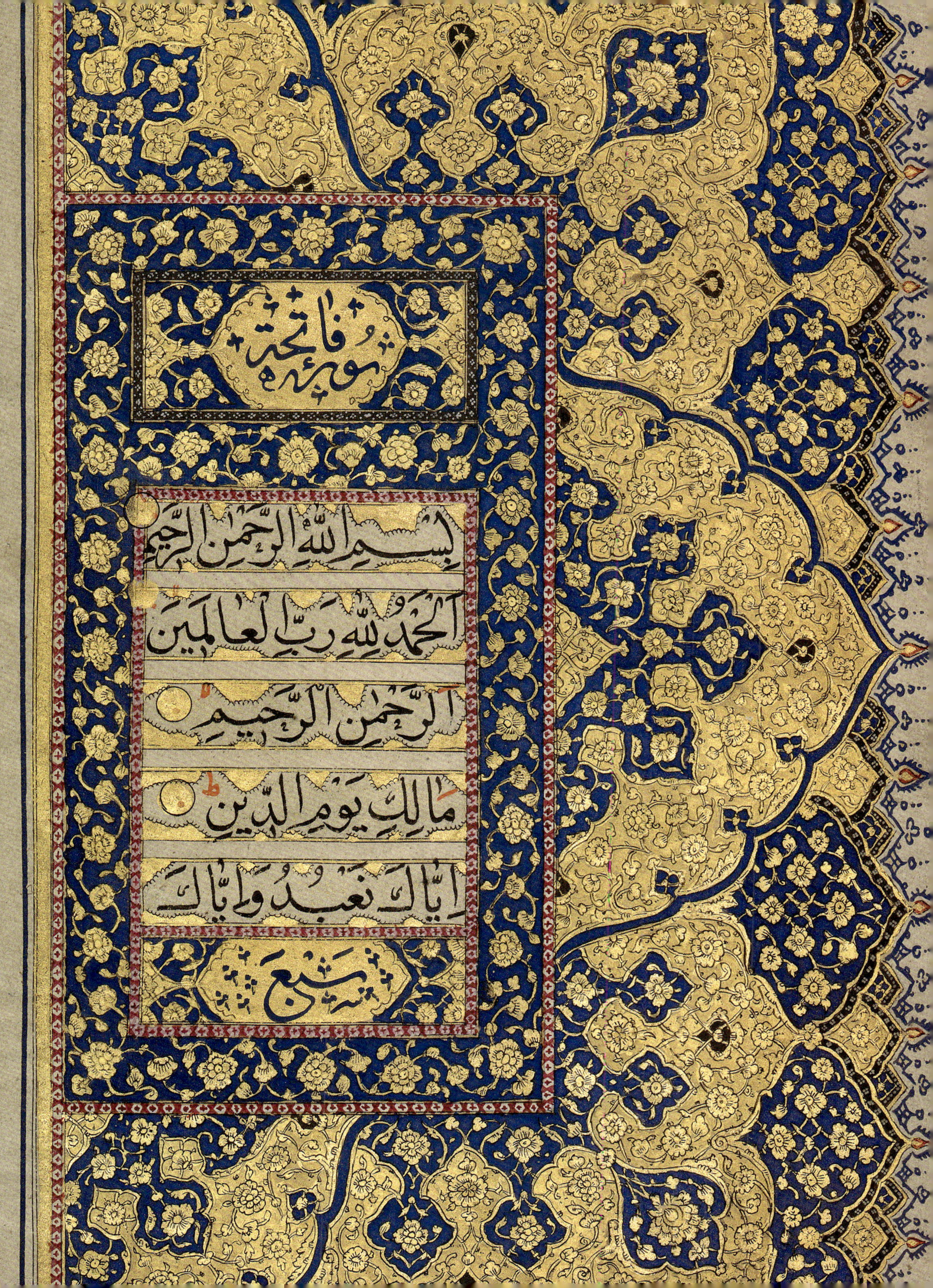
سورة فاتحة
بسم الله الرحمن الرحيم
الحمد لله رب العالمين
الرحمن الرحيم
مالك يوم الدين
اياك نعبد واياك
سبع

FOLIO FROM A QUR'AN WITH AN ELABORATE *SURA* HEADING

Spain, Nasrid, late 13th–early 14th century
Ink, opaque watercolor, and gold on parchment, 21 1/16 x 22 in. (53.5 x 55.9 cm)
Rogers Fund, 1942 (42.63)

This folio comes from a magnificent two-volume luxury Qur'an in a square format produced in Spain. It is notable for its large size, especially given the use of parchment as a support. It bears text on both sides (recto and verso) and contains the first four verses and most of verse 5 of *sura* 39 (*al-Zumar*, "Of the Crowds"). The recto is particularly notable for its first line, which highlights the *sura* heading in bold *kufic*, penned in gold and outlined in red. The heading also states that the number of verses is seventy-two, which may correspond to a specific division of the text used in the Maghrib region. The large medallion in gold outlined in blue that projects from the left side of the *sura* heading is a work of art in its own right, demonstrating the virtuosity of the illuminator (detail). It consists of a complex and intricate scrolling vegetal pattern in gold, subtly outlined in red. The disks of interlacing geometric designs that mark the end of a verse enclose the words *'ashr* (ten) and *khamsa* (five), written in white on a blue ground.

The seven lines of text are written in a balanced variant of the *maghribi* script and include diacritical and vocalization marks in blue, orange, and green ink. *Maghribi* diverged early on from the proportional cursive scripts practiced farther east, rendering letters and words in a rather "freehand" manner. Attention here is given to the harmony of the words as they appear on the line and the overall layout of the page rather than on the execution of individual letters. The letters are characterized by thin, spidery forms that vanish at the tips, and deep, sweeping curves that extend below the baseline. Along with the elaborate illuminations, the variation of *maghribi* used here exudes elegance and sumptuousness fit for a king or prince.

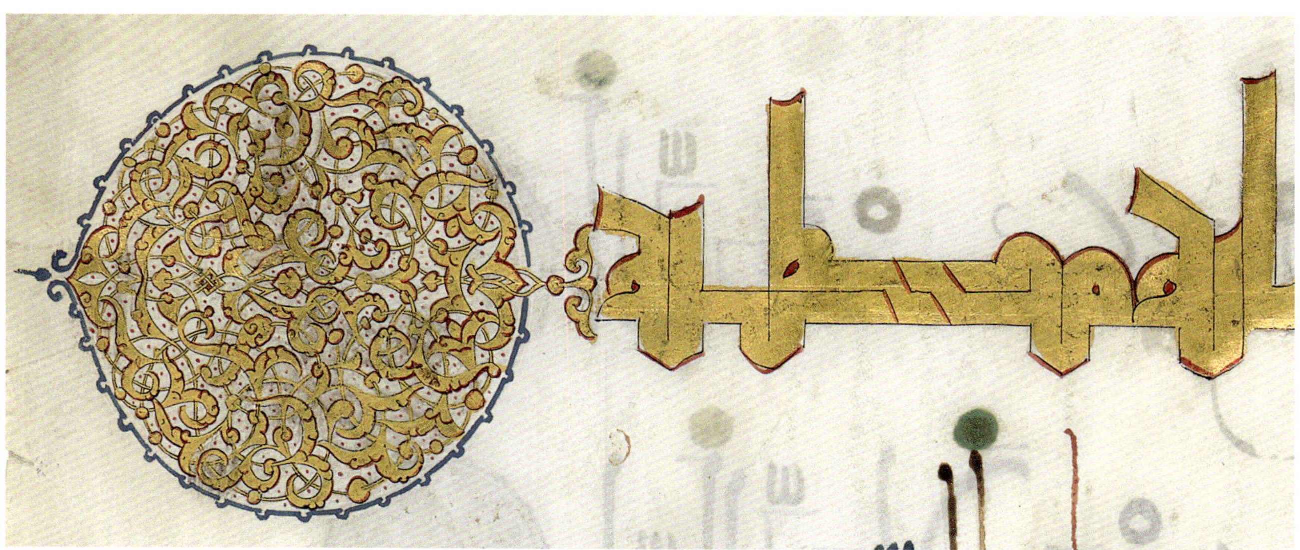

Detail of gold-illuminated medallion and *sura* heading

سورة الزمر ثنتان وسبعون آية

بسم الله الرحمن الرحيم

تنزيل الكتب من الله العزيز الحكيم ۝

إنا أنزلنا إليك الكتب بالحق فاعبد

الله مخلصا له الدين ۝ ألا لله الدين

الخالص والذين اتخذوا من دونه أولياء

ما نعبدهم إلا ليقربونا إلى الله زلفى إن

21

EMBROIDERED QUR'AN CASE

Spain, possibly Granada, second half 15th century
Leather; embroidered with gilt-silver wire, 4¼ x 4⅞ in. (10.8 x 12.4 cm)
Rogers Fund, 1904 (04.3.458)

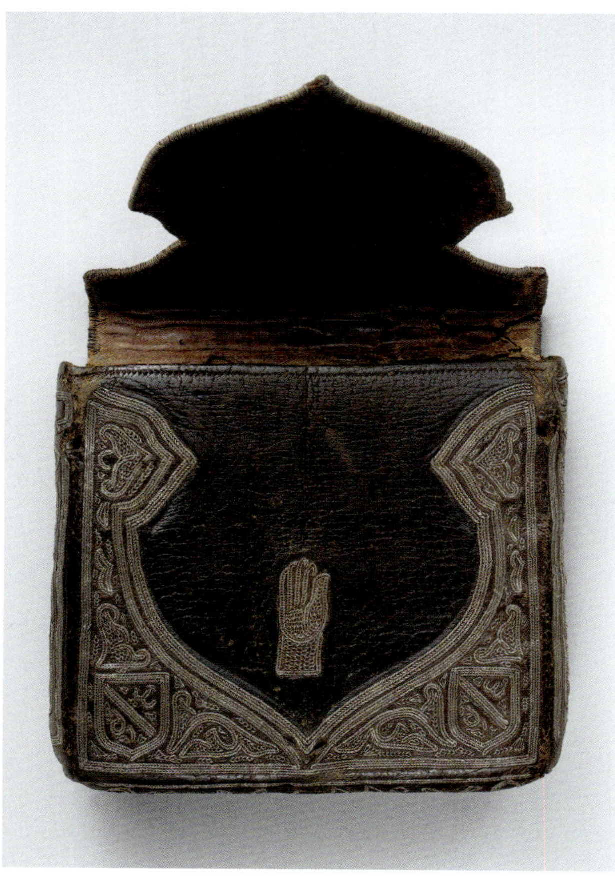

Detail of the *khamsa* motif

One of the few embroidered leather objects to have survived from the Nasrid period, this rare pouch bears the Nasrid dynastic shield and motto, "There is no victor but God." It probably held a section of a small Qur'an, likely a *juz'*. The square format and size are typical of those found in Spain and North Africa from the twelfth century onward. An inscription in French on a piece of paper found inside the pouch at the time of its acquisition claimed that it belonged to the last sultan of Granada, Muhammad XII (Boabdil, r. 1486–92).

With a shield-shaped opening flap, the pouch is decorated on the front with vegetal interlacing scrolls and the Nasrid motto, all embroidered in gilt-silver wire. Similar foliate designs surround the silver crescents that flank the inscription. On the back are interlacing star and curvilinear motifs, and another repetition of the motto. Under the flap is an image of the *khamsa*, an open hand with the palm facing outward (detail). This talismanic motif, believed to ward off the evil eye, was popular not only with the Nasrids but also with the Almohads, a Muslim dynasty of Berber origin.

The embroidered motifs on this Qur'an case belong to the larger decorative repertoire associated with Nasrid Granada. Metal embroidery on leather appears on Nasrid armor coverings and other ceremonial objects, and the dynastic shield and motto are found on objects as varied as silk textiles and architectural tilework. With their fanning terminals, vertical ascenders, and blocklike lettering, these inscriptions, all embroidered with gilt-metal wires, suggest a royal provenance.

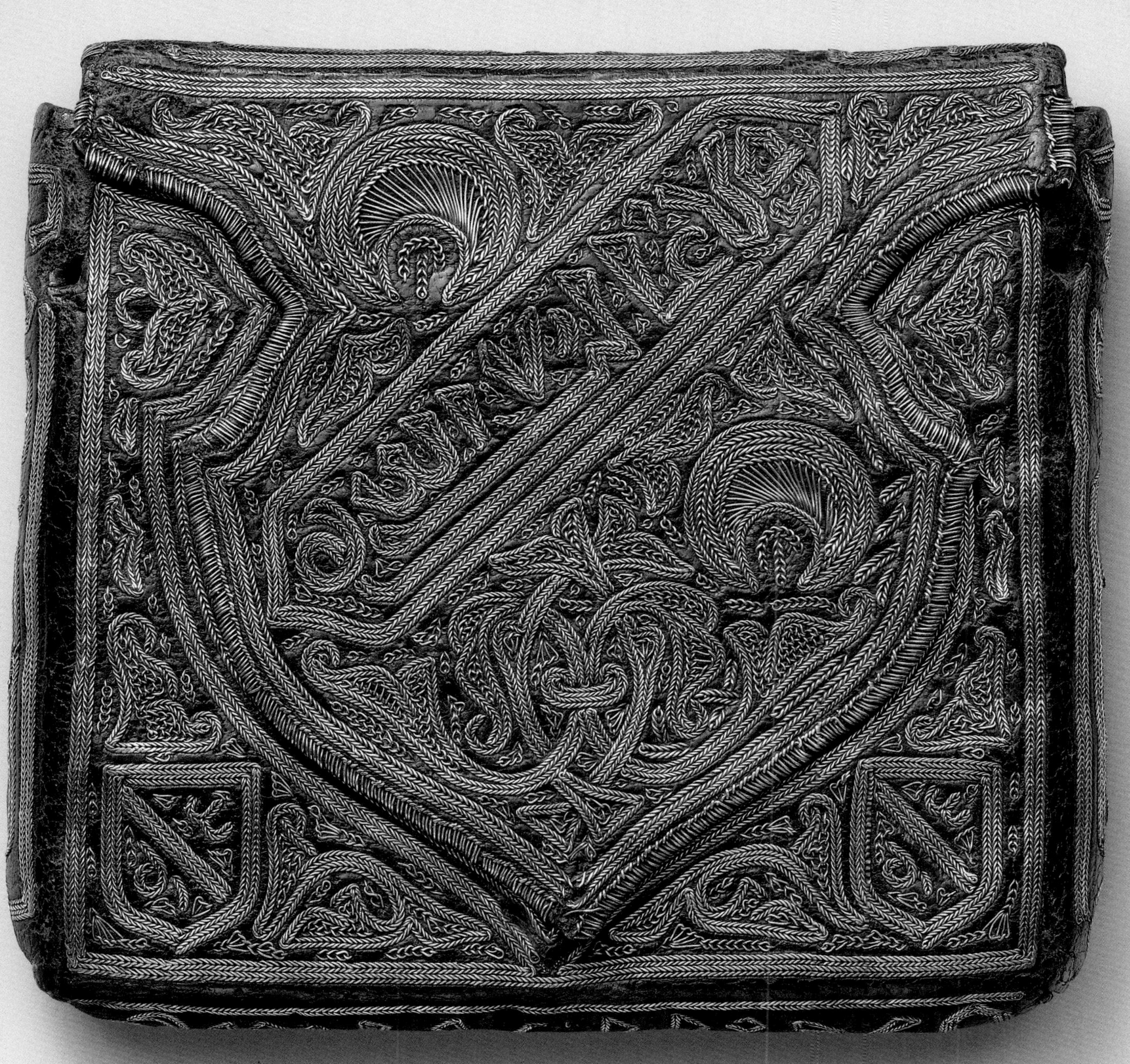

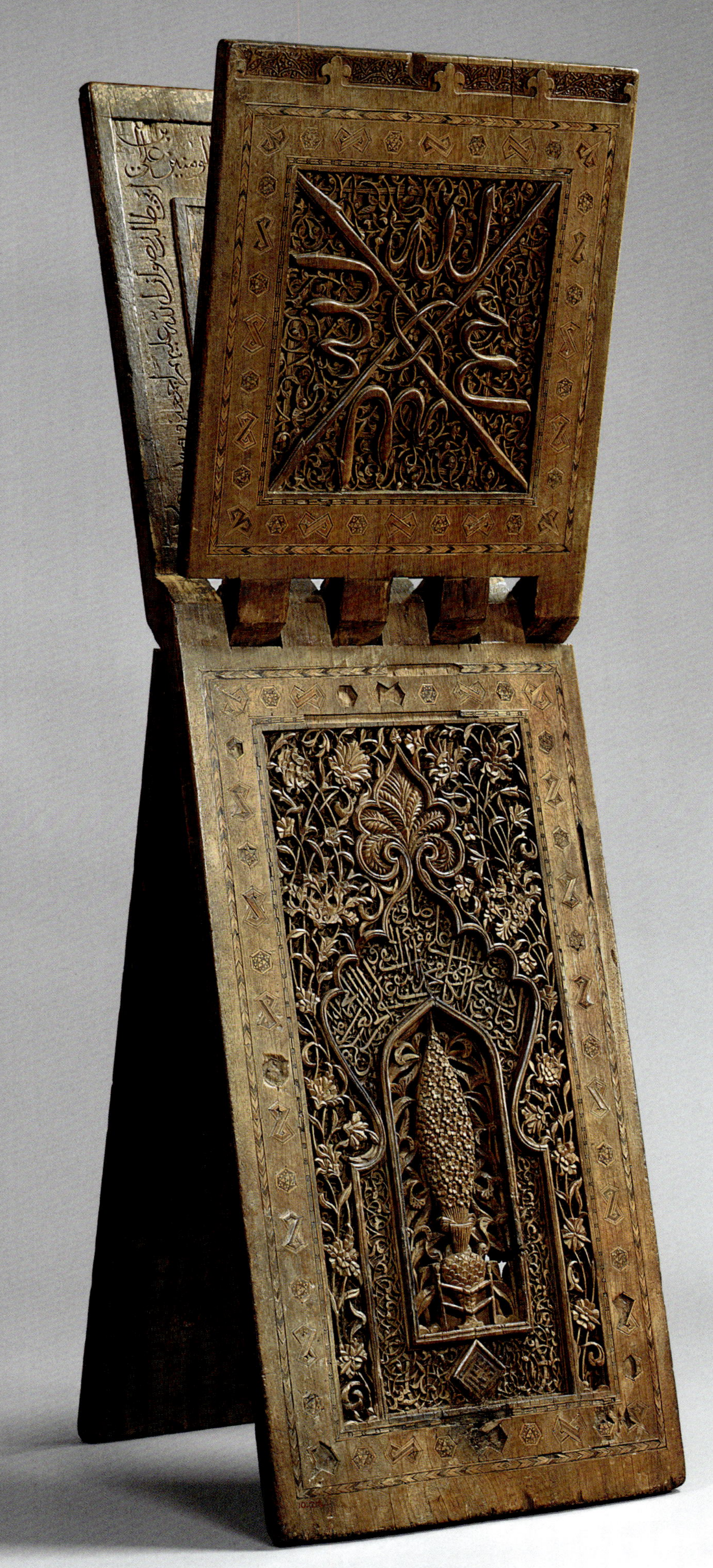

22

STAND FOR A QUR'AN (*RAHLA*)

Maker: Zain(?) Hasan Sulaiman Isfahani
Iran, dated A.H. 761/A.D. 1360
Wood (teak); carved, painted, and inlaid, closed: 51¼ x 16⅛ x 16½ in. (130.2 x 41 x 41.9 cm);
open: 45 x 50 x 16½ in. (114.3 x 127 x 41.9 cm)
Rogers Fund, 1910 (10.218)

When open, this stand, or *rahla*, forms an X, a perfect shape to hold a large copy of the Qur'an. This example is notable for its superb craftsmanship and intricate woodcarving (in Persian, *munabbat-kari*). It is made of a single slab of teak and framed by inlays of various other woods in shades of brown. The stand's decorative program is distinguished by layers of vegetal and geometric motifs, as well as by calligraphic inscriptions in three different scripts.

The panels can be divided into upper and lower segments. The outer surface of the square upper segments contain the word *Allah* repeated fourfold in elegant *thuluth* over a ground of vegetal scrolls and an obscure layer of carving beneath (possibly containing a hidden inscription; detail). The lower parts feature an elaborate composition, with a cypress tree at the center within an ogival niche, which is pierced and casts a shadow when the *rahla* is open. The niche is crowned by an inscription in *muhaqqaq* script that invokes Allah and bestows blessings on the Prophet and the Twelve Shi'i Imams, starting with 'Ali and ending with Mahdi (the twelfth, absent Imam). The text is framed within a polylobed cartouche surrounded by a flower-bearing plant, which originates at the base and rises upward. The maker's name, Zain(?) Hasan Sulaiman Isfahani, appears on the outer surface, just above the foot of the stand. Small square-*kufic* inscriptions refer to God's power and rule.

What survives of the incised inscription on the upper inner surface once contained blessings on the Prophet and his immediate successors, the four Rightly Guided Caliphs. However, the names of the first three caliphs, Abu Bakr, 'Umar, and 'Uthman, have been excised, leaving intact only the name of 'Ali, the fourth caliph and first Shi'i Imam. In Iran, inscriptions praising both the Rightly Guided Caliphs and the Twelve Imams are characteristic of the fourteenth century. However, after the adoption of Shiism as the official state religion by the Safavids in the early years of the sixteenth century, this practice was abandoned. 'Ali was thereafter regarded as the only legitimate successor of the Prophet, and the first three caliphs were rejected and never mentioned. It is for this reason that their names on this *rahla* were scratched out.

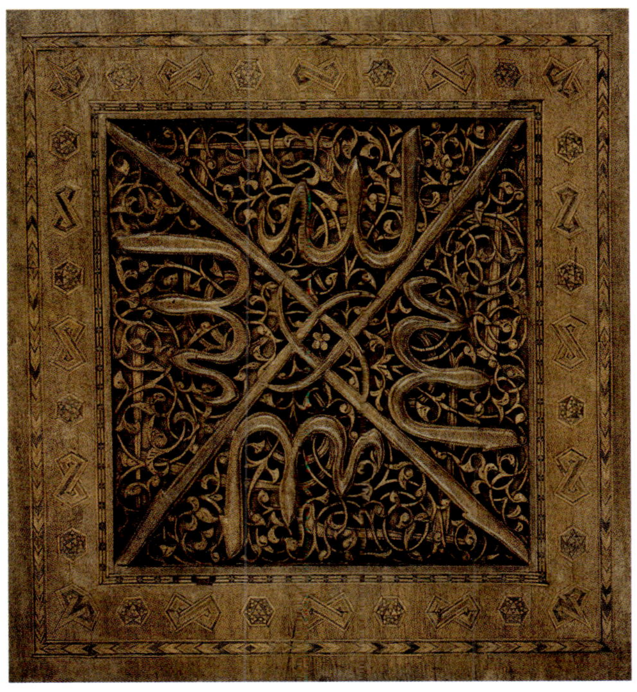

Detail of the repeated inscription *Allah*

23

MOSQUE LAMP OF AMIR QAWSUN WITH "LIGHT VERSE" FROM THE QUR'AN

Maker: 'Ali ibn Muhammad al-Barmaki(?)
Egypt, ca. 1329–35
Glass, colorless with brown tinge; blown, applied foot, enameled, and gilded,
H. 14⅛ in. (35.9 cm); max. Diam. with handles 10⁵⁄₁₆ in. (26.2 cm)
Gift of J. Pierpont Morgan, 1917 (17.190.991)

Used to illuminate the interiors of buildings such as mosques, tombs, and madrasas, mosque lamps were suspended from the ceiling by chains. They were intended not to hang alone but, rather, as integral elements in an overall lighting program. One can just imagine the rows of floating lamps, their lights flickering in unison. The significance of light as a symbol of the divine is a recurring theme in Islamic culture, particularly in mysticism or Sufism, in which man's union with God is the ultimate aim, and the interplay between light and shadow is a powerful metaphor.

This enamel-painted and gilded example is covered in inscriptions in a large, refined *thuluth* script. In addition to benedictory phrases, the inscription on the body tells us that the lamp was made for Qawsun (d. 1342), an amir at the court of the Mamluk sultan al-Nasir Muhammad (r. 1294–1340). It repeats his blazon, or heraldic symbol, six times—a red stemmed cup, representing his position as the sultan's cupbearer (*saqi*). It was among the most prestigious positions at court, and for this reason a number of extant glass, ceramic, and metal objects bear this emblem. The lamp was probably intended for either a mosque built in 1329 or a tomb-hospice erected by the sultan in 1335 in Cairo.

The inscription on the neck contains the beginning of the "Ayat al-Nur," or Light Verse (Qur'an 24:35), one of the most cherished and frequently quoted *ayas* from the Qur'an. Likening the light emanating from the lamp to the divine light of God, it reads: "Allah is the Light of the heavens and the earth. The parable of His Light is as if there were a Niche and within it a Lamp: the Lamp enclosed in Glass: the Glass as it were a brilliant star." Enameled painted glassware was exported to Europe, particularly Venice, where it inspired the production of local variants.

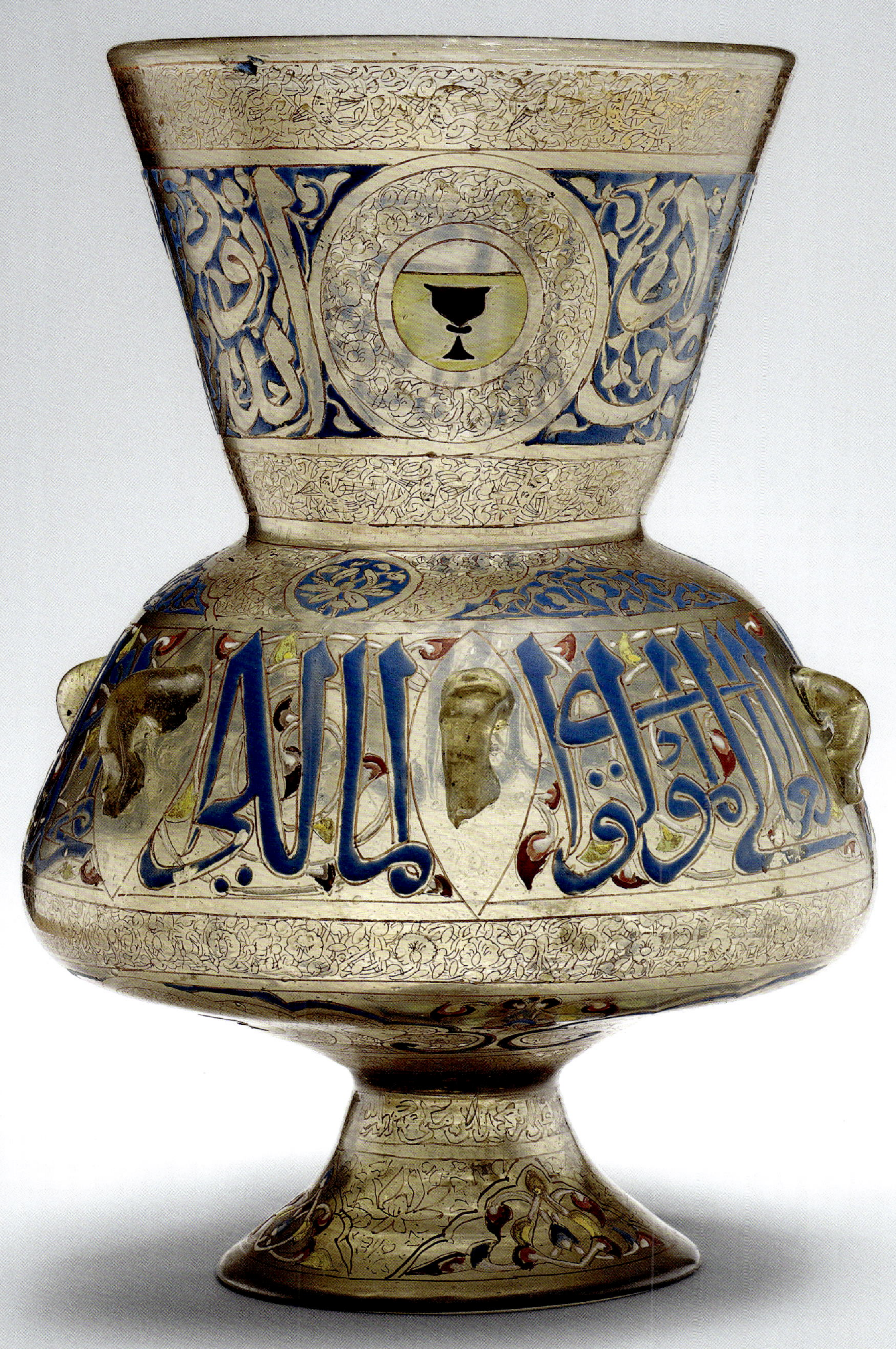

TILE FROM A *MIHRAB* WITH AN INSCRIPTION ON THE IMPORTANCE OF PRAYER

Iran, dated A.H. 722/A.D. 1322–23
Stonepaste; modeled, painted under transparent glaze, 27⅜ x 26 in. (69.5 x 66 cm)
Gift of William Mandel, 1983 (1983.345)

This tile was once the upper segment of a *mihrab*—the niche in the wall of a mosque or religious building that indicates the *qibla*, the direction toward the holy city of Mecca that worshippers face while praying. The inscription around the rim is from *sura* 11 (*Hud*), which stresses the importance of prayer and directly references the *mihrab*'s function. It reads, "In the name of God, the Merciful, the Compassionate. And perform the prayer at the two ends of the day and nigh of the night; Surely the good deeds will drive away evil deeds. That is a remembrance unto the mindful" (Qur'an 11:114). The fragment also provides the date of the tile's manufacture, A.H. 722 (A.D. 1322–23), which could also be when the mosque to which it once belonged was constructed.

The scrolling vegetation at the center is hand-modeled, creating a rich visual effect in combination with the blooming white peonies and framing calligraphy, gleaming beneath a lustrous transparent glaze. The designs are outlined in black with touches of turquoise, setting off a striking contrast to the bright cobalt-blue background. The vegetal and floral motifs follow a Chinese aesthetic and recall glazed tilework of the same period produced in Kashan, a major Iranian production center for tiles.

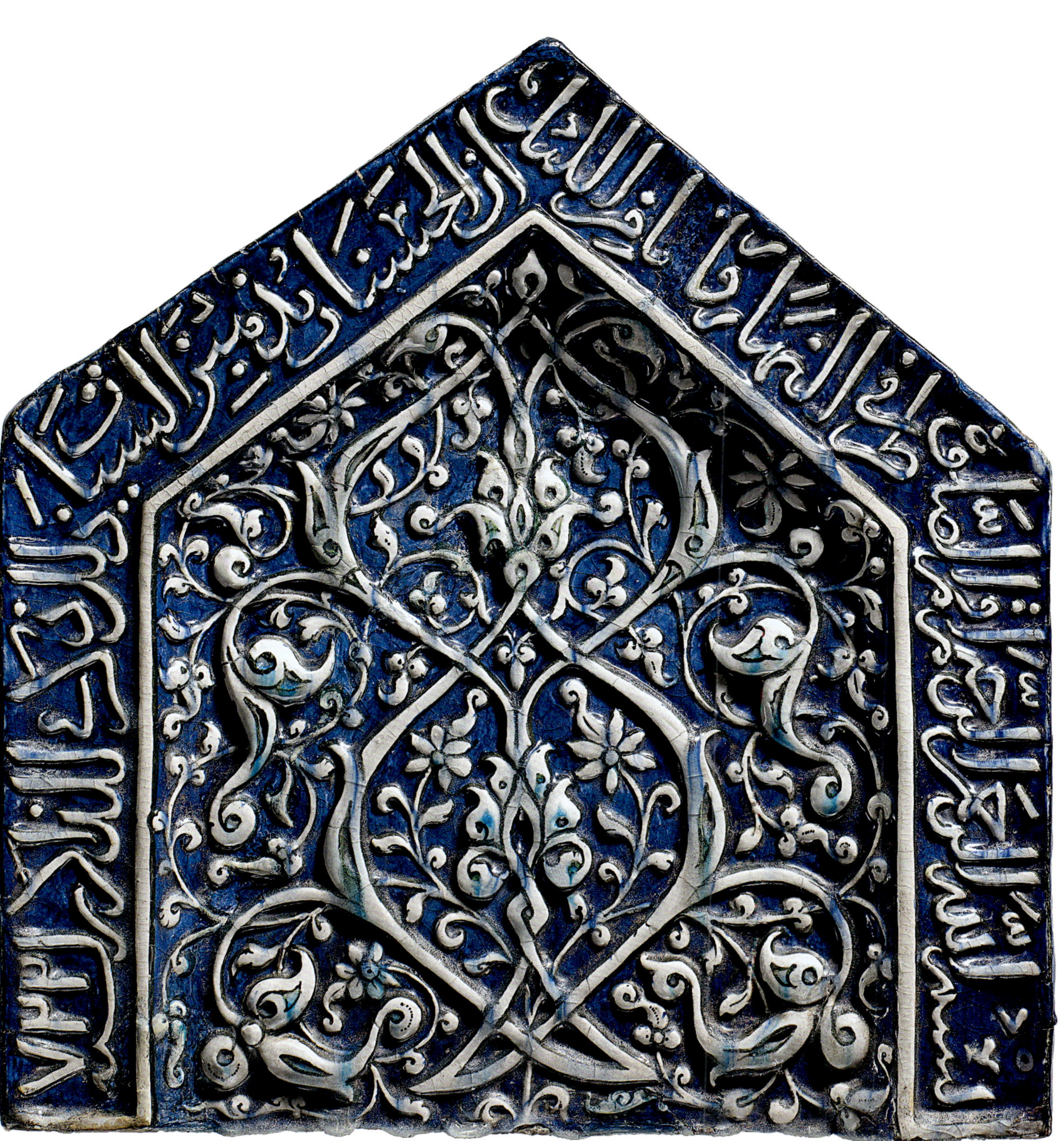

25a

FOLIO FROM AN EARLY MINIATURE QUR'AN

Central Islamic Lands, Abbasid, 9th century
Ink, opaque watercolor, and gold on parchment, 1½ x 2⅞ in. (3.8 x 7.3 cm)
Rogers Fund, 1962 (62.152.2)

25b

FOLIO FROM AN OCTAGONAL MINIATURE QUR'AN

Turkey or Iran, 17th century
Ink and gold on paper; leather binding, 1¼ x 1¼ in. (3.2 x 3.2 cm)
Gift of Joseph W. Drexel, 1889 (89.2.2156)

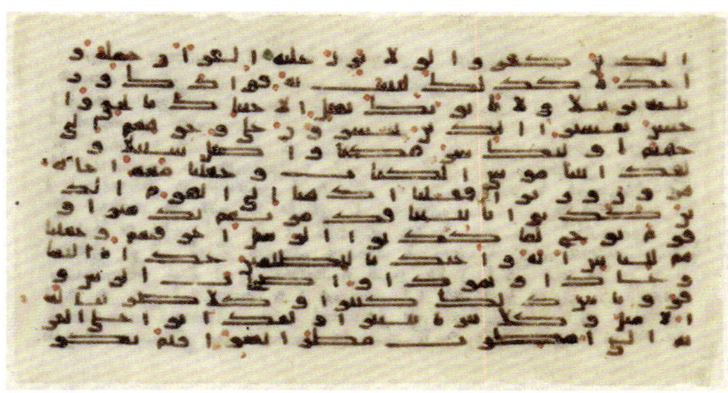

Actual size

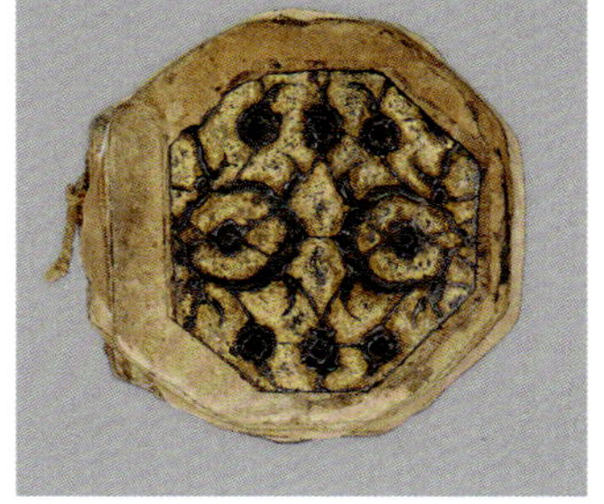

Actual size

Each of these miniature Qur'ans probably functioned as an amulet. The oblong format of the parchment example (cat. 25a) is similar to that of its full-size counterparts. Its size and shape suggest that it could have been carried close to the body in a pouch, pocket, or sleeve. The densely packed text is written in a diminutive variation of *kufic* characterized by thin, consistent strokes that extend horizontally along the baseline, with red dots marking short vowels. Here, the amuletic use of the text and its readability reinforce the "intimacy" between the object and its owner. Interestingly, in miniature Qur'an manuscripts, no matter how tiny the script, readability is never compromised, even though literacy is not required for benefit to be accrued. In fact, the reduction in scale serves to further concentrate or distill its power.

The octagonal example on paper (cat. 25b) is of a type that was popular in Turkey and Iran during the seventeenth through nineteenth centuries. Many were carried in lockets or leather cases, and they were used for various purposes. They were sometimes attached to armbands (*bazubands*) worn by rulers, princes, statesmen, and soldiers, or hung around a warrior's neck. Historical texts and paintings reveal that, in Ottoman Turkey, tiny manuscripts similar to this one, referred to as *sançak* Qur'ans, functioned as talismanic pendants that were placed in metal boxes or pouches and attached to the shafts of military standards (*'alams*). Whether affixed to a weapon or used as a ceremonial object, these Qur'ans were thought to empower and protect the sultan and his troops both on and off the battlefield.

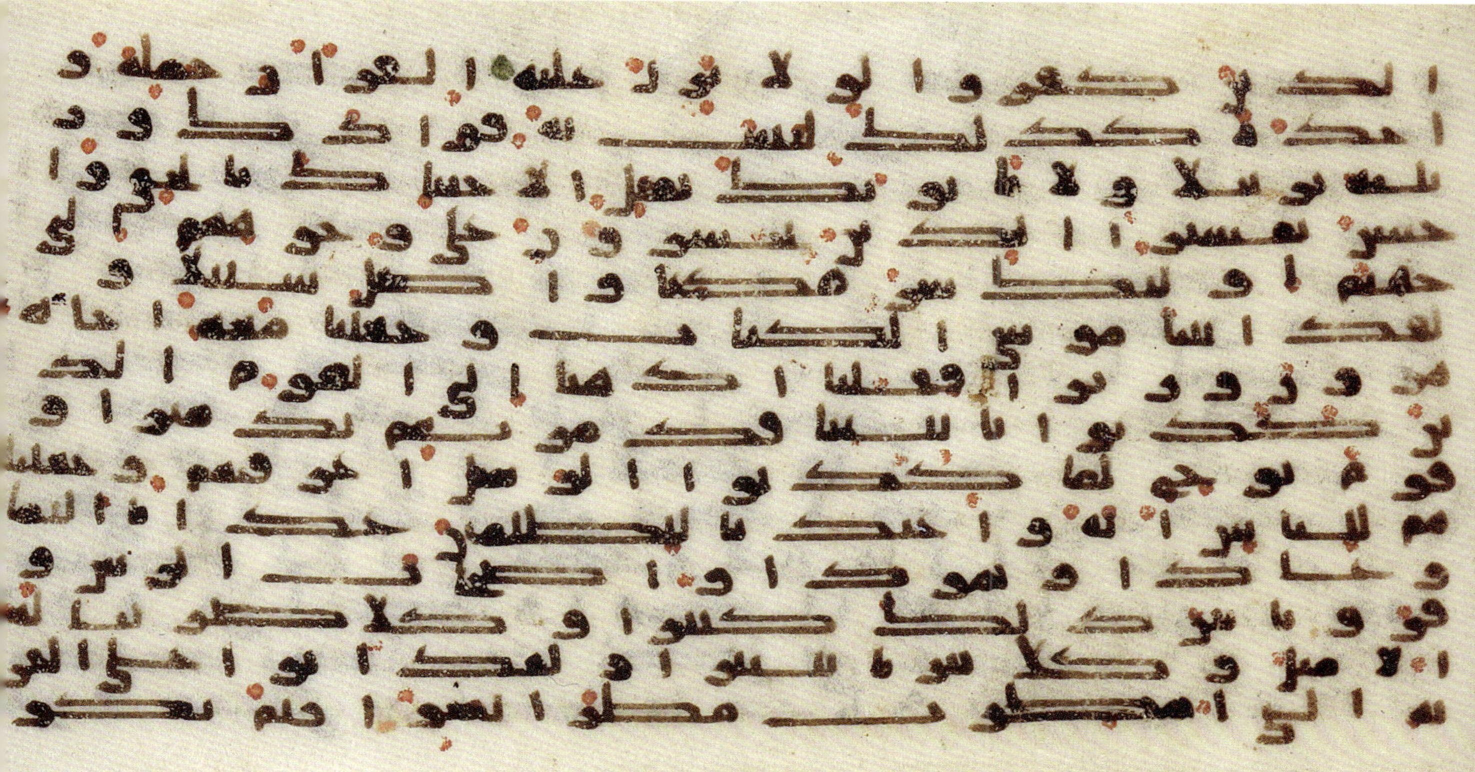

CUIRASS (*CHAR-A'INA*) WITH PROTECTIVE INSCRIPTIONS

Indian or Iranian, late 18th–early 19th century
Steel, gold, and textile, H. breastplate 13 in. (33 cm), backplate 15½ in. (39.4 cm), each side 9⅝ in. (24.5 cm);
W. overall 11¼ in. (28.5 cm); Diam. 9½ in. (24 cm); Wt. 7 lb. (3.16 kg)
Gift of Harry G. Friedman, 1948 (48.92.1)

Divine protection was especially desired by men at war, to ensure safety and success on the battlefield. Inscriptions transformed weapons, armor, and other martial objects into conduits between an owner-worshipper and holy personages and/or the divine. These talismans present a paradox, since they were meant to empower and provide courage, but they also reflect the owner's sense of vulnerability and a fear of danger and the unknown.

This steel cuirass consists of five plates bound together by hinges. Each plate is embellished with scrolling vines and flowers within a border containing inscriptions, applied in gold using a damascene-like technique (whereby a dark metal is inlaid with gold to obtain a rich contrast). The larger front and back plates terminate in parrot's-head finials. The inscriptions, which include Qur'anic verses, Shi'i prayers, and the names of the Fourteen Infallibles, imbue the cuirass with protective powers. The interplay of the steel plates and the Qur'anic verses accentuates the imagery of light, which is particularly appropriate for gold-embellished armors of the "four mirror" (*char-a'ina*) type. The "mirrors" in this context refer to the reflective surfaces of the plates prior to their decoration, believed to deflect the evil eye away from the warrior, keeping him safe.

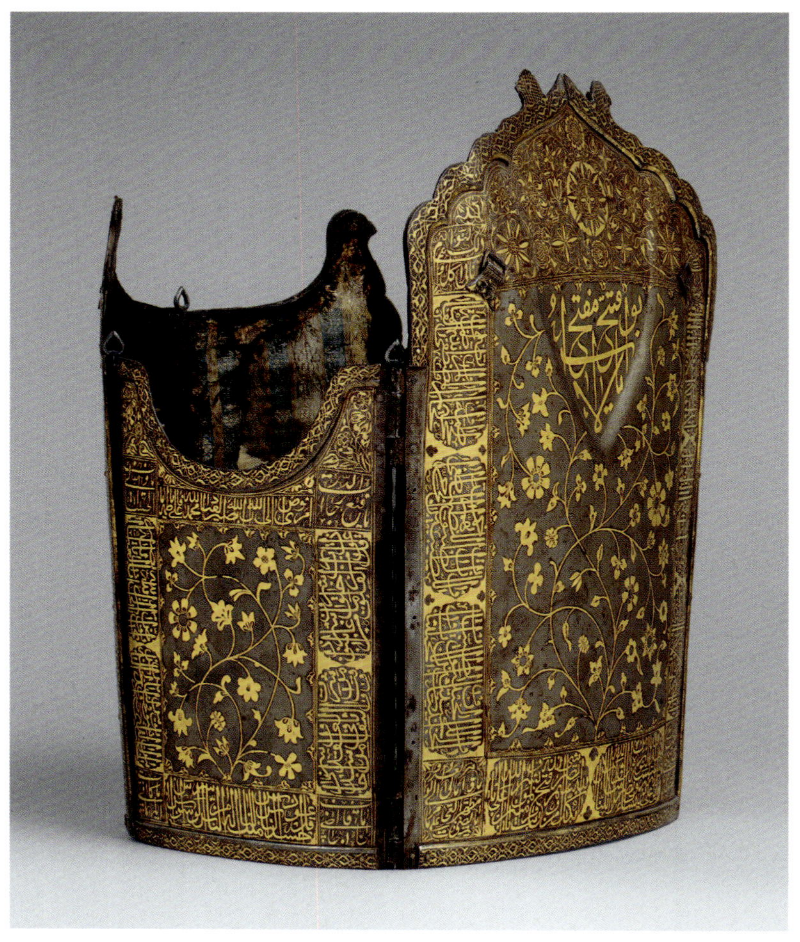

Back

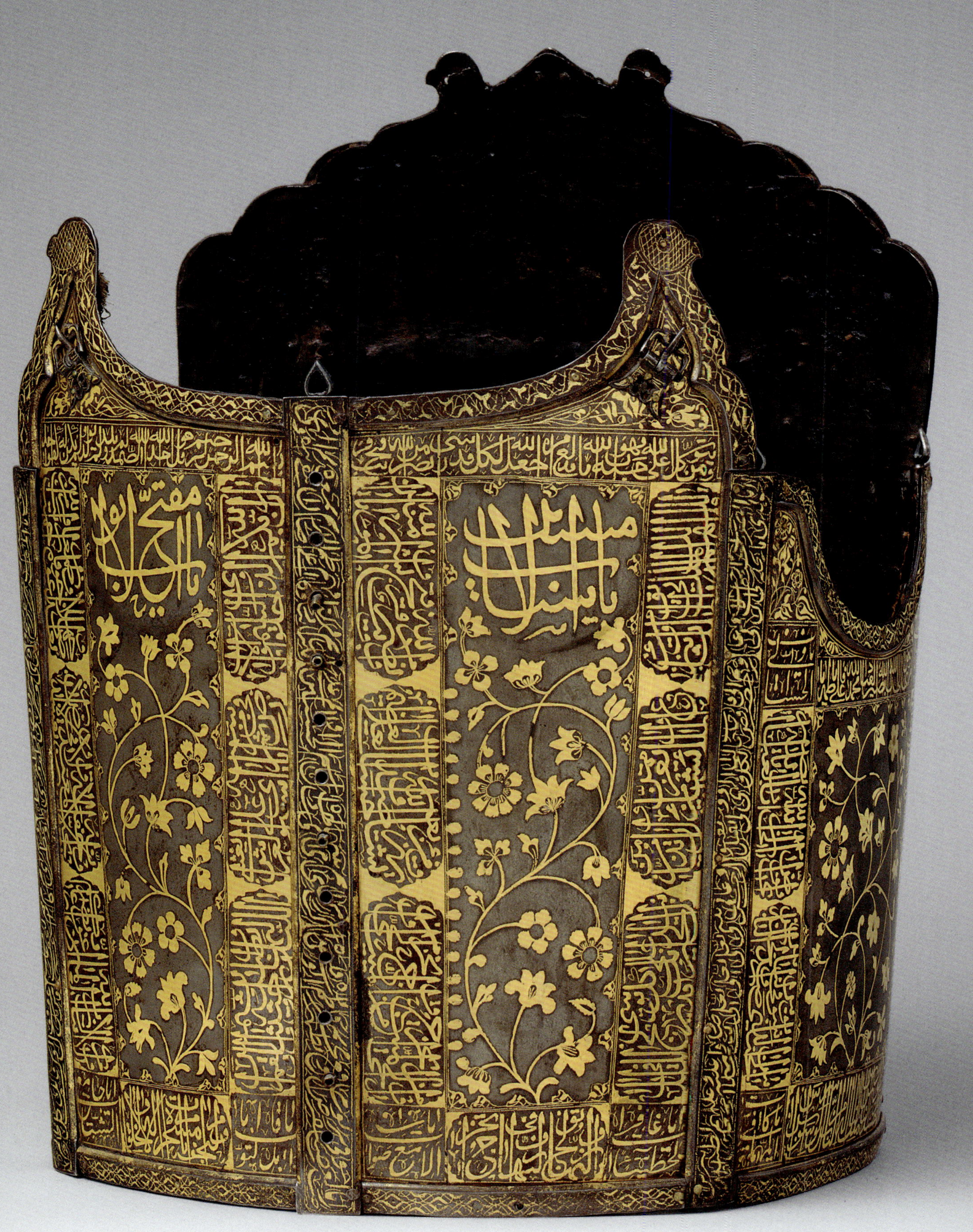

27

TALISMANIC SHIRT BEARING THE FULL TEXT OF THE QUR'AN

Northern India or Deccan, Indian Sultanate period, 15th–early 16th century
Cotton, ink, and gold; plain weave, painted, 25 x 38¾ in. (63.5 x 98.4 cm)
Purchase, Friends of Islamic Art Gifts, 1998 (1998.199)

The full text of the Qur'an is contained within the squares, medallions, and large rectangular sections that adorn the outer surface of this talismanic shirt (detail). Bordering these areas are the ninety-nine beautiful names of Allah (*asma al-husna*), written in gold against an orange background. A panel at the center of the reverse contains an inscription in gold stating, "God is the Merciful, the Compassionate," an invocation known as the *bismallah*.

Shirts of this type were worn under armor and were thought to protect a warrior in battle. They might also be worn off the battlefield, by an individual seeking relief from illness. While talismanic shirts were produced and used in Iran, Turkey, and India, the practice of transcribing the entire Qur'an onto a garment is seen only in those from Mughal and Deccan India. This example, attributed to the Deccan, is particularly rare because of its early date. Although technically a garment, designed and made to be worn, it also has close associations with the arts of the book, since its decoration consists entirely of calligraphy and illumination. The shoulder cartouches, decorated with roundels, contain checkerboard patterns bearing the name of God, and the two breast roundels repeat the *bismallah*.

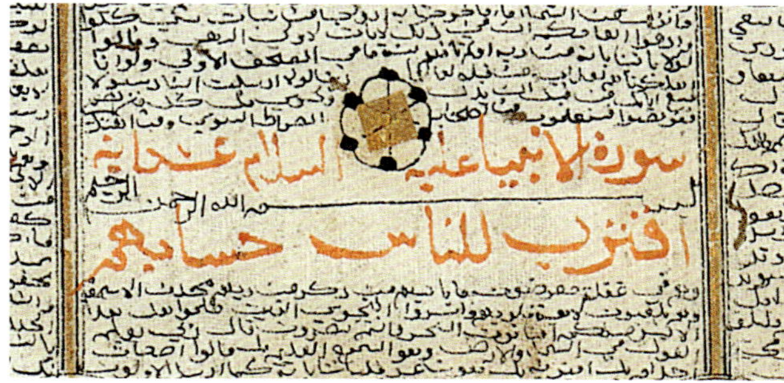

Detail of Qur'anic inscriptions

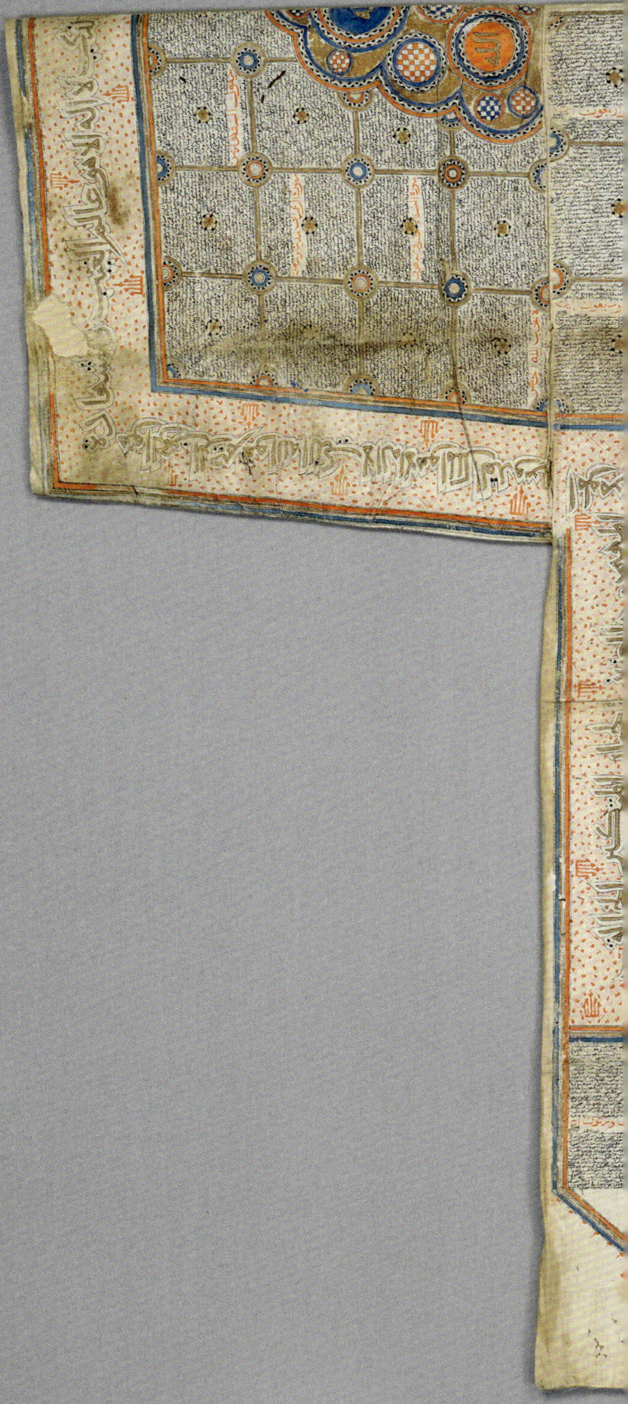

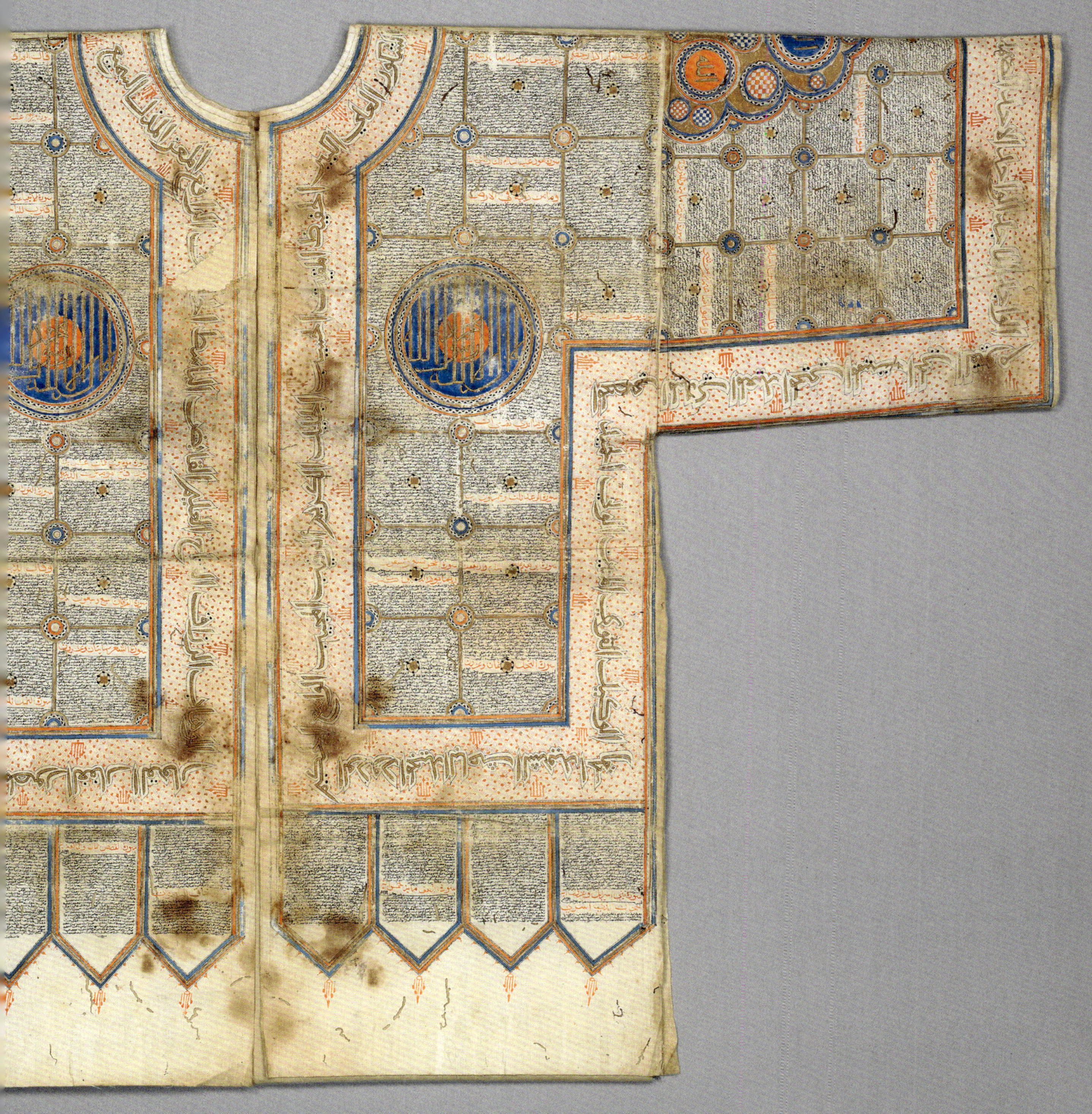

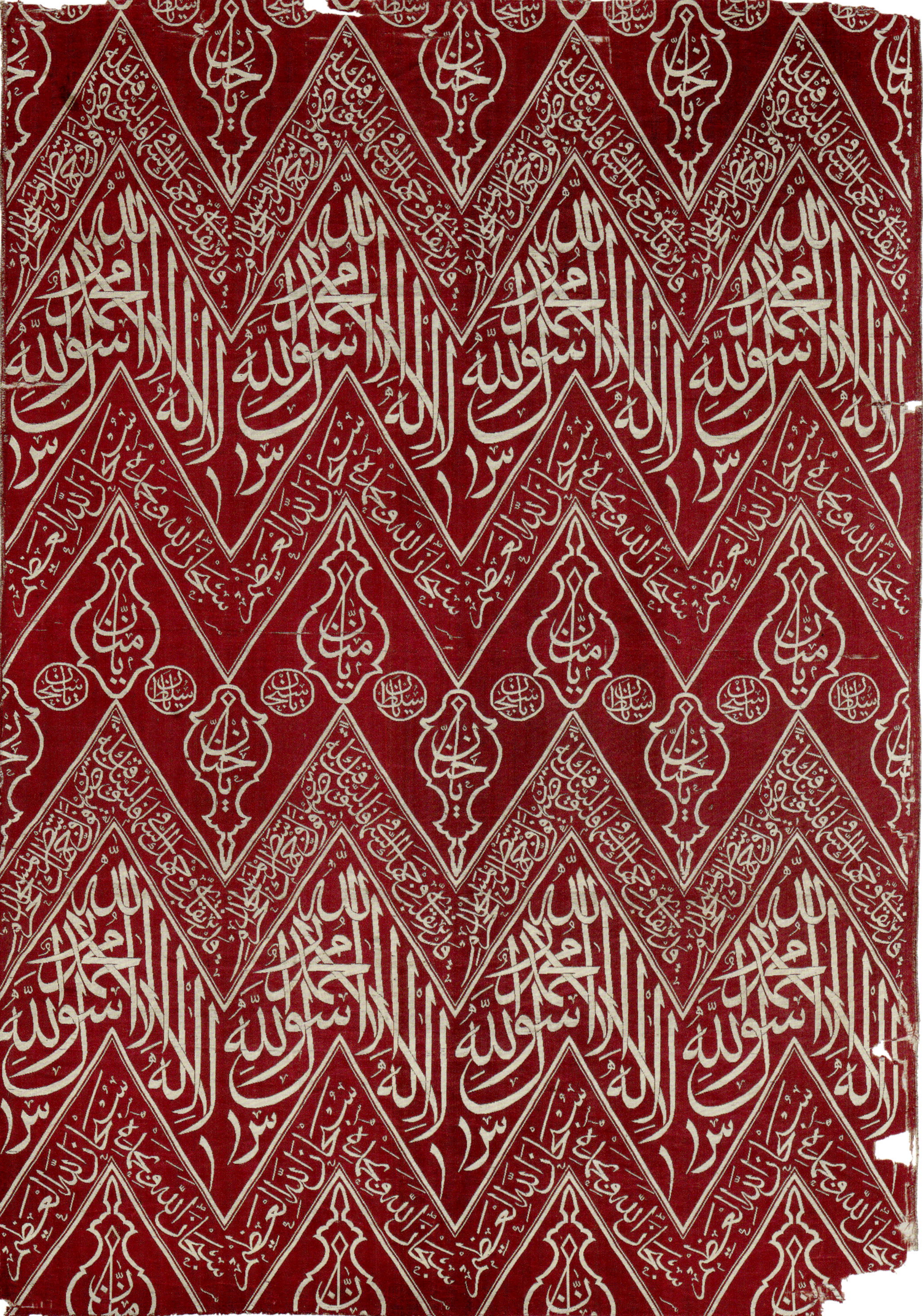
لا اله الا الله محمد رسول الله
يا حنان
يا منان

FRAGMENTARY CENOTAPH COVER WITH QUR'ANIC VERSES

Turkey, Ottoman, 17th–18th century
Silk; lampas, 38¼ x 26¾ in. (97.2 x 67.9 cm)
The Friedsam Collection, Bequest of Michael Friedsam, 1931 (32.100.460)

This silk textile is woven with Qur'anic verses, invocations to God, and the *shahada*, or Muslim profession of faith ("There is no God but God, and Muhammad is his Messenger"), all in elegant *thuluth* script. The Qur'anic verses include excerpts from *sura* 2 (*al-Baqara*, "The Cow") that state, "Indeed we see the turning of your face to heaven, so we shall surely turn you to *qibla* [the direction toward Mecca], which you shall like. Turn then your face toward the sacred mosque. . . ." The verses may allude to the intended use of this textile in a funerary context.

Muslims equated draping a cenotaph with holy verses to covering the deceased with blessings, or *baraka*. Furthermore, since such textiles traditionally had come into contact with holy places, they were thought to be carriers of divine grace. The present example is of a type used to cover the stone cenotaphs of Ottoman royalty and the elite. It recalls the similarly designed but much larger *kiswa* fabrics that Ottoman sultans sent to Mecca to adorn the Ka'ba—the cubic structure in the courtyard of the Great Mosque that all Muslims face when praying—as well as to Medina to drape over the Prophet's tomb and the graves of his companions. Such textiles were replaced annually, meaning they could be cut into fragments and reused as furnishings, garments, Qur'an pouches, and other objects.

The chevron (zigzag) pattern seen on this textile was established during the Mamluk period. It echoes the triangular shape of cenotaphs, as illustrated in a painting by the nineteenth-century Turkish painter Osman Hamdi Bey. In it, not only does the green tomb cover bear the same chevron pattern, but a similar design is painted on the cenotaph itself, under the textile (fig. 39). Although earlier examples were produced in Egypt, these silk textiles were likely woven in the imperial workshops in Istanbul and other Ottoman cities in the eighteenth century.

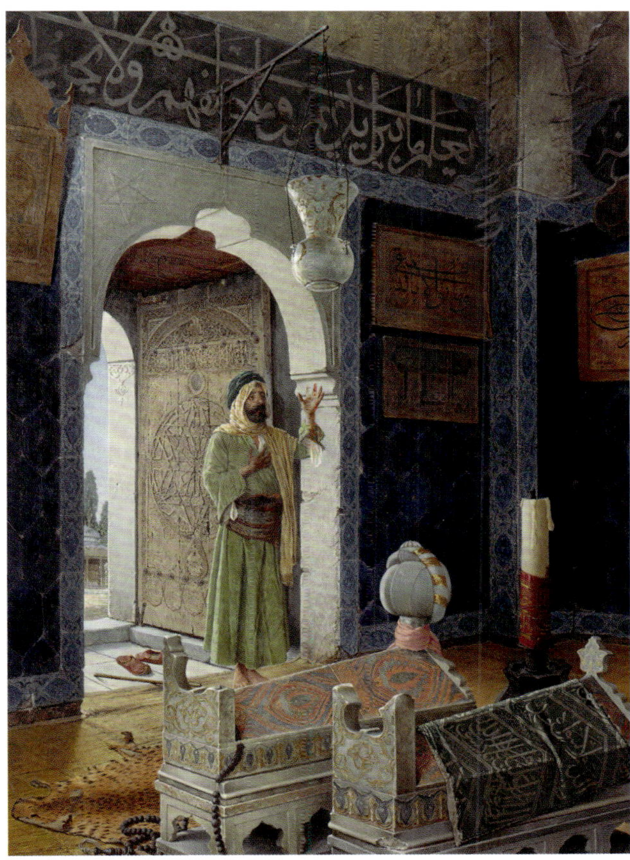

Fig. 39. Osman Hamdi Bey (Turkish, 1842–1910). *Old Man before Children's Tomb*, 1903. Oil on canvas, 184¼ x 152⅜ in. (72.5 x 60 cm). Musée d'Orsay, Paris (20736)

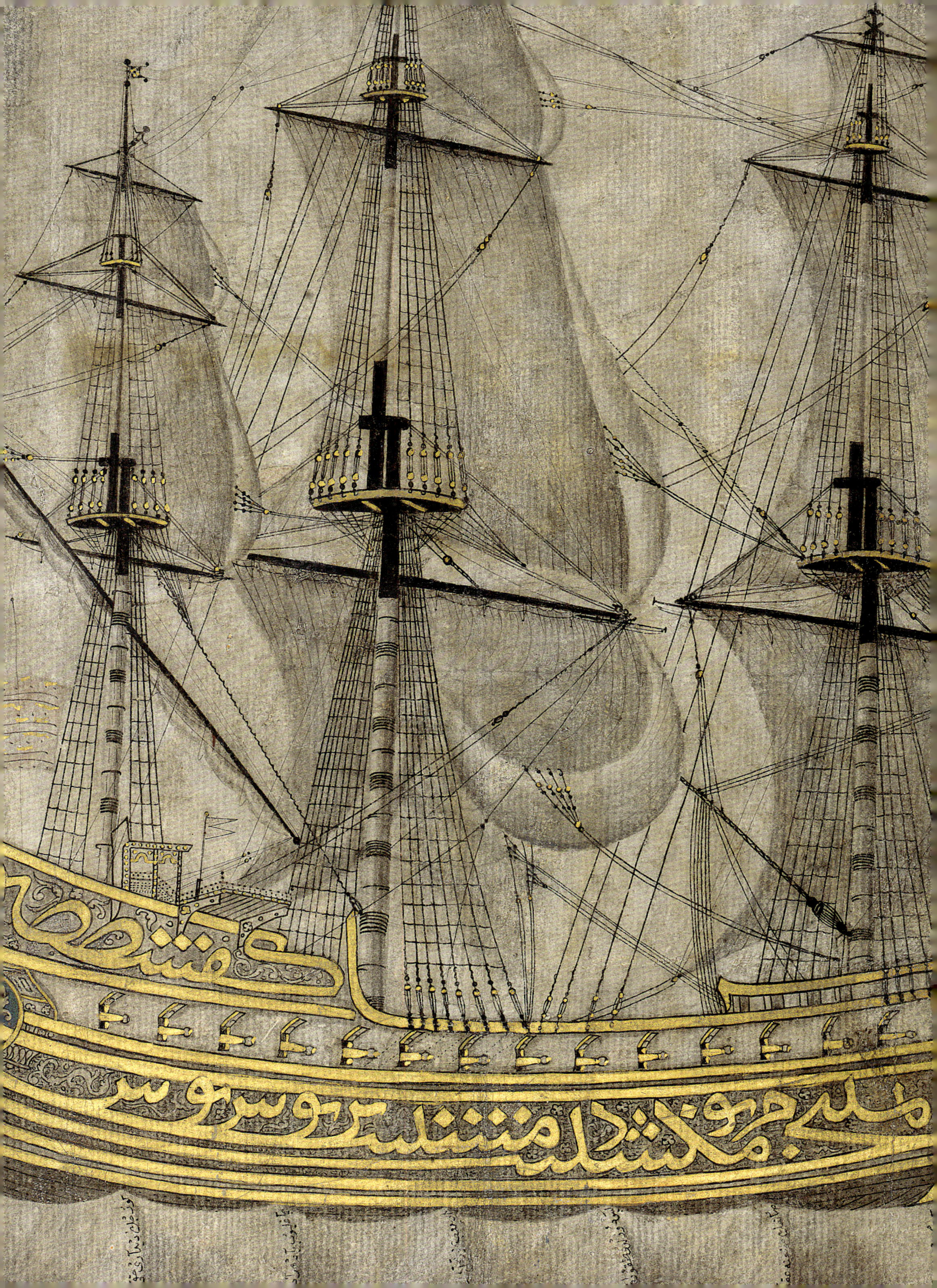

ORNAMENT AND ABSTRACTION

THE TRIUMPH OF FORM OVER CONTENT

From the early years of the Islamic era, calligraphers and artists recognized the artistic potential of the Arabic alphabet. Indeed, the ninth-century philosopher al-Kindi noted, "I do not know of any other form of writing in which the letters undergo so much beautifying and refining as they do in Arabic writing." Interest in exploring the decorative properties of writing was closely connected to the need or desire to embellish the text of the Qur'an, and this penchant for variety flourished and intensified with the passage of time across the Islamic world. The earliest forms of Arabic writing had appeared on stone and, subsequently, two-dimensional supports such as papyrus and parchment. Within a few decades after the codification of the Qur'an, however, Arabic writing occurred on virtually every support, from architecture, ceramics, and metalwork to textiles and wood. The primary challenge for the calligrapher/artist was what scholar Sheila Blair refers to as "an ambiguity of purpose"—that is, to strike a balance between the rigors of the calligraphic discipline, the communication of information, and the desire to instill wonder in the viewer. Another challenge was to adapt inscriptions to an array of shapes, formats, and media. For example, weaving an inscription into a textile required a very different set of skills than painting it on a ceramic vessel or carving it in wood or stone. Although calligraphers and craftsmen deemed it important to follow the prescribed canon of scripts, many took liberties, sometimes breaking with tradition

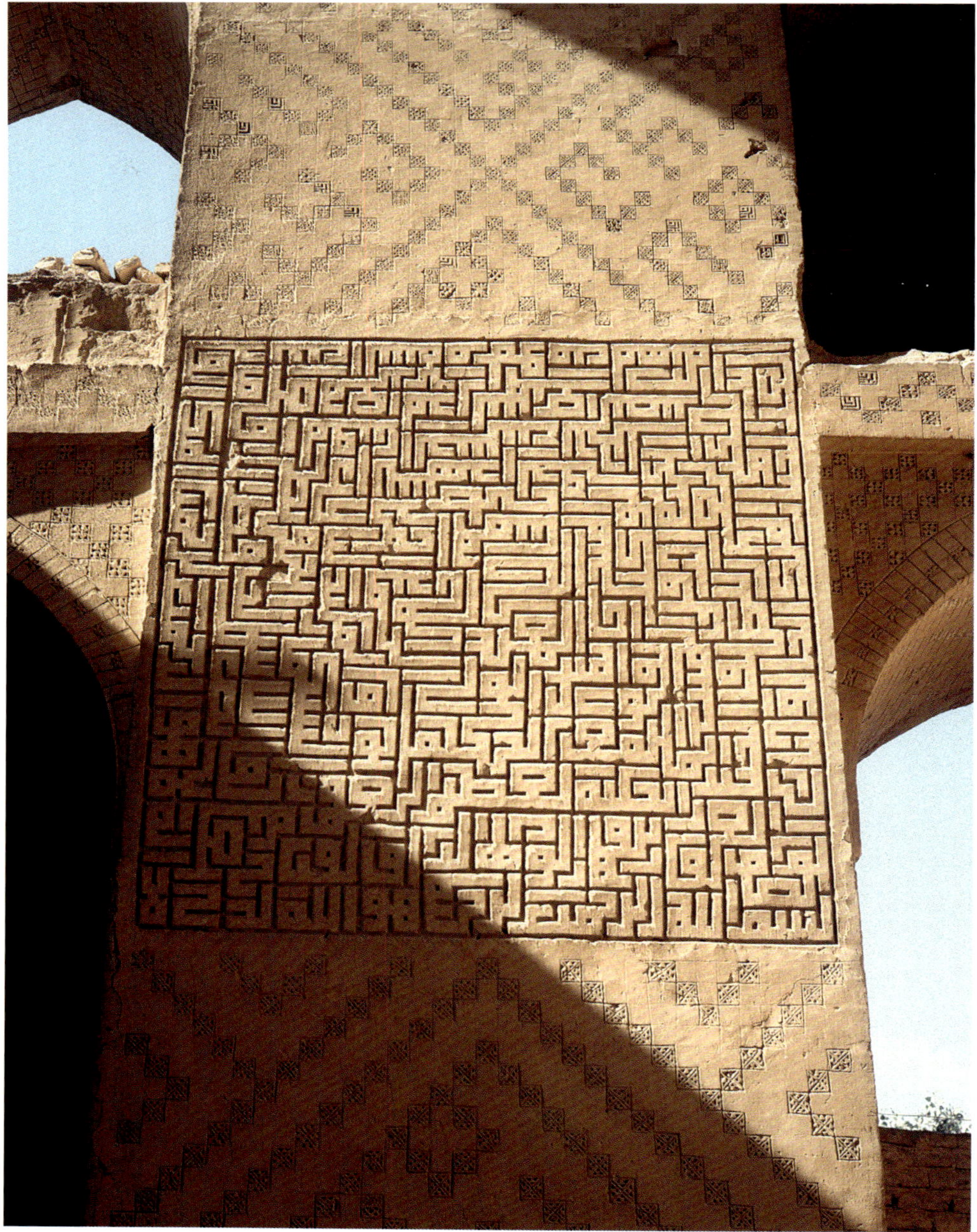

Fig. 40. Carved stucco inscription in square *kufic*, Pir-i Bakran shrine, Linjan, Iran, 14th century

and allowing their imagination, sense of humor, and desire to induce awe to take over. The result was an art form with unparalleled variety, creativity, and complexity across time and place.

Experimentation and innovation in Islamic calligraphy reached new heights in the sixteenth century and continued to evolve into the modern period, exhibiting an increasing tendency toward abstraction and ornamentation that moved to eliminate verbal clarity altogether. Such stylization could sometimes make inscriptions difficult to decipher, relegating meaning subordinate to aesthetics and allowing form to overshadow content. The inherent tension between textual design, decoration, readability, and verbal clarity raises several fascinating questions: Were these texts meant to be read in a literal sense? How were they perceived by their creators, patrons, and viewers, or in non-Arabic-speaking regions, where the majority of the population was unable to read them? Although we may not have definitive answers, scholars continue to develop interesting hypotheses.

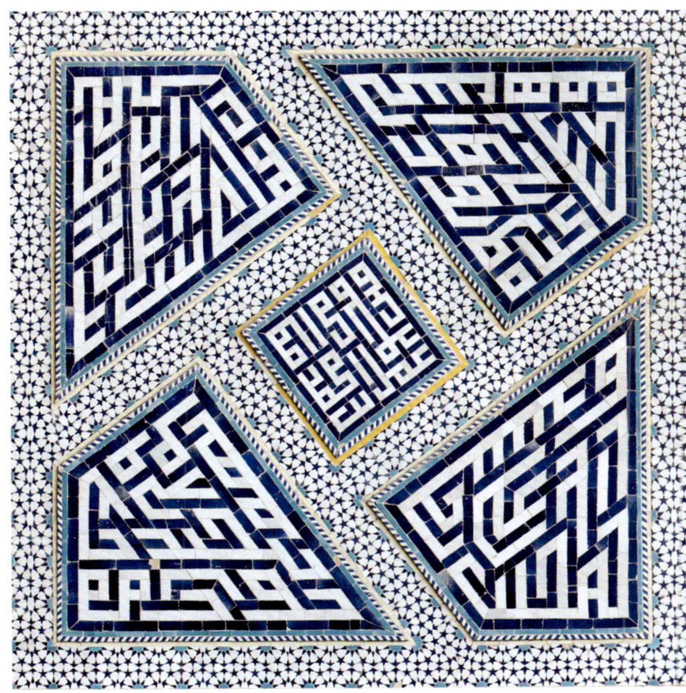

Fig. 41. Tile with an inscription in geometric *kufic*, Shah Mosque, Isfahan, Iran, 17th century

The Question of Abstraction

Abstraction of calligraphic scripts appeared in the Islamic world within a century or two after the emergence of Islam, well before the advent of twentieth-century Western modernism. In the earliest, parchment copies of the Qur'an, the writing was highly stylized and used only the armature of the letters (*rasm*), with no short vowels or diacritical marks, rendering them difficult to read even for a highly literate person (see cats. 15a, b). The earliest instances of abstracted square *kufic* can be found on brick structures in Iran; it would also appear later in other regions, such as Turkey and Egypt, in media including stucco and marble. One impressive example is a panel bearing the names of the Fourteen Infallibles (the Prophet, his daughter Fatima, and the Twelve Shi'i Imams), on the fourteenth-century tomb of a Sufi saint at Pir-i Bakran, at Linjan, near Isfahan (fig. 40). Another notable example, a glazed tile panel in the seventeenth-century Safavid Shah Mosque in Isfahan, bears the names Allah, Muhammad, and 'Ali (cousin and son-in-law of Muhammad, and the last Rightly Guided Caliph), as well as a poem and the name of the tile maker (fig. 41). On a smaller scale, square *kufic* features on a fourteenth-century marble tombstone from Yazd, now in The Met's collection (fig. 42), in inscriptions that include passages from the Qur'an (3:18 and 40:16), a segment of the *shahada*, or profession of the faith ("There is no God but Allah"), and the names of Allah, Muhammad, and 'Ali.

These are just a few examples demonstrating that the meaning of a calligraphic inscription relies as much

Fig. 42. Detail of geometricized *kufic* inscription on a tombstone. Yazd, Iran, A.H. 753/A.D. 1352. Marble; carved, 32¾ x 21¾ x 3½ in. (83.2 x 55.3 x 8.9 cm). Rogers Fund, 1935 (35.120)

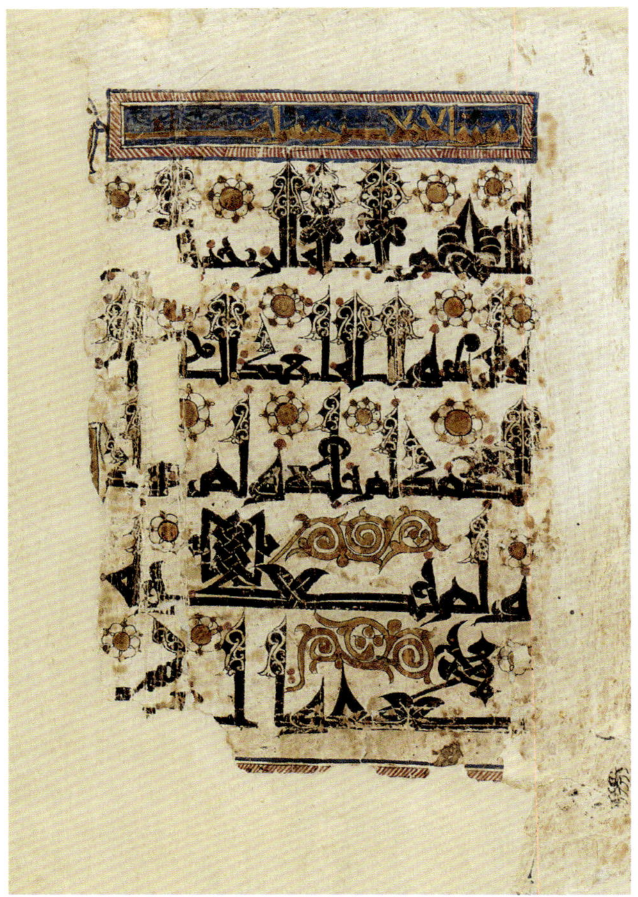

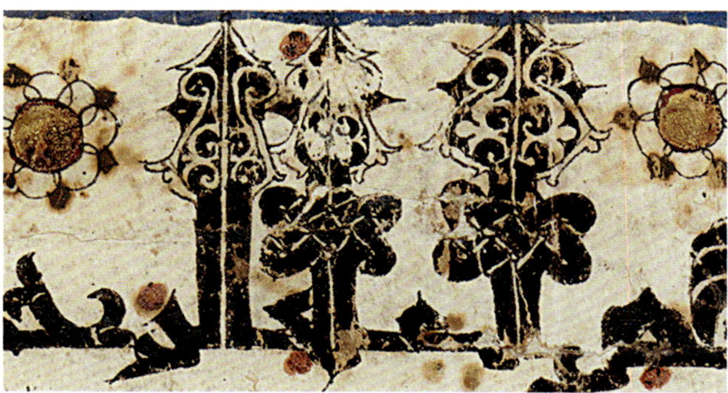

Fig. 43. Folio with plaited script. Iran or Central Asia, Seljuq, 11th century. Ink, opaque watercolor, and gold on paper, 9⅞ x 7⅛ in. (25.1 x 18.1 cm). Rogers Fund, 1945 (45.140). Detail of plaited *kufic*

on nonverbal elements such as script type, scale, spatial organization, ornamental features, and legibility as it does on its content. They also illustrate the blurred boundaries between text and image and raise questions about the ways in which inscriptions were experienced and perceived. Scholars have suggested that abstract and decorative inscriptions, particularly Qur'anic and other religious ones, acted as signifiers, the primary purpose of which was to affirm belief and serve as a focus for meditation and devotion, rather than as texts to be read word for word. Therefore, the very presence of inscriptions on buildings, objects, and folios rendered them efficacious and, in some cases, talismanic. They appear to have sometimes functioned as signs and coded images whose mystery and sacred potency were facilitated and enhanced by their indecipherability.

Decorative Scripts

In the early decades of the Islamic era, calligraphers and artists rendered the Arabic scripts more decorative by shaping them to accentuate the page format—they stretched letters horizontally along the baseline or elongated the shafts of upright letters, leaving the weight of the text in the lower half of the line. They created attractive variations of the *kufic* and new-style scripts and experimented with color and contrast, as seen in the interior mosaics of the Dome of the Rock (see fig. 14) and in the Blue Qur'an (cat. 16), both of which set gold lettering against a vivid blue ground. By the tenth century, in the eastern reaches of the Islamic world, artists were plaiting or interlacing the vertical shafts and horizontal bars of letters (fig. 43 and detail) and transforming the terminals and sometimes medial letters into palmettes, floral motifs, tendrils, and scrolls.

Scholars have studied the use of these decorative devices in an attempt to categorize and date them. Their findings demonstrate that the development of ornamental styles did not follow a linear path from simple to complex. In fact, in the absence of dated evidence, creating an accurate chronology is almost impossible: there was no formula. In some instances, the extent of ornamentation was dictated by the content of the inscriptions. While legibility was maintained for important dedicatory, foundation, or pious inscriptions, we can see in examples such as a tenth-century textile from Yemen (cat. 32) and a twelfth-century metal ewer from Iran (cat. 31) that liberties were taken for benedictory and other, less weighty texts. In other instances, inscriptions formed part of a more elaborate program of decoration and were placed in registers, bands, compartments, and cartouches that provided structure. Furthermore, in addition to animating the letters themselves, artists filled backgrounds and

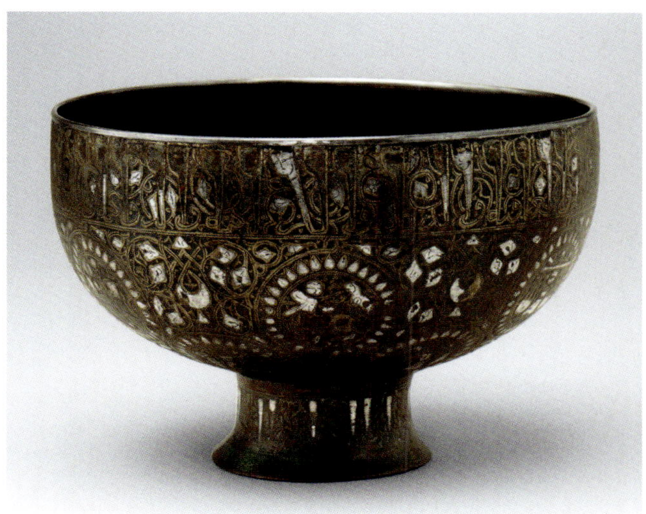
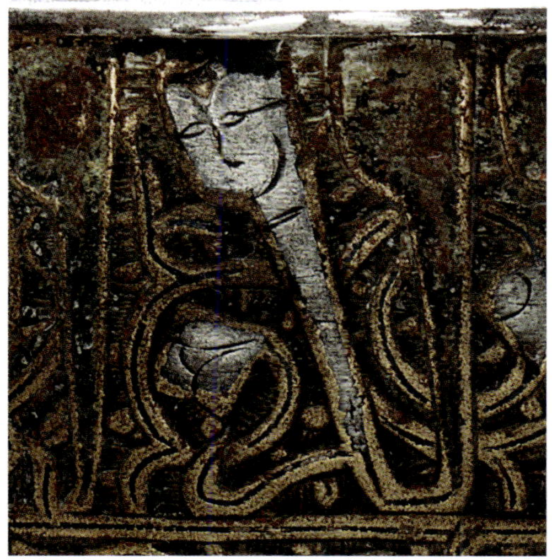

Fig. 44. Footed bowl with anthropomorphic script. Attributed to Iran, early 13th century. Bronze; inlaid with silver and black compound, H. 4⅜ in. (11.1 cm); Diam. 6¹⁵⁄₁₆ in. (17.6 cm). Edward C. Moore Collection, Bequest of Edward C. Moore, 1891 (91.1.543). Detail of human-headed *naskh* script

interstitial spaces with vegetal and floral scrolls. The scholar Lisa Volov Golombek has interpreted the use of such devices as an infusion of a sense of humor and charm into an otherwise sober epigraphic program.

From the tenth century onward, calligrapher-artists exercised even greater freedom, experimenting with techniques and creating novel styles of writing. One curious type involved transforming letters, usually in *kufic* or *naskh*, into human-, bird-, and animal-like forms. This playful use of writing was unique to metalwork from Khurasan, in northeastern Iran, and, in the twelfth and thirteenth centuries, from Mosul, in present-day Iraq. Blurring the lines between text and image, zoomorphic and anthropomorphic inscriptions vary widely. In some cases, the upright letters terminate in heads with the usual facial features (fig. 44 and detail), while in others, they act as the arms and legs of figures—some even carry weapons. Animated letters could be generously spaced or very compact. By the end of the thirteenth century in Syria, animated calligraphy had disappeared and was replaced by the austere *thuluth*, *muhaqqaq*, and *naskh* scripts. Images of animals and humans were extracted from the inscription fields and placed instead in separate registers.

Mirror-Image Writing and Pseudo-Inscriptions

Referred to in Arabic as *muthanna*, mirror-image writing can be defined as an inscription that is arranged symmetrically so that one side "mirrors" the other. It is seen on architecture, furnishings, and textiles in Iran, Fatimid Egypt, Ottoman Turkey, and Deccan India (cat. 33). Although the technique's origins are unknown, it has been suggested that the earliest examples, which date to the mid-eighth century and are in a utilitarian, nondecorative script, are carved on rocks in Ghar al-Hamam, at Tayma, on the Arabian Peninsula. In the Ottoman empire, mirror-image writing was most often associated with the Bektashi Sufis, an order with strong Shi'i leanings founded in the early fourteenth century. By the seventeenth and eighteenth centuries, the sect controlled a network of dervish lodges (*tekkes*) throughout the empire. Mirror writing was associated with the Bektashi belief that ʿAli and the Prophet Muhammad were mirror reflections of the exoteric, or *zahir*, and esoteric, or *batin*, aspects of the divine—that is, complementary manifestations of the same sacred reality. In the fifteenth century, mirror writing reached Deccan India from Turkey and Iran, probably due to an influx into the subcontinent of talented Iranian and Ottoman calligraphers, painters, and artisans.

Another curious, and somewhat baffling, category of script is what art historians refer to as pseudo-calligraphy or pseudo-epigraphy. These inscriptions, occurring mainly in ceramics, textiles, carpets, and paintings, appear to be Arabic words or phrases but are, in fact, random groups of indecipherable and illegible letters. This is not attributed to the artist's illiteracy or lack of proficiency in Arabic; rather, they were likely never meant to be read. The intention and meaning of pseudo-inscriptions seem to rely largely on context. For example, pseudo-epigraphy on a fifteenth-century luster dish from Spain (cat. 34) can be interpreted as an indicator of the refinement, taste, and status of the patron, or perhaps of the prestige and popularity associated with "things Arab" long after Muslim political control in the region had ended. Some pseudo-inscriptions had a protective function, as seen in a seventeenth-century Turkish prayer rug (fig. 45). It bears a perfectly legible inscription at its borders but relies on pseudo-inscriptions at the foot. Here, the placement of the pseudo-writing is well thought out. To protect the sacred texts from being stepped on and violated, the designer rendered them illegible.

Pseudo-*kufic* is also present in several European paintings of the tenth to sixteenth century, appearing on the halo crowning the Virgin Mary (fig. 46) or on rugs and textiles depicted in the painting. We do not know if the Europeans knew that these inscriptions were illegible. It is possible that artists and patrons wanted to express a cultural universality for the Christian faith, by blending together various written languages at a time when the church had a strong international presence. Arabic pseudo-inscriptions were also thought to imbue objects intended for rulers or church officials with a degree of luxury, opulence, and refinement.

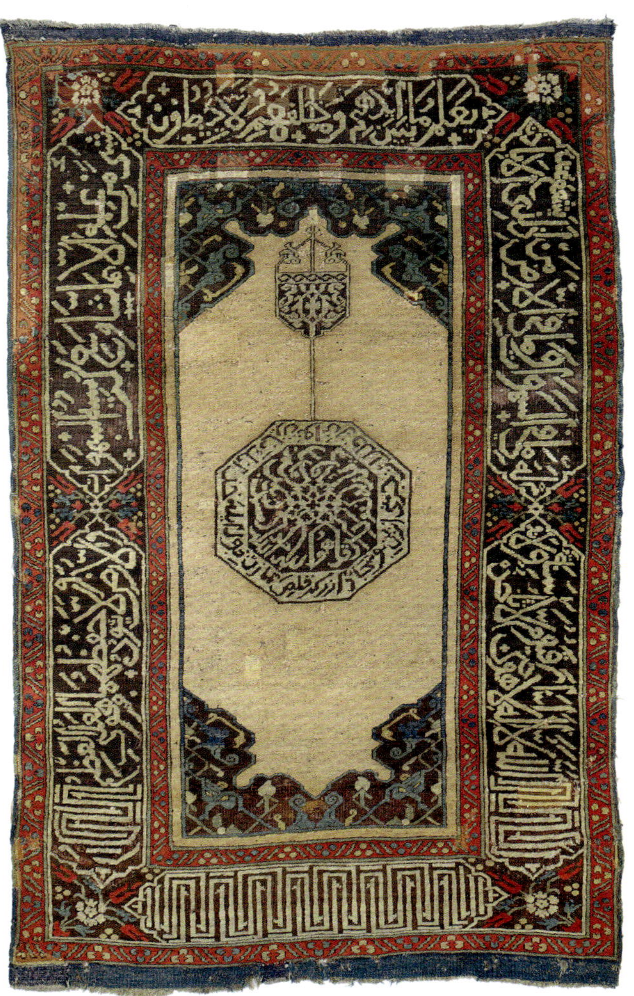

Fig. 45. Carpet with pseudo-*kufic* border. Attributed to Turkey, probably 17th century. Wool; symmetrically knotted pile, 64 x 41 in. (162.6 x 104.1 cm). The James F. Ballard Collection, Gift of James F. Ballard, 1922 (22.100.123)

Words as Tiny as Dust

Calligraphers were always looking for ways to arouse awe and wonder in a viewer. One way they achieved this was through the manipulation of scale. Texts could be monumental, as seen in the abovementioned Qur'an folio copied with an oversize pen by 'Umar Aqta' (cat. 18)—the *alif* alone is fourteen centimeters high—or so tiny that they could be read only with the aid of a magnifying glass. It was considered a great feat to be able to write an entire Qur'anic verse on a kernel of rice or to

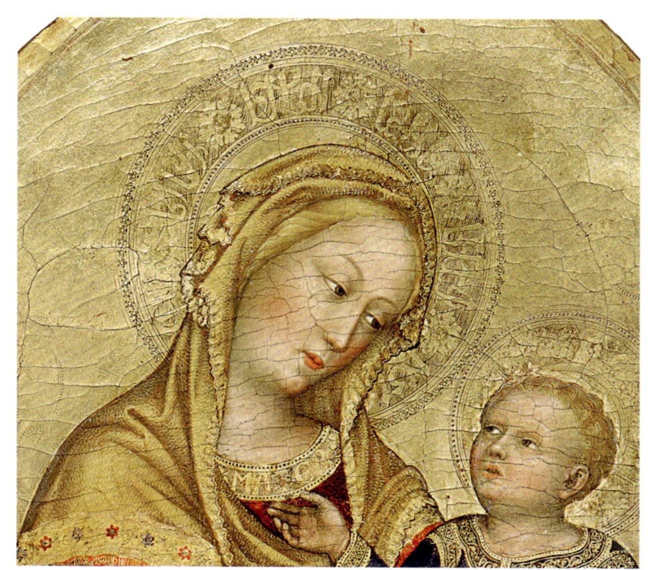

Fig. 46. Gentile da Fabriano (Italian, ca. 1370–1427). *Madonna and Child Enthroned*, ca. 1420, detail of pseudo-kufic "inscription." Tempera on poplar, 37¹¹⁄₁₆ x 22¼ in. (95.7 x 56.5 cm). National Gallery of Art, Washington, D.C., Samuel H. Kress Collection (1939.1.255)

transcribe the complete text of the Qur'an onto a scroll or talismanic shirt.

Ghubar, or "dustlike," script was typically encountered in small Qur'ans, prayer books, and scrolls and on an array of talismanic objects that could be worn or carried close to the body. The practice is referred to by one scholar as "textual intimacy," wherein the words are activated through bodily contact. However, in these works legibility is never compromised by the reduced size of the writing. Micrography is not unique to the Islamic world, although it is said to have been originally devised in the ninth century to send messages on small sheets of paper by pigeon post, tied to the bird's wing or leg.

Pictorial Calligraphy

For centuries calligraphers and artists from the Islamic world have straddled the boundary between text and image, writing and picturing, revealing their inextricable intertwinement. An intriguing phenomenon that epitomizes the fusion of text and image is the calligram, or pictorial calligraphy. This art form gained popularity in Iran, Ottoman Turkey, and Deccan India in the eighteenth and nineteenth centuries. Here, letters, words, and phrases are shaped into a range of animate and inanimate forms such as animals, humans, ships, swords, and countless others. In some cases, word(s) and image share the same referent, while in others they are distinct. Form and content can be conflated or independent.

In the Ottoman context, pictorial calligraphy was closely connected to the Sufi orders, particularly the Bektashis, who were noted practitioners of mirror writing. For example, since 'Ali has traditionally been referred to as Asadullah, or Lion of God, calligrams in the shape of lions often include invocations to 'Ali. Pictorial calligraphy is also encountered in the art of seventeenth- and eighteenth-century Deccan India, which had large communities of Shi'i believers. Examples include a prayer to 'Ali in the form of a pierced metal standard in the shape of a falcon (fig. 47) and a calligram in the form of a human face composed of the names of the members of the Prophet's family, or the *ahl al-bayt* (fig. 48). An eighteenth-century *hilya*, or votive plaque, from Ottoman Turkey in The Met's collection can also be seen as a calligram (cat. 38). Here, the physical attributes of the Prophet

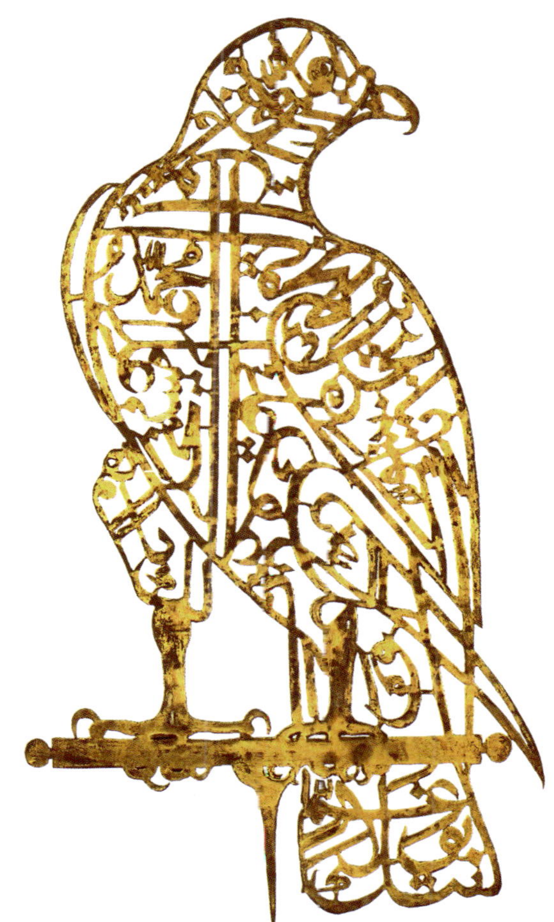

Fig. 47. Calligram in the shape of a falcon. India, Golconda, 17th century. Gilt copper; pierced, 7⅓ x 4¼ in. (18 x 10.7 cm). Victoria and Albert Museum, London (IM-163-1913)

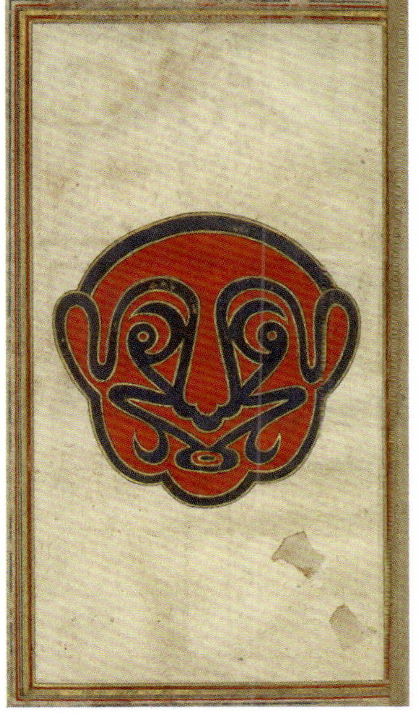

Fig. 48. Calligram from *Nan va Halwa* (Bread and Sweets) in the shape of a man's head. Maker: Muhammad Baha' al-Din al-'Amili (1547–1620). India, Aurangabad, Deccan, ca. 1690. Ink, opaque watercolor, and gold on paper, 9¼ x 5½ in. (23.5 x 14 cm). Purchase, Friends of Islamic Art Gifts, 1999 (1999.157)

are represented as a verbal/textual "portrait" that visually alludes to the human form with head, body, belly, and limbs.

The Art of *Siyah Mashq*

The emergence of the calligrapher's practice page as a popular art form in its own right is another fascinating manifestation of calligraphic abstraction. Traditionally, calligraphers copied letters or groups of letters over and over in order to strengthen their hand, instill discipline, and perfect their craft. The result was a heavily blackened surface with little of the underlying support showing through (fig. 49). Referred to as *mashq* or *siyah mashq* ("exercise" or "black exercise"), these sheets were integral to the process of creating a finished, polished folio of calligraphy. Regarded as the most immediate and intimate trace of the calligrapher's pen—an extension of his hand, mind, and soul—*mashq* pages were typically devoid of meaning and were intended to be enjoyed solely for their aesthetic merits. Cherished as works of art, they were collected, exchanged as gifts, sometimes set in elaborate borders, and included in albums along with paintings and drawings.

The art of *siyah mashq* first emerged in Iran in the late sixteenth century and surged in popularity in the eighteenth and nineteenth centuries in both Iran and Ottoman Turkey (where it was called *karalama*). *Siyah mashq* pages were produced by calligraphers from all walks of life, often renowned masters, many of whom were in the service of the court. Occasionally, the rulers themselves penned *mashq* pages as gifts or for inclusion in royal albums (cat. 39).

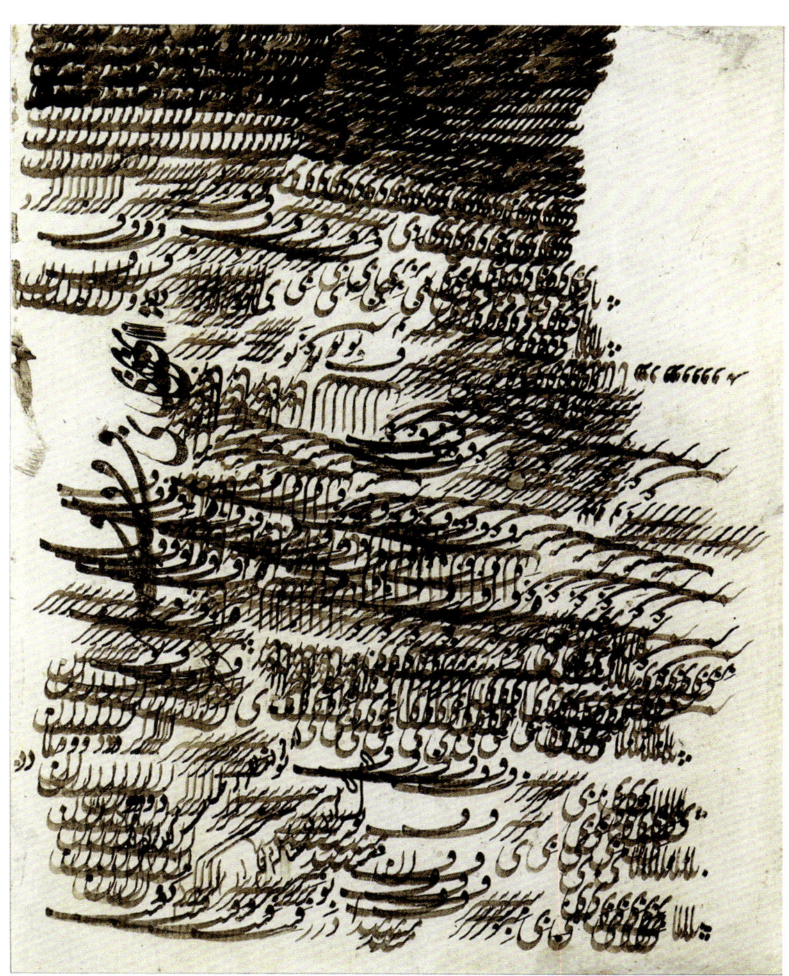

Fig. 49. Calligraphic practice sheet (*siyah mashq*). Collection of the author

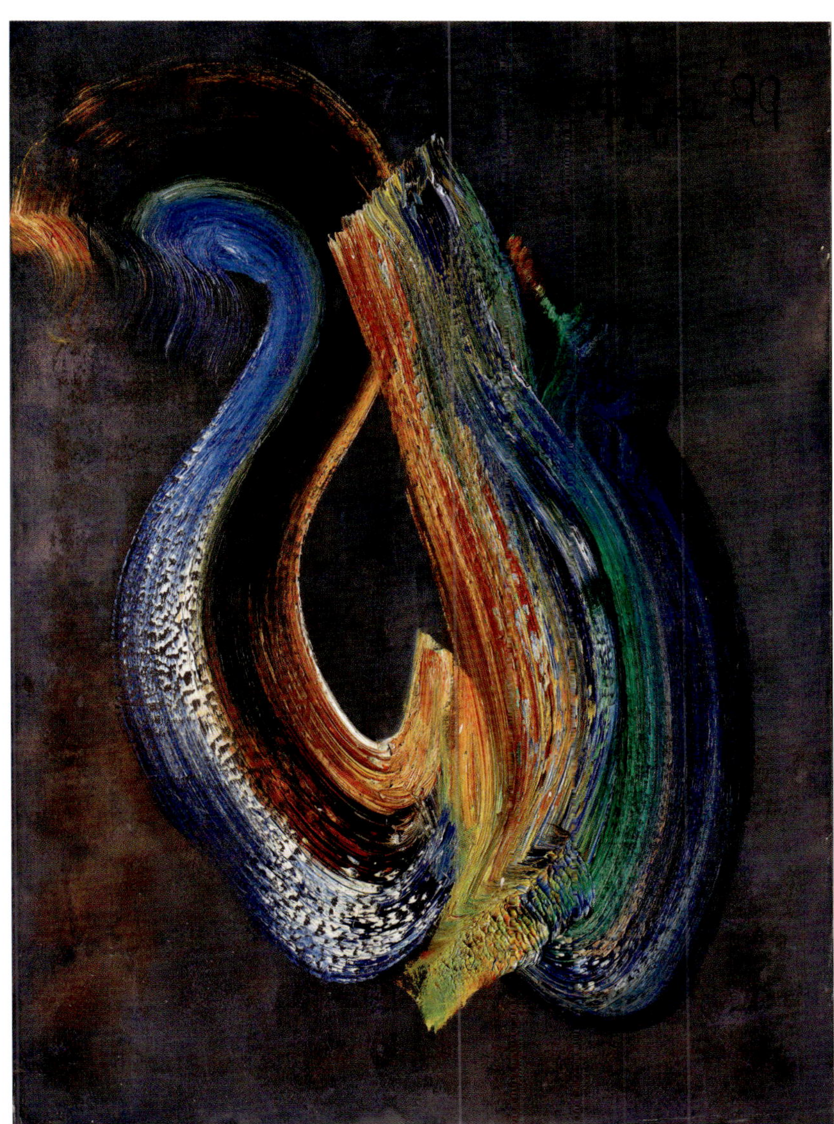

Fig. 50. Ismail Gulgee (Pakistani, 1926–2007). *Allah*, 1999. Oil on canvas, 48 x 36¼ in. (121.9 x 92.1 cm). Gift of Amin Gulgee, 2014 (2014.597)

Calligraphic Abstraction in the Modern Era

The mid-1950s marked a new chapter in the development of calligraphic abstraction in the various regions of the Islamic world, triggered by the global phenomena of modernism and postcolonial nationalism (fig. 50). Calligraphy became an instrument of protest and a means of reclaiming national identity and heritage, which many felt had been diluted and "invaded" by Western domination. For many artists, writing was a vehicle for voicing sociopolitical and economic concerns, as well as issues of personal identity and gender. Furthermore, writing became a space in which artists negotiated their place within the international art scene and worked through the desire to be members of a global community while remaining faithful to, and proud of, their cultural roots. Many had visited or studied in Western Europe, where they had come into contact with European artists and observed their practices. They had visited museums, attended fairs or biennials, and learned about international movements such as Letterism, minimalism, conceptualism, Dada, and Abstract Expressionism. Calligraphic abstraction of the modern era is thus best understood through these filters. Today, the dialogue between "writing" and "picturing" is very much alive and will no doubt give voice to further aesthetic preferences, sociopolitical concerns, and personal convictions and aspirations. Pages 140–45 explore a handful of calligraphic compositions by postwar artists from Iran, Pakistan, and Turkey whose work speaks to this subject and reveals the vibrancy of this art form today.

29

FOLIO FROM A QUR'AN IN PLAYFUL FLORIATED SCRIPT

Iran or Central Asia, Seljuq, 11th century
Ink, opaque watercolor, and gold on paper, 12⅞ x 9 in. (32.7 x 22.9 cm)
Rogers Fund, 1940 (40.164.2a)

Copied in floriated new-style script, this Qur'an folio demonstrates the balancing act performed by the calligrapher who sought to highlight the importance of design and composition while communicating the content of sacred verses. Its composition is unusual in that the fourth line of text is noticeably larger and more elaborate than the rest. Given its highly decorative quality, one would expect it to be a *sura* heading, but it is actually a phrase from the *shahada*, or profession of faith, stating that "Muhammad [is] God's Messenger." The actual chapter heading, dwarfed by comparison, is written in gold at the bottom of the page. Here, the calligrapher has taken the liberty of visually stressing the importance of this phrase, perhaps to remind the reciter to raise his voice or to enunciate the words while reading.

The vertical shafts of the letters terminate in lively vegetal and floral sprays accentuated with meandering gold scrolls. The creative treatment is further expressed by the elongation and stacking of certain letters, such as *kaf*, along the baseline, creating a certain cadence. This playful use of floriated and plaited new-style script is a feature also seen on Seljuq objects and architectural decoration, for instance, on the inner dome of the Karatay Madrasa in Konya (fig. 51).

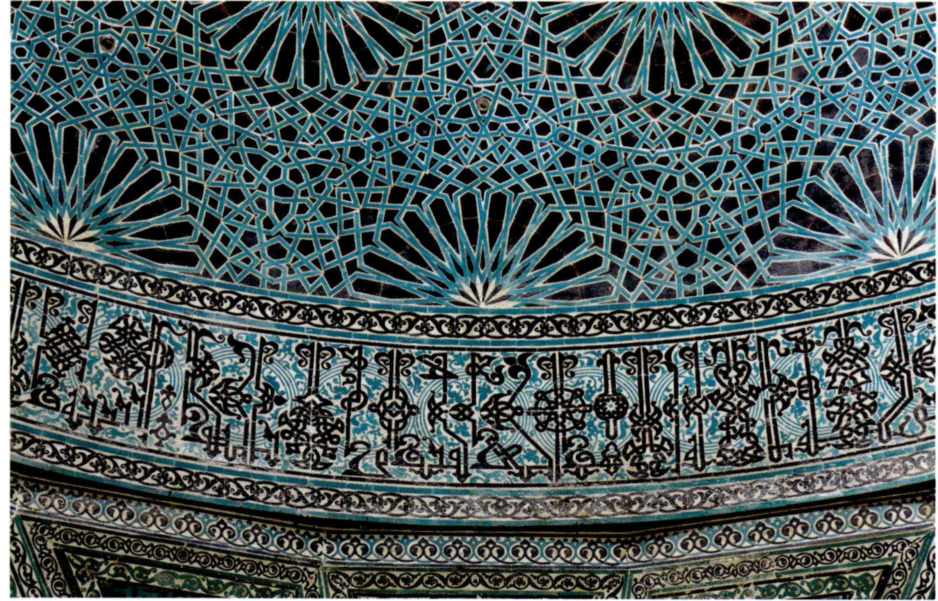

Fig. 51. Mosaic tiles on the dome of Karatay Madrasa with inscriptions in plaited new-style script, Konya, Turkey, A.D. 1250–51

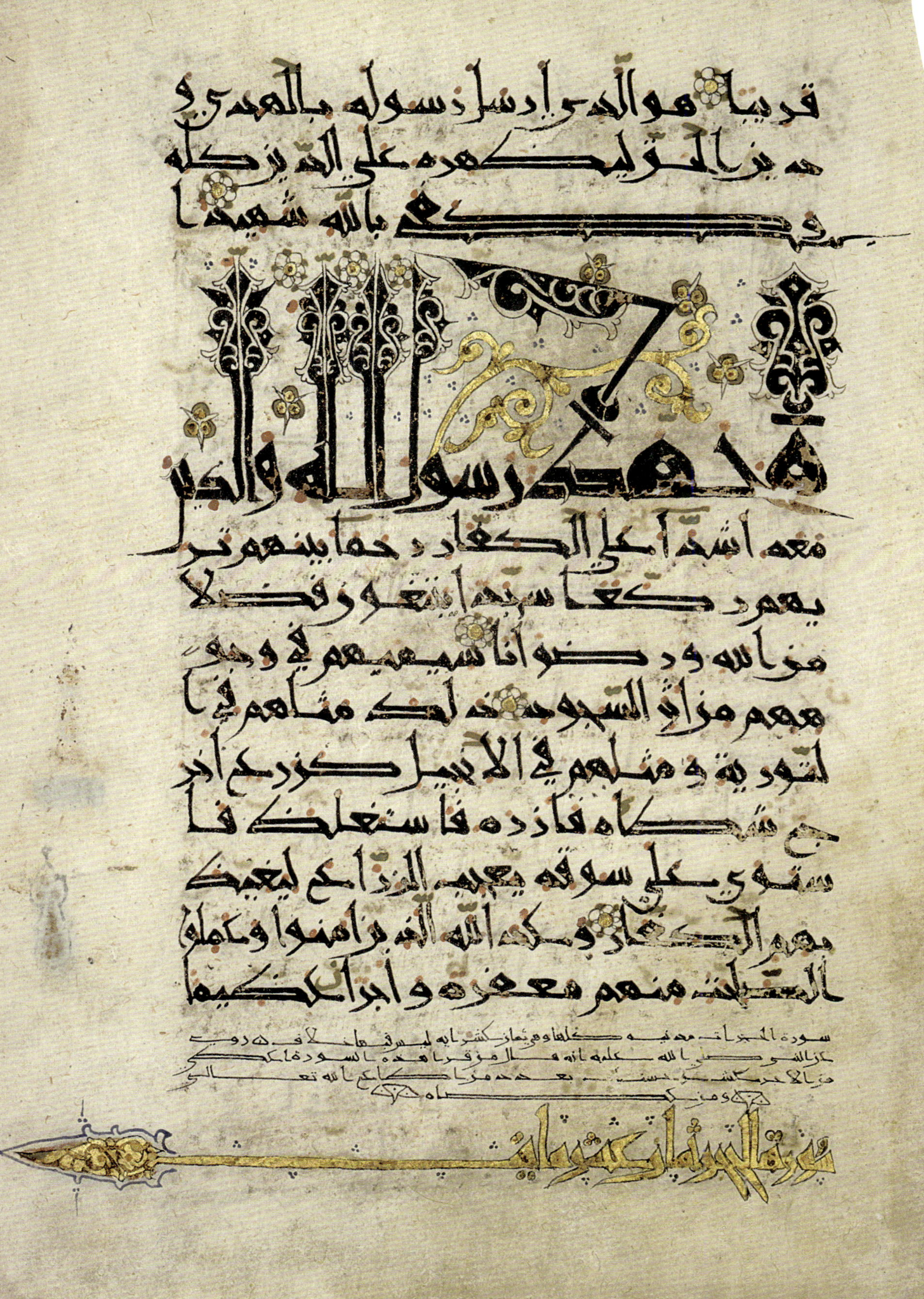

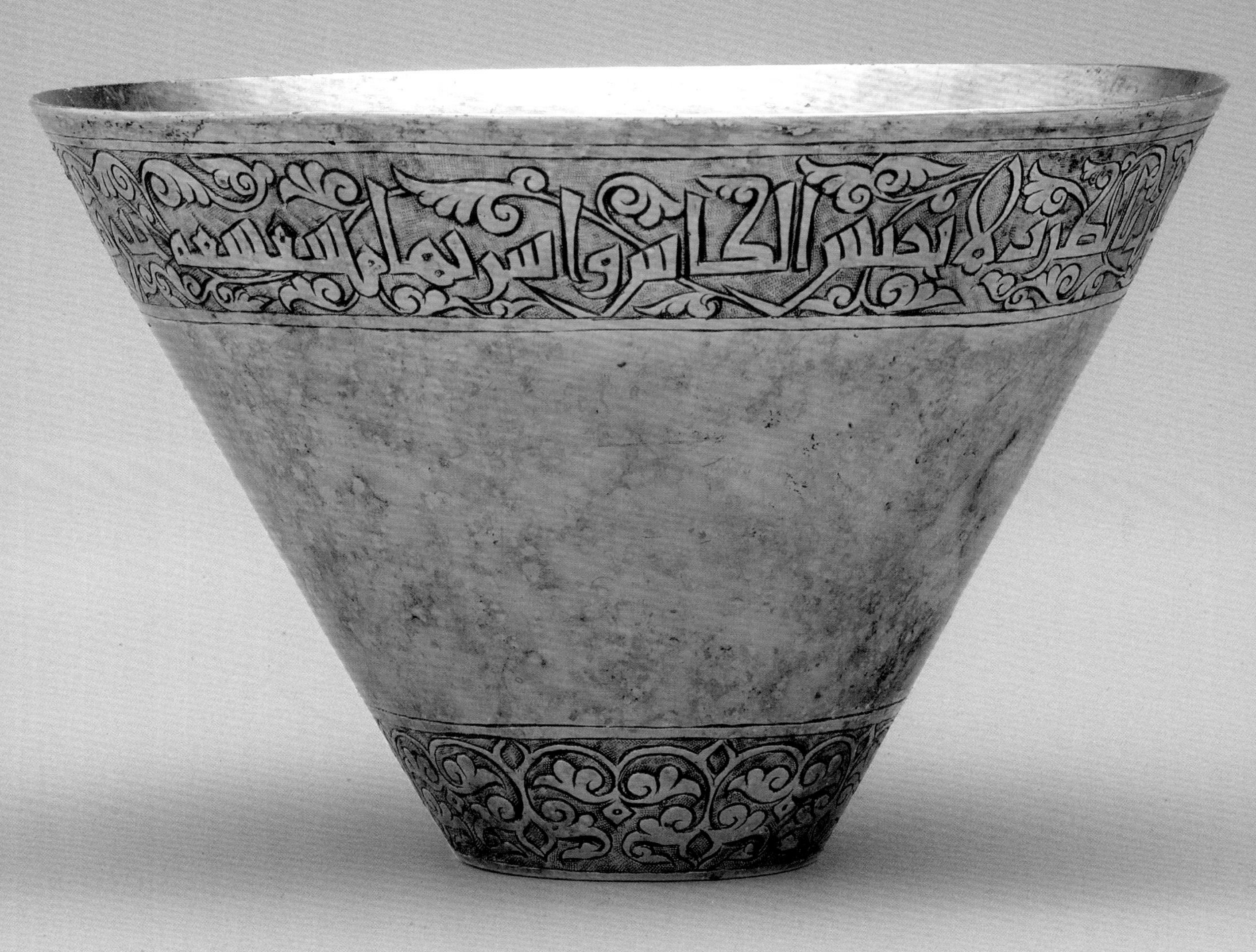

30

CUP WITH A POEM ON WINE IN FLORIATED *KUFIC*

Poet: Ibn Sukkara al-Hashimi (d. A.H. 385/A.D. 995–96)
Iran, second half 10th–11th century
Silver; fire-gilded, hammered, chased, H. 3¼ in. (8.3 cm); Diam. 5 in. (12.7 cm)
Harris Brisbane Dick Fund, 1964 (64.133.2)

Characterized by straight, flaring sides and a narrow base, this silver cup has a band of poetic verses in *kufic* script engraved around its outer rim. The inscriptions, set against a ground of scrolling vegetal forms, are outlined with a black paste that enhances their readability. Drawn from the *divan*, or anthology of poems, of Ibn Sukkara al-Hashimi, a satirical poet who lived in Baghdad in the second half of the tenth century, the inscription begins with an invitation to drink, but then cautions the owner to refrain from drinking in excess. It reads:

> Drink! For this day has a special boon, which if you had known about it
> [You would have hurried up with entertainment and hastened with rapture!]*
> Don't hold the cup back, but drink it diluted, until you die from it without reason!

The cup invokes the setting of a traditional celebratory feast or drinking party (*bazm*), during which a ruler, prince, or member of the elite would gather with his guests to eat and drink, recite or listen to poetry and music, and enjoy entertainments such as dancing or acrobatics. According to the Hadith, however, Muslims are forbidden to use gold and silver vessels for eating and drinking, a prohibition that is further confirmed in a twelfth-century encyclopedic work that devotes an entire chapter to licit and illicit uses of gold and silver wares. Yet the material evidence provided by this and other vessels, along with many textual and visual references contained in literary sources, demonstrate that actual practice often contradicted well-established proscriptions.

* *The couplet in brackets does not appear on the cup but is present in the original poem.*

31

EWER WITH HUMAN-HEADED *NASKH* SCRIPT

Present-day Afghanistan, Khurasan, probably Herat, ca. 1180–1210
Brass; raised, repoussé, inlaid with silver and a black compound, H. 15¾ in. (40 cm); Diam. 7½ in. (19.1 cm)
Rogers Fund, 1944 (44.15)

With its many benedictory inscriptions and copious figural and astrological imagery, this fluted ewer would have been regarded as a highly desirable luxury object of great talismanic and cosmological value. It belongs to a group of silver-inlaid brass vessels of similar shape and size that all exhibit fluted bodies, crowned harpies on their shoulders, and repoussé (hammered) lions on their necks. One of its most striking features is the use of animated calligraphy on the neck and shoulder. Benedictory in nature, these inscriptions—which invoke glory, prosperity, dominion, health, happiness, and longevity—exhibit the playfulness and inventiveness of the artist, who placed human heads atop the upright and other letters (details). Here, the legibility of the inscriptions is not impeded by such decorative treatment, but other examples of anthropomorphic calligraphy have proved difficult to decipher, as the human forms and their activity have overshadowed the content of the inscriptions. Interestingly, animated calligraphy is never used when inscribing the name of a ruler, a date, or even the name of an artist, all of which are always highly legible.

Scholars have had different interpretations for the meaning of animated script. Some believe that it emerged from a strong figural tradition that flourished in the Eastern Islamic world during the age of the Seljuqs. Others trace its origins to literature, seeing it as a metaphor for the *waq-waq* tree from the story of Alexander in the Iranian national epic, the *Shahnama* (Book of Kings) of Firdausi. Still others believe that it developed as a result of exchanges between Iran and neighboring Christian regions in the Caucasus, such as Georgia, where the initial letters of words in illuminated manuscripts were frequently embellished and transformed into vegetal forms.

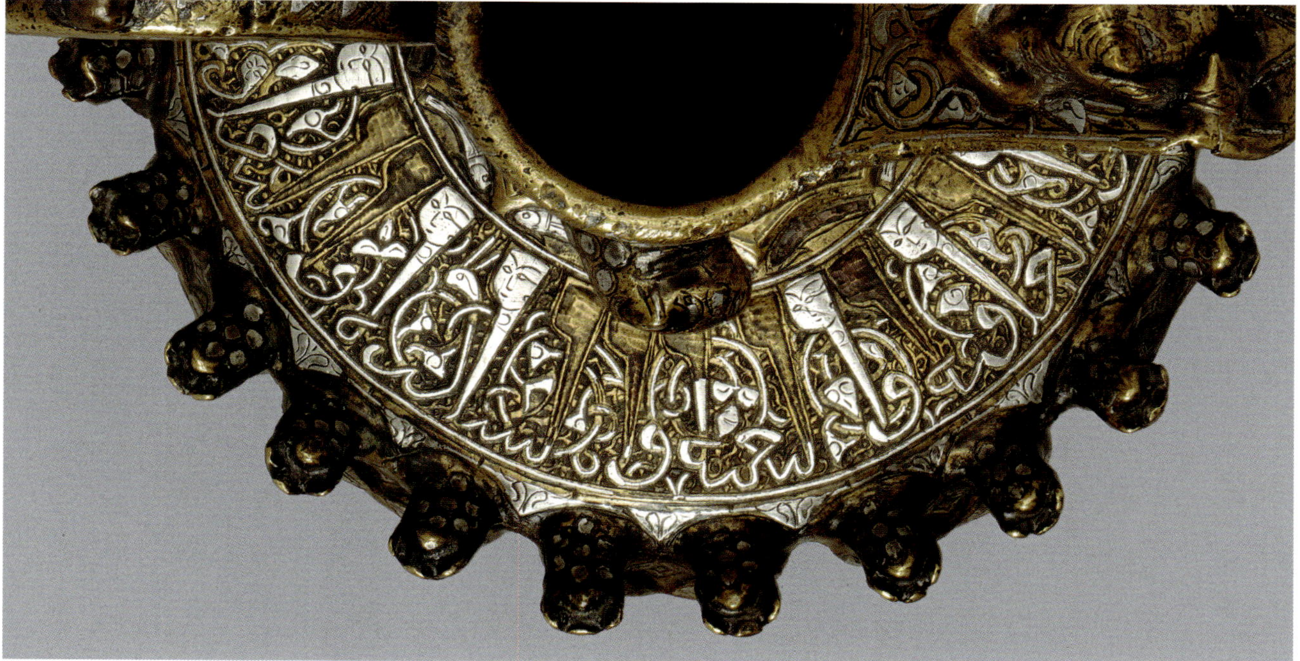

Detail of shoulder with anthropomorphic script

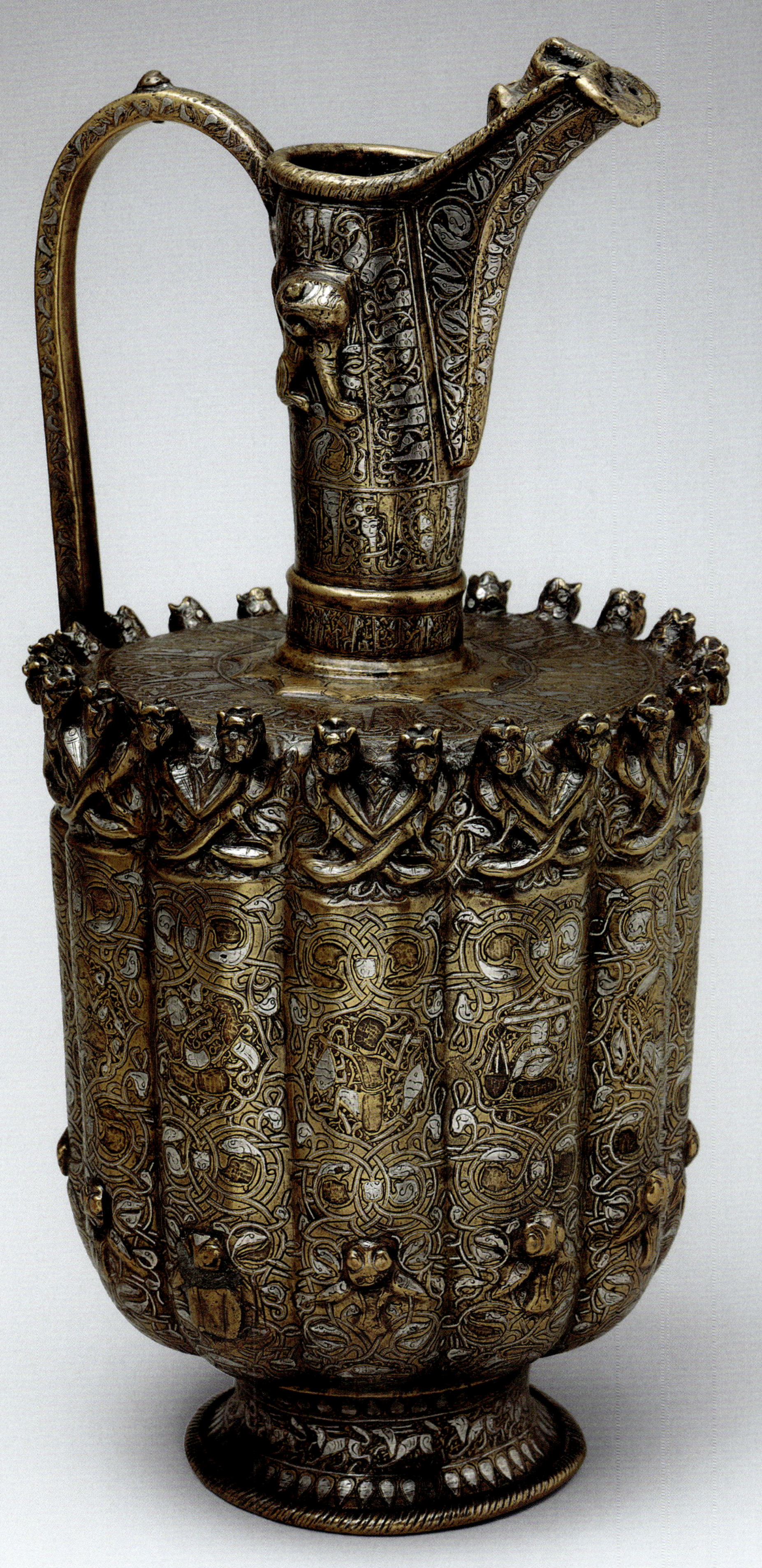

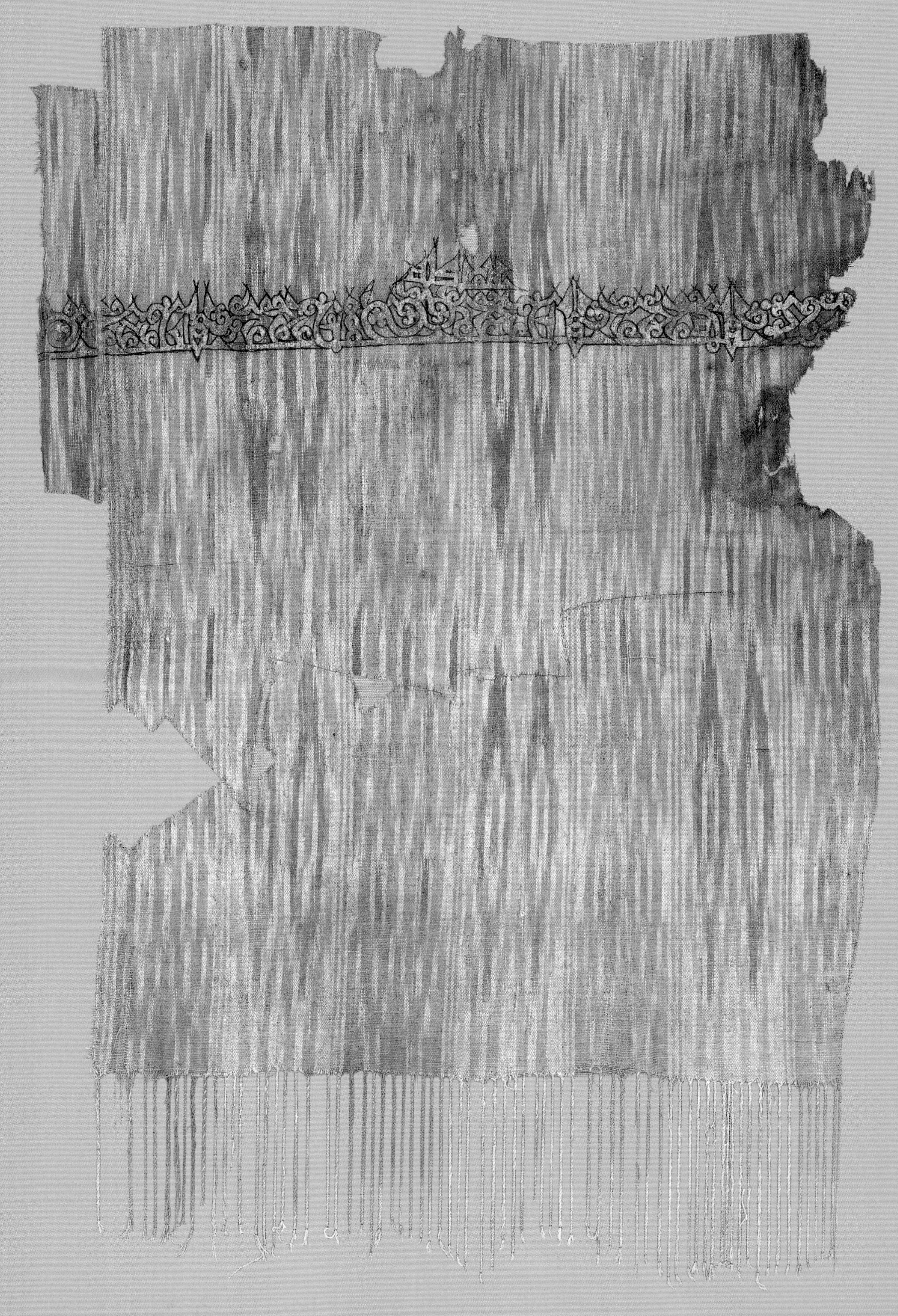

TIRAZ TEXTILE FRAGMENT WITH ORNATE INSCRIPTION

Probably Yemen, late 9th–early 10th century
Cotton, ink, and gold; plain weave, resist-dyed (*ikat*), painted;
inscription: black ink and gold leaf, painted, 23 x 16 in. (58.4 x 40.6 cm)
Gift of George D. Pratt, 1929 (29.179.9)

Historical sources of the early Islamic period confirm that *ikat* textiles from Yemen were prized throughout the Islamic world. They were made via a complex technique that involved weaving individually resist- or tie-dyed cotton threads into a pattern of arrowheads and lozenges. Most surviving Yemeni textiles are embroidered with the names of the Abbasid caliphs; some also mention the Yemeni capital of Sana'a as a place of production. Inscribed *ikat*s were considered markers of wealth and status both in and beyond areas under Abbasid control, as well as important luxury items linking the trade routes of the Red Sea and the Indian Ocean.

The fragment seen here is a fine example in its materials and manufacture, in the regularity of its weave and distinctive pattern, and in its benedictory inscription in ornamental *kufic*, applied in gold leaf and outlined in black (detail). The Arabic letters are highly embellished, and spaces between words have been omitted, making the text difficult to decipher, but it can be read as "Dominion belongs to [God]." Similar fragments bear the name of Amir Abu Ibrahim, son of the Abbasid caliph al-Muntasir (r. 861–63), who reportedly held governorships of several Arab provinces, possibly including Yemen.

*Ikat*s with gilded inscriptions outlined in black are rare; in fact, The Met's example is one of only two that survive. Both illustrate the collaboration that took place between weavers and calligraphers. Here, for instance, the application of the gold-leaf inscription resembles techniques used in manuscripts on parchment or paper, thus raising the possibility that a calligrapher was involved in the production of this and other, related inscribed Yemeni *ikat*s.

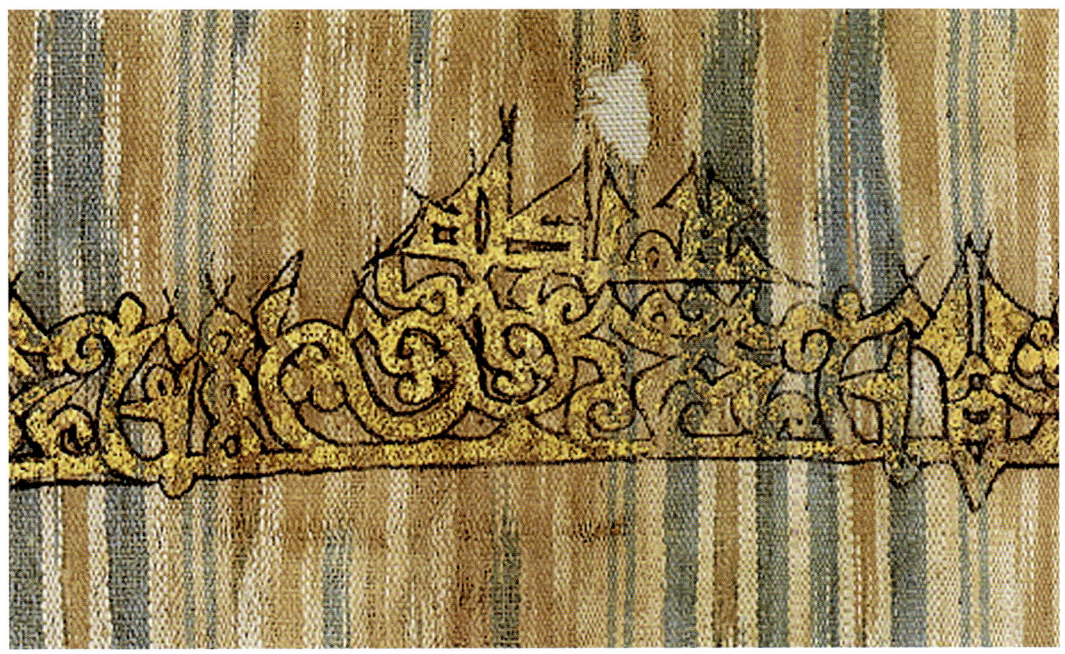

Detail of inscription, applied in gold and outlined in black ink

33

ROUNDEL WITH INSCRIPTIONS IN MIRROR-IMAGE WRITING

India, probably Hyderabad, Deccan, late 16th century
Wood and gesso, painted and metal-leafed with gold and silver, Diam. 19⅞ in. (50.5 cm)
Purchase, Richard S. Perkins and Alastair B. Martin Gifts and Rogers Fund, 1991 (1991.233)

This carved wood roundel contains two of the ninety-nine beautiful names of Allah (*asma al-husna*), first written vertically and then in mirror image (*muthanna*) and repeated eight times. Two rows of flamelike lappets encircle the text. Residue of green paint suggests an original palette in a range of vibrant pigments that have since worn off, leaving only the gold and brown intact. While not many wood roundels survive, this one is related to a group of now heavily repainted examples affixed to the upper walls of the Badshahi ʻAshurkhana, a Shiʻi shrine in Hyderabad, in the Deccan region of India (erected 1593–96). Calligraphic roundels in mirror image are primarily found on architecture, but they also appear on works in other media, such as metal *ʻalam*s (processional standards). In a few cases, mirror-image writing appears as illumination in manuscripts or on album pages.

Calligraphic roundels are not exclusive to the Deccan or northern India. As early as the fourteenth century, they could be found on the exteriors and interiors of buildings as far west as Egypt and Turkey and as far east as Iran. However, the compositional characteristics of Deccan examples distinguish them from the others in their persistent use of calligraphy in mirror image. Although the origins of this form remain unclear, the type probably entered the Deccan from Iran and Ottoman Turkey in the fifteenth century with the influx of talented Iranian and Ottoman calligraphers, painters, and artisans into the region.

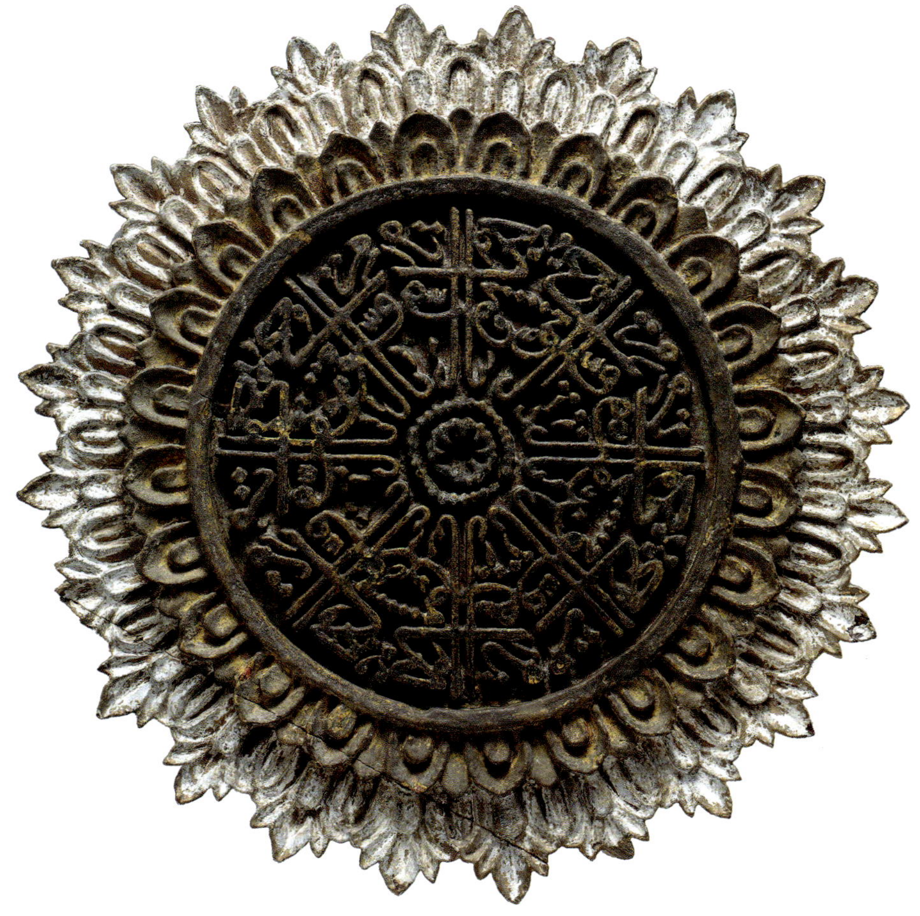

DISH WITH PSEUDO-*KUFIC* INSCRIPTION

Spain, probably Manises or Valencia, ca. 1430
Tin-glazed earthenware, stained and luster-painted, Diam. 17¾ in. (45.1 cm)
The Cloisters Collection, 1956 (56.171.162)

Lusterware produced in early fifteenth-century Manises (near Valencia, in southeastern Spain) exhibits a taste for the Muslim aesthetic, namely, the use of a copper-tone luster and cobalt-blue glaze on a red earthenware body. In this deep dish (*brasero*), a tree rendered in deep blue, perhaps an allusion to the Tree of Life, forms the central vertical axis of the inner roundel; it is surrounded by bands of pseudo-*kufic* and ovals, while delicately patterned lines, spirals, and palmettes fill out the background. A wide inner rim bearing a continuous scriptlike decoration is indecipherable.

As with other pseudo-inscriptions, whether for Muslim or Christian patrons, what was written here was not meant to be read. It served instead to convey the impression of elegance and wealth long associated with the Muslim arts of Spain. After the conquest of Valencia by the Christian forces of James I of Aragon (r. 1213–76) and the subsequent influx of Christians into the region, Islamic decorative styles continued to enjoy popularity for more than two centuries. Muslim potters, particularly in the small town of Manises, were commissioned by the kings of Aragon, secular and ecclesiastical officials, and merchants to produce lusterware for the court and for export to other regions in Europe, particularly Italy. It was a lucrative trade, which testifies to an enduring taste for Islamic and Islamic-style artifacts in Spain.

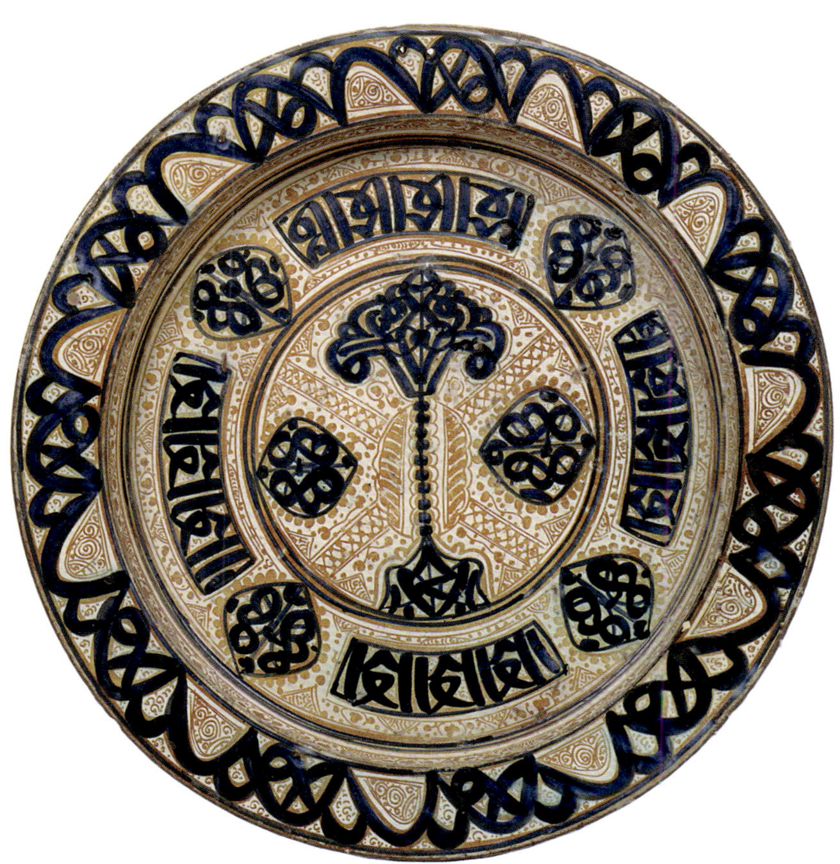

35a

PRAYER BOOK WITH IMAGES IN *GHUBAR* SCRIPT

Calligrapher: ʻAbd al-Qadir Hisari
Turkey, Ottoman, dated A.H. 1180/A.D. 1766
Ink, opaque watercolor, and gold on paper; leather and gold binding, 6 x 4 in. (15.3 x 10.2 cm)
Purchase, Friends of Islamic Art Gifts, 2014 (2014.44)

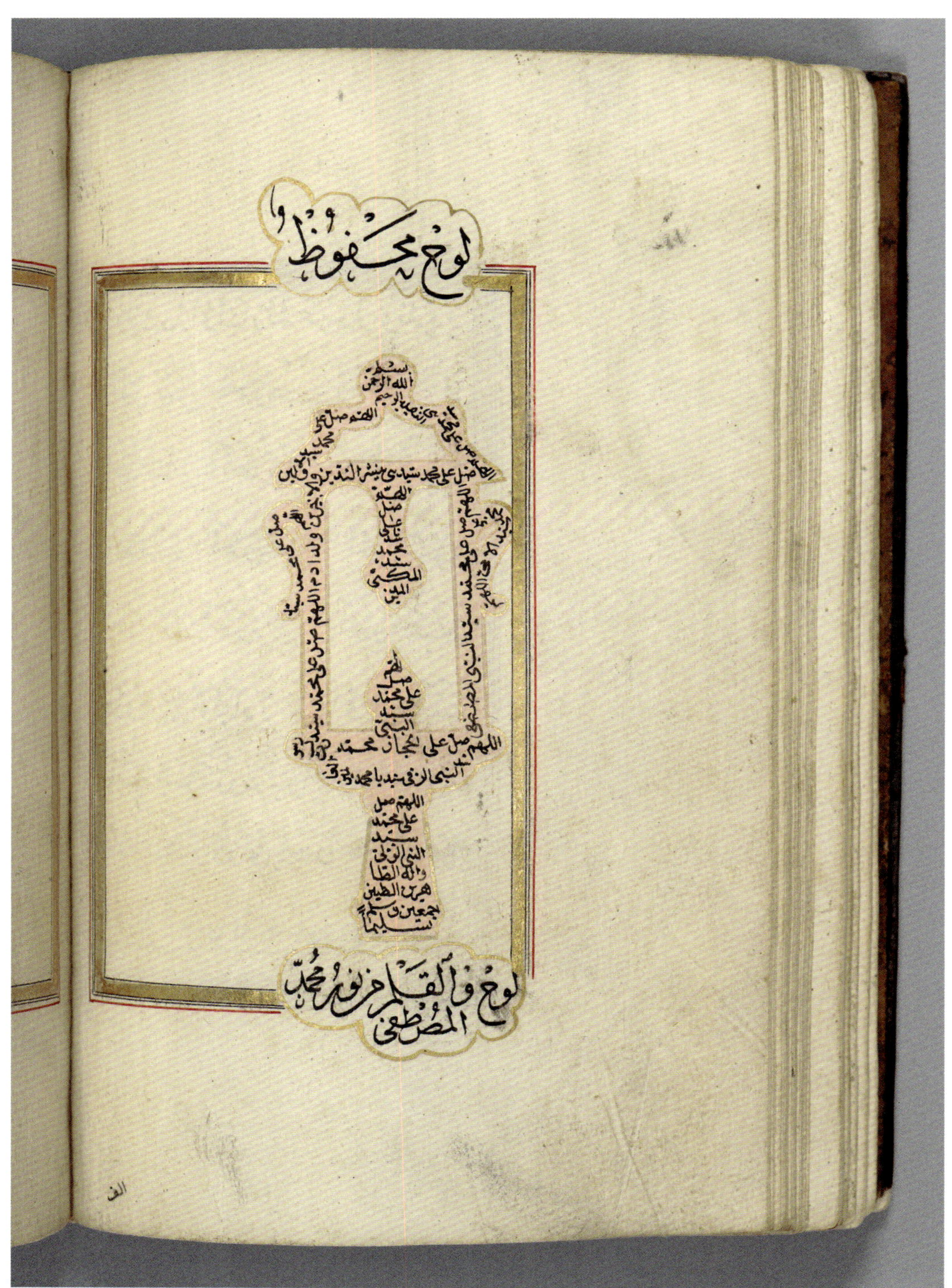

35b

CALLIGRAPHIC COMPOSITION IN *GHUBAR* SCRIPT INVOKING FIVE SHI'I LUMINARIES

Iran, second half 19th century
Ink, opaque watercolor, and gold on paper, 10 x 15½ in. (25.5 x 39.5 cm)
Purchase, Friends of Islamic Art Gifts, 2015 (2015.140)

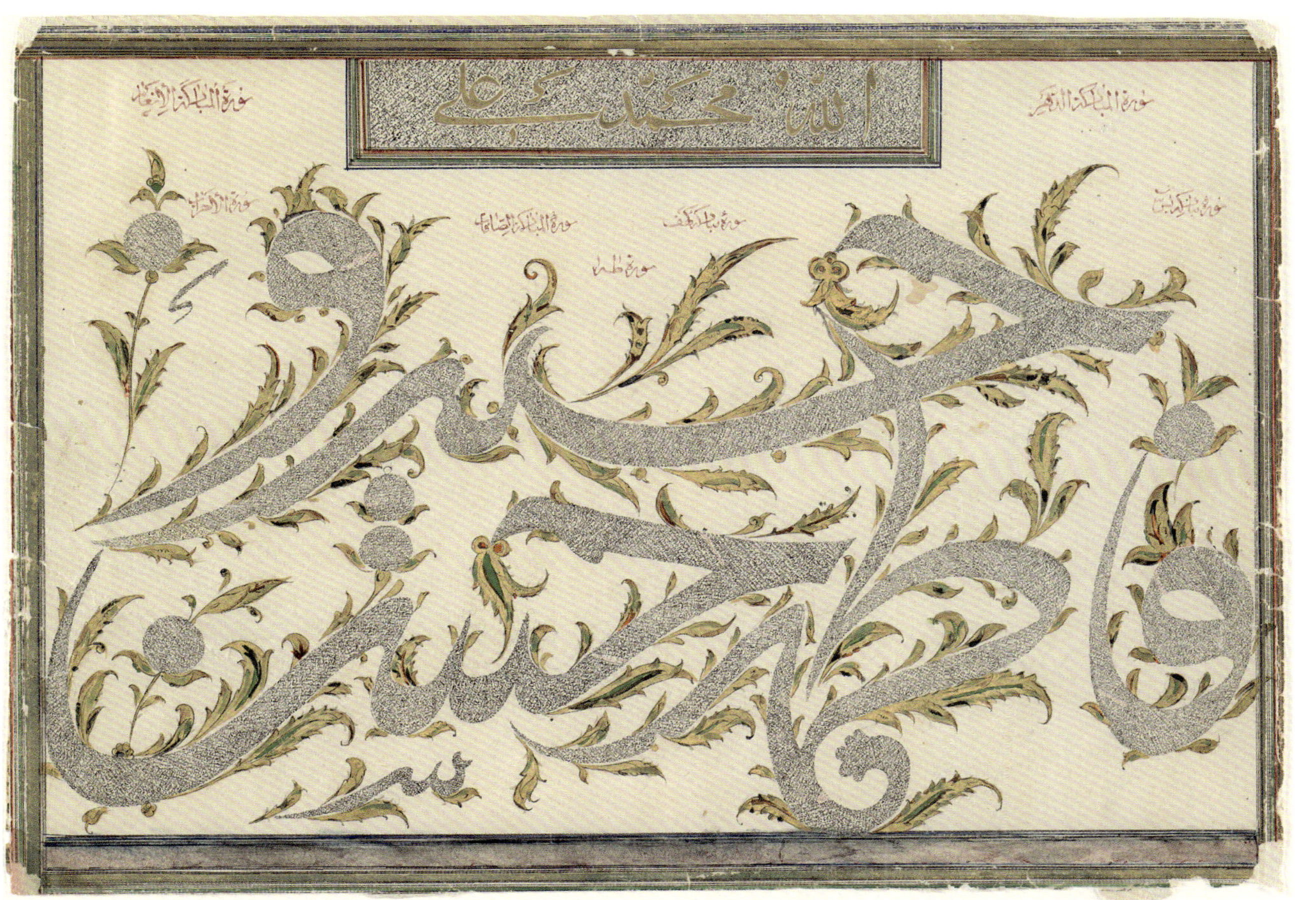

The written word held power in the Islamic world even when rendered at a minute scale. Here, we see two fine examples of *ghubar*, or "dustlike," script. The first (cat. 35a), a small prayer book, or *du'anama*, belongs to a body of illustrated devotional texts produced in the Ottoman empire in the eighteenth and nineteenth centuries. It was a time of religious revivalism, and prayer manuals enjoyed wide popularity throughout the empire. Used for individual prayer, they were also believed to protect, comfort, and heal their owners.

Most Ottoman prayer books of the period were unillustrated, but this one contains twenty-nine renderings of traditional Islamic themes and subjects, outlined in gold and filled in with prayers in *ghubar naskh* script. Among these representations are the footprints (*kadem*) of the Prophet, the Seal of Solomon, and, shown here, the Lawh al-Mahfuz (Preserved Tablet), as identified by inscriptions above and below it. A *lawh* is tablet of wood or stone used for writing, and *mahfuz* means "secure," "preserved," or "something that cannot be apprehended

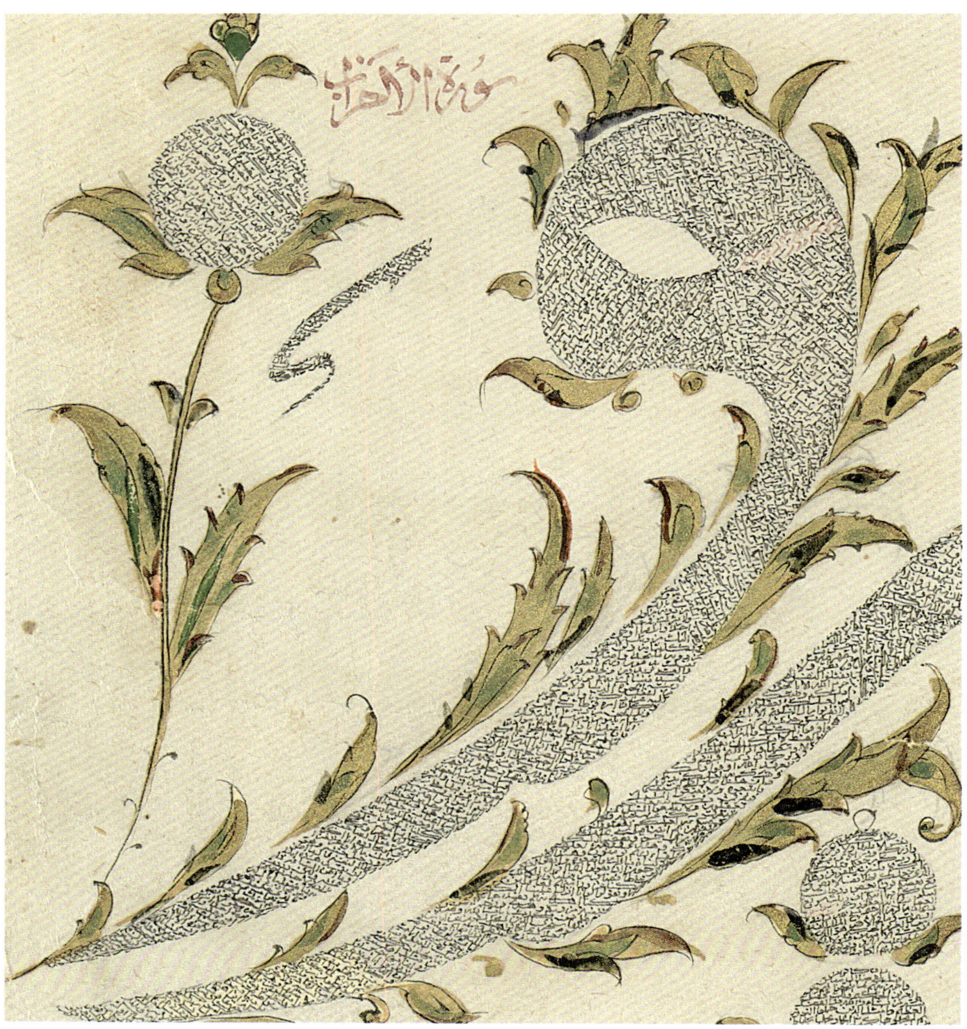

Detail of the minute *ghubar* inscriptions in cat. 35b

by unauthorized persons." In Islam this term represents the infallible and unalterable knowledge of God, which is implied to be "the only true knowledge." Verses in *sura*s 13 and 85 examine this theme: "Allah erases out whatever He pleases and writes (whatever He pleases); and with Him is the mother of the book" (13:39). This "mother of the book" is referred to as "*lawh mahfuz*" in verse 85:22: "Nay, it is the glorious Qur'an, in the guarded tablet." The book is signed and dated by ʻAbd al-Qadir Hisari, a prominent calligrapher known for his pictorial calligraphic compositions (see also cat. 37).

The second example, a nineteenth-century album page from Iran (cat. 35b), presents the names of the *ahl al-bayt*, the five holy figures central to Muslim (particularly Shiʻi) belief: Muhammad, ʻAli, Hasan, Husayn, and Fatima. Inscriptions bearing the names of these protectors of the Muslim faith are believed to have talismanic properties and therefore appear on a wide range of objects, including vessels, weapons, and military accoutrements, from Iran, India, and other regions, particularly those with large Shiʻi populations. At the top of this composition, a rectangular cartouche bears the words "Allah," "Muhammad," and "ʻAli" against a ground of micrographic Qur'anic verses. Below, the names of ʻAli's wife Fatima (the youngest daughter of the Prophet) and of her and ʻAli's sons, Hasan and Husayn, are rendered in large, ornate letters, which themselves enclose Qur'anic verses in tiny *ghubar* script (detail). The seven inscriptions in red at the top of each name identify the corresponding *sura*s featured within the contours of the letters.

36

CALLIGRAPHIC COMPOSITION IN THE SHAPE OF A PEACOCK

Folio from the Bellini Album
Turkey, Ottoman, ca. 1600(?)
Ink, opaque watercolor, and gold on paper, 9$\frac{9}{16}$ x 7$\frac{1}{16}$ in. (24.3 x 17.9 cm)
Louis V. Bell Fund, 1967 (67.266.7.8r)

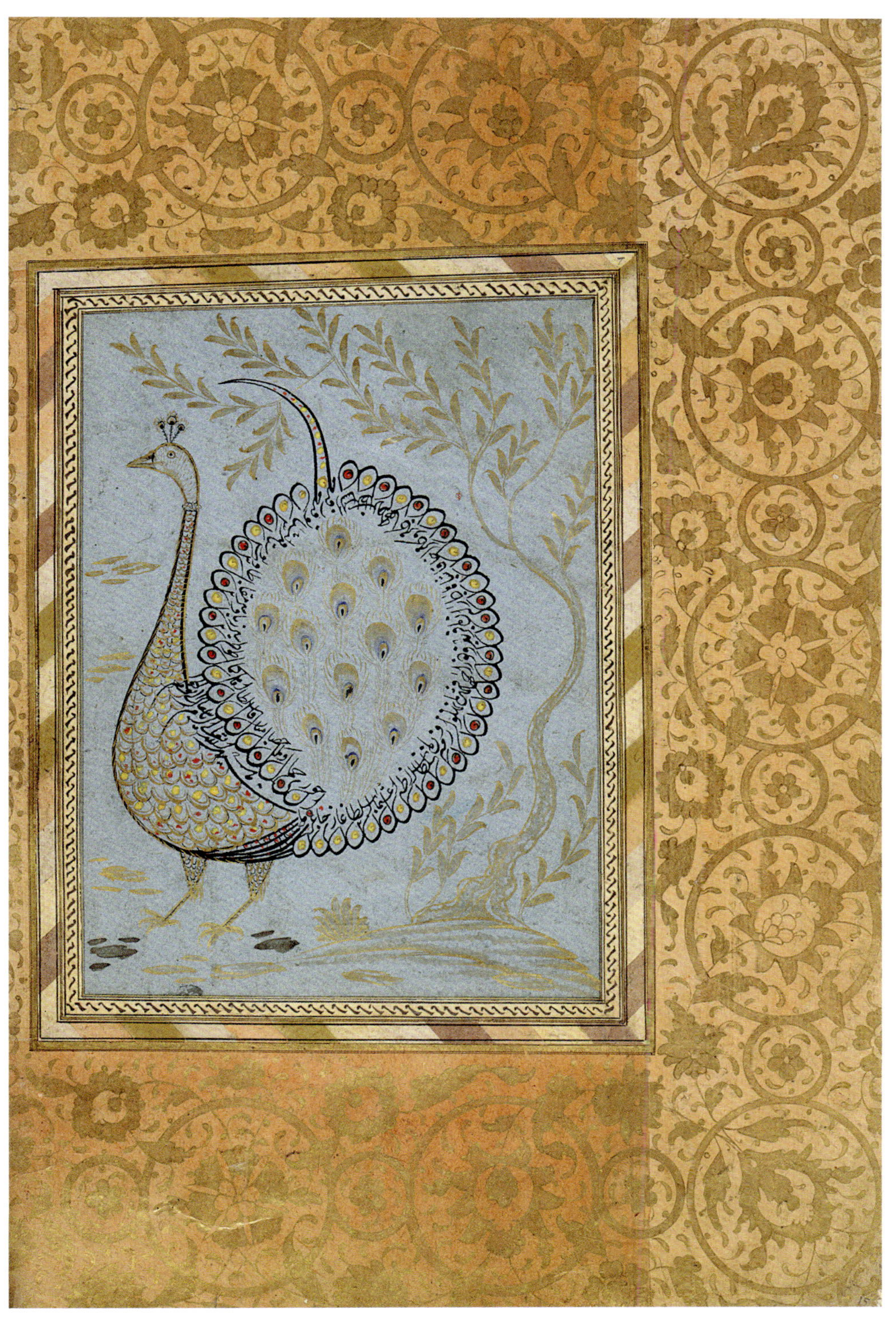

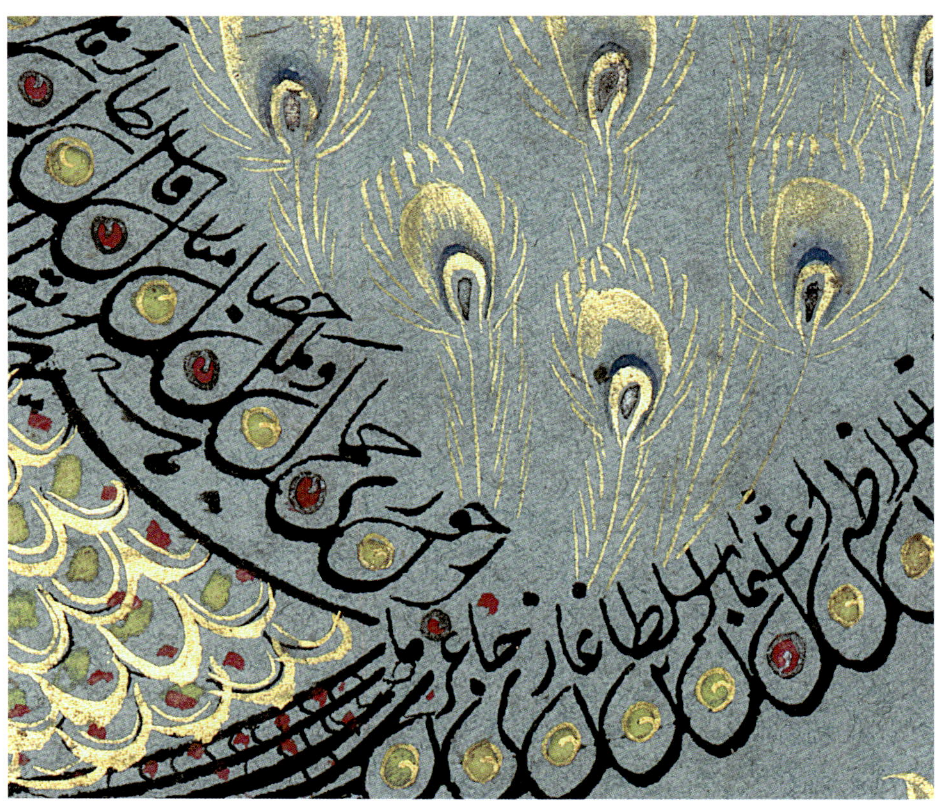

Detail of the elaborate inscription forming the peacock's tail

The playful practice of weaving an inscription into the form of an animal, bird, flower, or inanimate object remains a tour de force of Islamic calligraphers to this day. Also referred to as calligrams, these works are most closely associated with Ottoman Turkey and Deccan India, although examples of the art form are sometimes found in Iran and other regions, as well. In this folio, the eye of the viewer is immediately drawn to the peacock's stunning tail. An inscription in the chancellery *divani* script follows its outer curve and reverses direction midway (detail). Composed of blessings and praise for an unnamed sultan, it reads:

> Beautiful as a *houri*, of angelic character, of auspicious omen, envy of the perfect ones, parrot of sweet tongue and sweet speech, peacock of the garden of [. . .] the lofty decree, sultan of the sultans of the world, fortunate and august, *khaqan* of the shahs, Darius of the time, Fereydoun of the age, hero of the world, [*text reverses direction*] champion of earth and time, sultans of the sultan of the family of ʿUthman ibn Sultan Ghazi Khan [. . .] may God extend the days of his [happiness] to the day of [judgment?].

The peacock is not mentioned in the Qur'an but appears in religious literature and folklore, where it functions as a metaphor for power, virility, sovereignty, and beauty. Here, the peacock is celebrated for its regal qualities and connotations. The bird, however, also had negative associations with vanity, and according to the *Qisas al-Anbiya*, or Stories of the Prophets, and other sources, the peacock was believed to have collaborated with Satan

(Iblis) by enlisting the serpent to slip him into the Garden of Eden, thus indirectly causing Adam and Eve's expulsion from Paradise. It is for this reason that the peacock was itself cast out of heaven, lost its beautiful voice, and, despite its spectacular tail, has ugly feet. The peacock also appears in Persian poetry and on medieval and Ottoman Turkish and Safavid Persian architecture and carpets, as well as on Iznik ceramics (fig. 52).

This folio belongs to The Met's Bellini Album, so called because it is thought to have once contained a portrait of a Turkish prince by the Italian Renaissance artist Gentile Bellini. The album also contains folios of Persian calligraphy in *nasta'liq* script by Mir 'Ali Haravi (1476–1544), a drawing by the Persian artist Riza-yi 'Abbasi (1565–1635), folios with an assortment of European prints, and even a Chinese painting of a goose preening its tail.

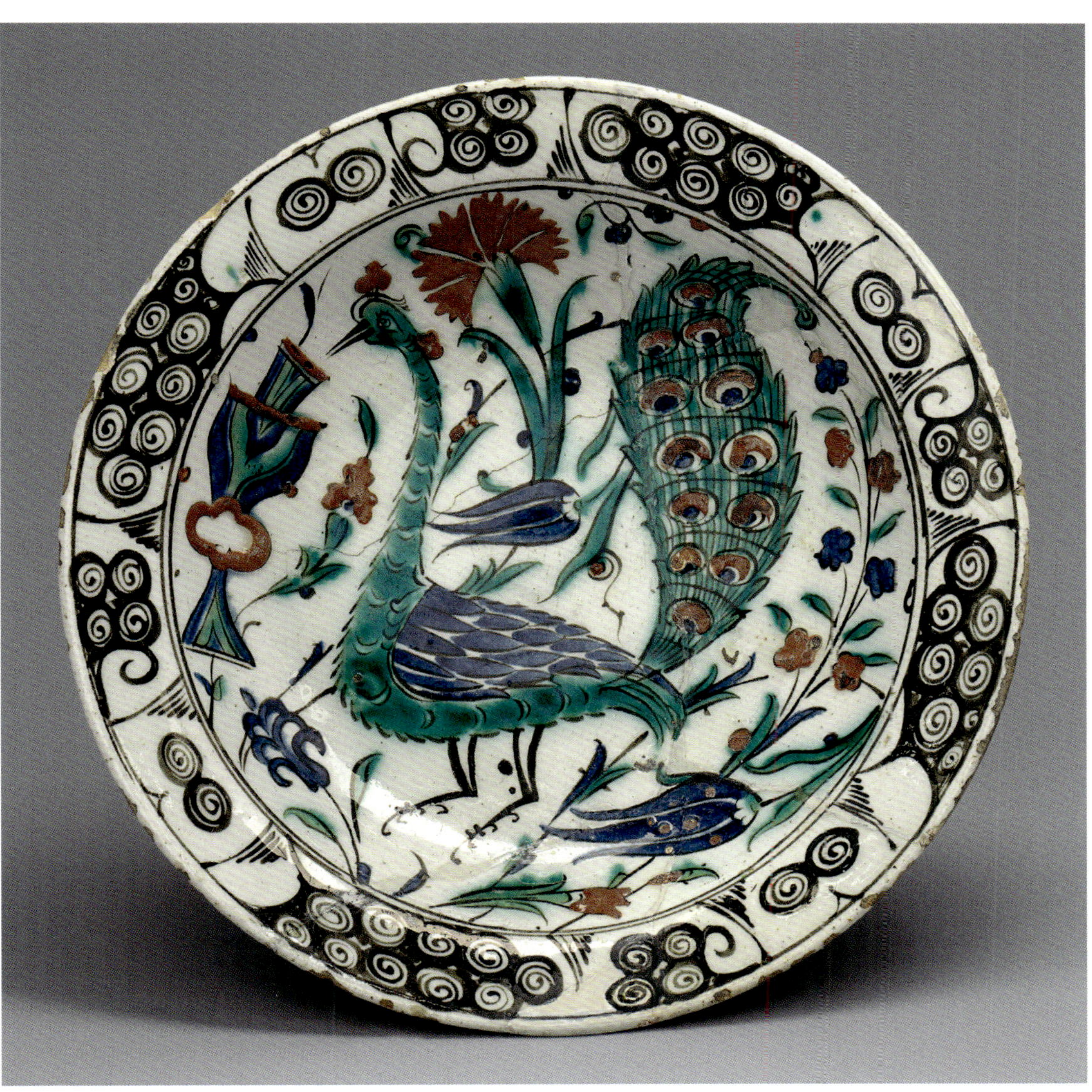

Fig. 52. Dish with peacock design. Turkey, Iznik, early 17th century. Stonepaste; polychrome painted under transparent glaze, H. 2½ in. (6.4 cm); Diam. of rim 11⅜ in. (28.9 cm). Gift of Edward J. Wormley, 1965 (65.103)

37

CALLIGRAPHIC GALLEON WITH THE NAMES OF THE SEVEN SLEEPERS

Calligrapher: ʿAbd al-Qadir Hisari
Turkey, Ottoman, dated A.H. 1180/A.D. 1766–67
Ink and gold on paper, 19 x 17 in. (48.3 x 43.2 cm)
Louis E. and Theresa S. Seley Purchase Fund for Islamic Art
and Rogers Fund, 2003 (2003.241)

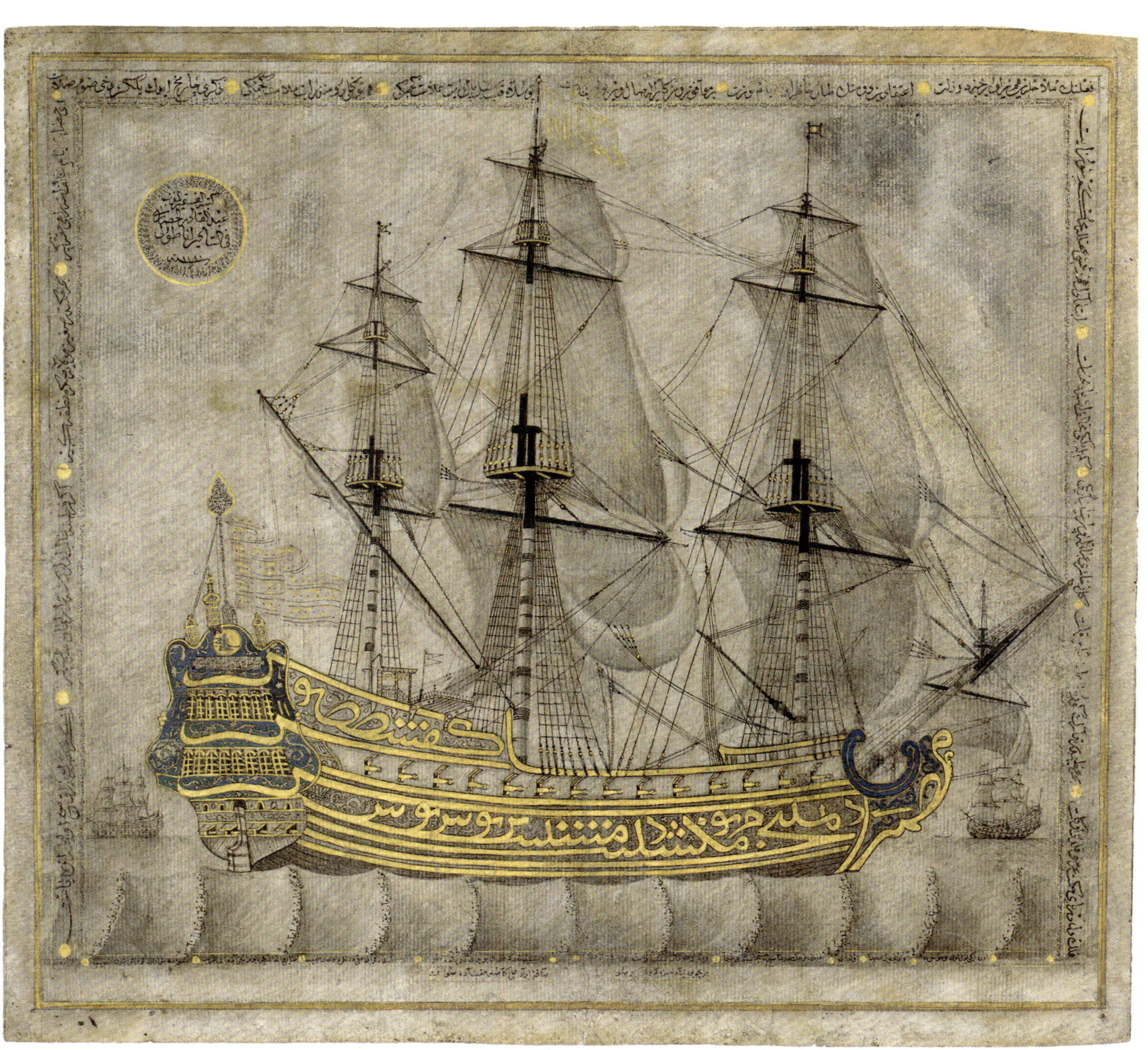

Ships were among the most popular subjects of calligrams in the Islamic world, particularly in Ottoman Turkey and South and Southeast Asia. This large example shows an imperial galleon in full sail, amid waves made of tiny *ghubar* inscriptions (detail). The hull and deck are composed of the names of the Seven Sleepers of Ephesus, a Christian story of seven youths who escaped persecution from the Roman authorities by taking refuge in a cave and sleeping there for a few hundred years. The name of their dog, Qitmar, outlines the prow. The story is reinterpreted in *sura* 18 of the Qur'an (*al-Kahf*, "The Cave"), in which neither the names nor the number of sleepers are mentioned, suggesting that the source of inspiration here was most likely Christian.

The dedication, "Al-Sultan ibn al-Sultan Mustafa Khan ibn Sultan Ahmad Khan," refers to Mustafa III, the 26th Ottoman sultan (r. 1757–73). It is copied within a panel above the grilled windows of the stern and surmounted by a gold disk containing the sultan's *tughra*. Affixed to the stern are three gilded lanterns and an imperial standard incorporating, in minute *ghubar* script, the popular "Throne Verse" (Ayat al-Kursi) from the Qur'an (detail).

The outer borders of the composition consist of two calligraphic panels written in black ink. The inner panel features repetitive prayers to the Prophet Muhammad in *ghubar* script, while the outer panel, together with the folds of the waves and a lower inner border, features Ottoman Turkish poetry in *naskh* and *thuluth* scripts. A *ghubar* inscription within a roundel at the upper left contains repetitive prayers to the Prophet and discloses the artist/calligrapher and the place and date of production: "Written by the humble sinner 'Abd al-Qadir Hisari in Akşehir, Anatolia, [in the] year 1180." We previously encountered 'Abd al-Qadir Hisari as the calligrapher of the Ottoman prayer book discussed earlier (cat. 35a). In fact, one of his images in that book is a textual rendering in *ghubar* script of another fabled ship, the Safina-yi Nuh, or Noah's Ark (fig. 53).

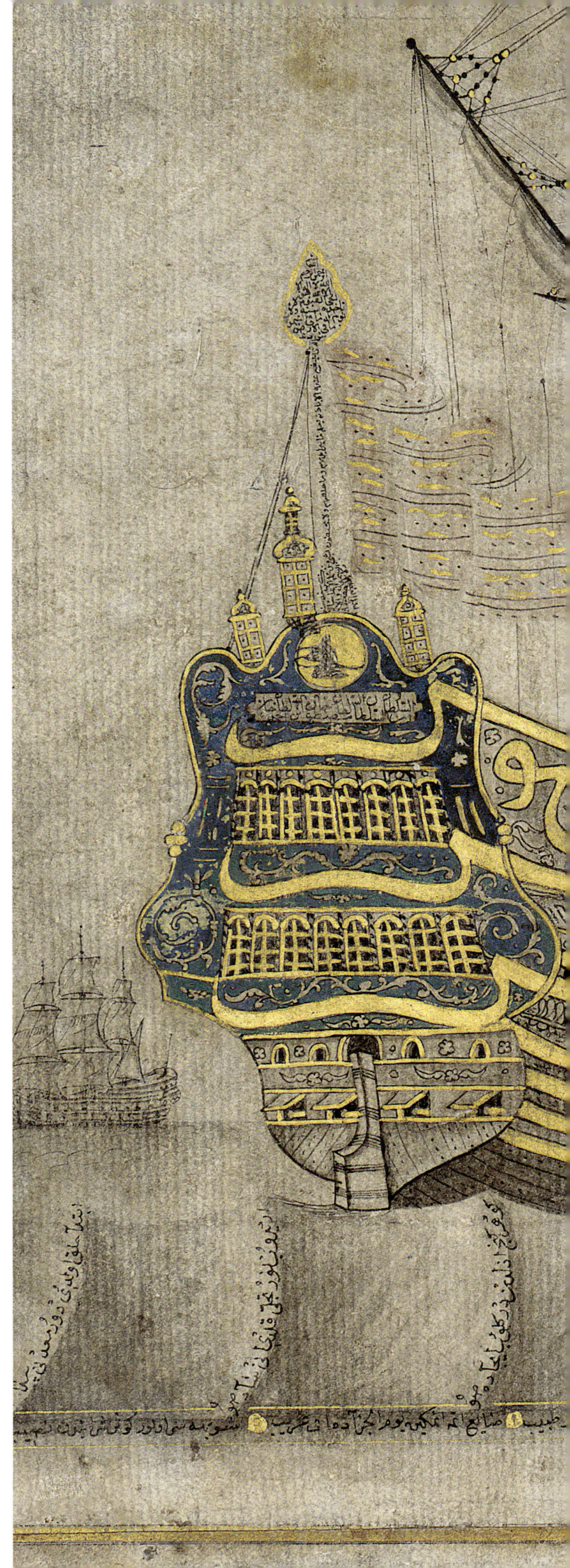

Detail of tiny *ghubar* script that comprises the waves and other elements of the ship

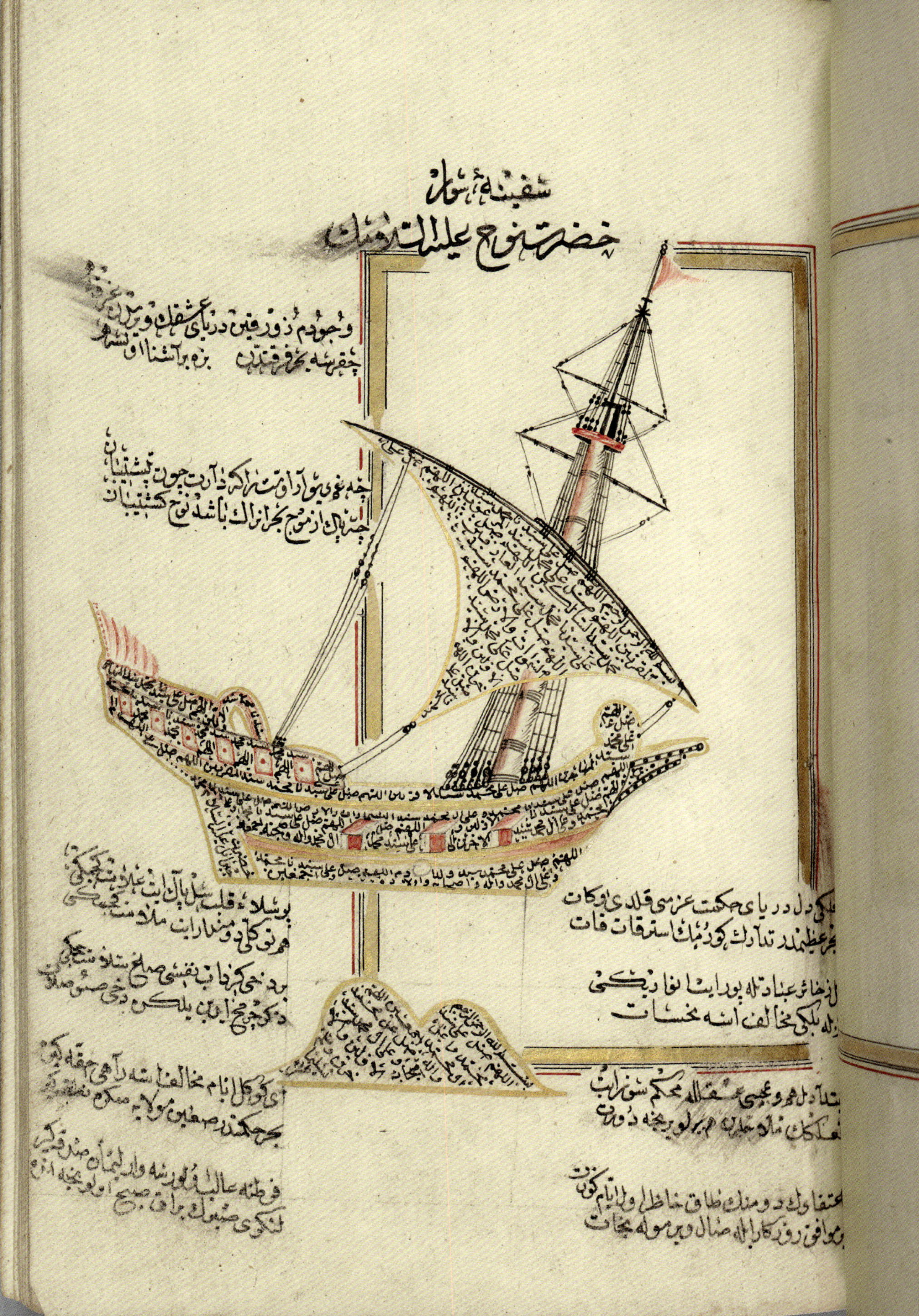
سفینهٔ شعار
حضرت نوح علیه السلامڭ

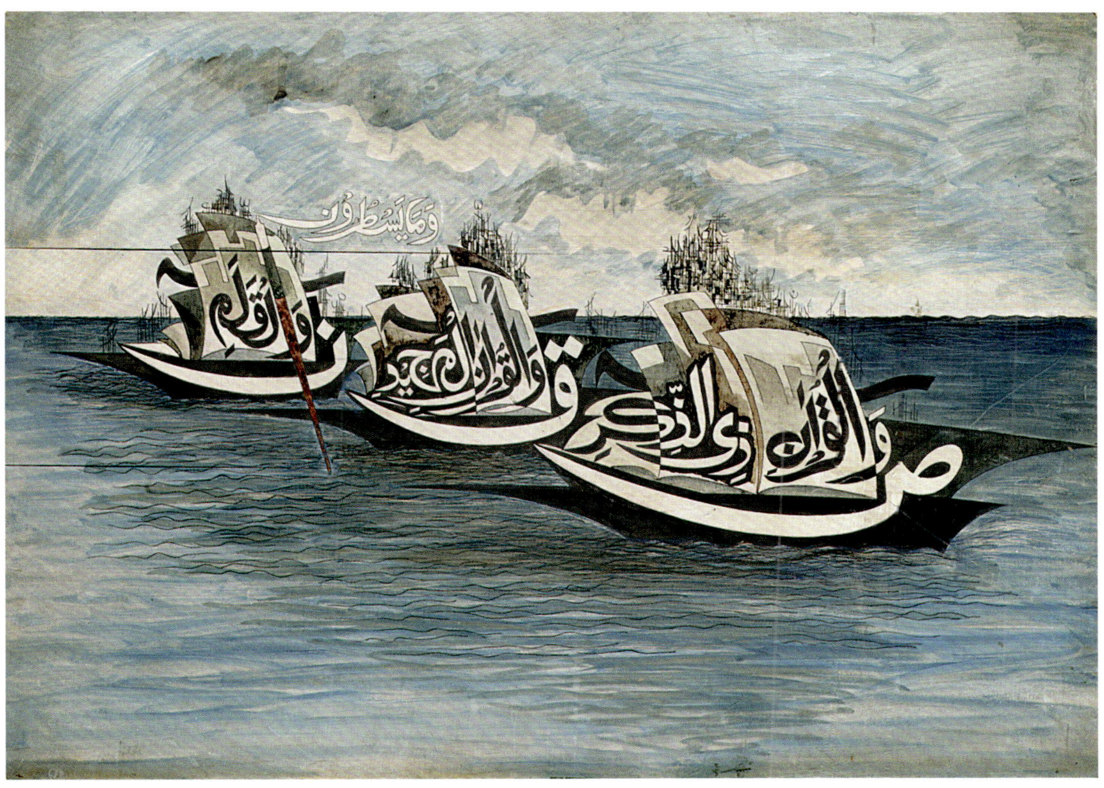

Fig. 54. Sadequain (Pakistani, b. India, 1930–1987). *Seascape with Three Boats*, 20th century. Oil on wood, 22½ x 32 in. (57.2 x 81.3 cm). Gift of the Government of Pakistan, 1980 (2016.12)

The Ottoman empire was at the height of its power from the sixteenth to the eighteenth century and prided itself on its maritime strength, so it is not surprising that majestic naval vessels figured so prominently in Ottoman art of the period. These works, in a range of media, celebrated the military achievements of a particular sultan, or they were commissioned by royals or high-ranking officers to record military triumphs and to protect against enemies and turbulent seas. That the inscriptions here refer to the Seven Sleepers renders this calligram an especially potent talisman, for the Sleepers were believed to protect ships from sinking. In fact, the Ottoman navy is said to have been dedicated to the Sleepers. While no mention of a ship is made in either the Christian or the Muslim version of the story, Ottoman artists have incorporated the Sleepers' names into depictions of ships since at least the seventeenth century.

Calligrams of ships remained popular subjects among artists well into the modern period. An example by the renowned Pakistani artist Sadequain (fig. 54) depicts a seascape with three boats whose forms are composed of the Arabic phrases "In the name of the memorable Qur'an. In the name of the glorious Qur'an. In the name of the pen [and anything it writes]." The three letters in the front of each boat, *sad*, *qaf*, and *nun*, may refer to the appearance of individual letters at the beginning of some *suras* of the Qur'an, and could also be a pun on the artist's own name, Sadequain. Here, the painter has used an age-old cipher of a boat as a symbol of safety and security.

Opposite: Fig. 53. Prayer book with Noah's Ark (Safina-yi Nuh) in *ghubar* script. Calligrapher: ʻAbd al-Qadir Hisari. Turkey, Ottoman, dated A.H. 1180/A.D. 1766. Ink, opaque watercolor, and gold on paper; leather and gold binding, 6 x 4 in. (15.3 x 10.2 cm). Purchase, Friends of Islamic Art Gifts, 2014 (2014.44)

38

VOTIVE TABLET (*HILYA*) BEARING A TEXTUAL "PORTRAIT" OF THE PROPHET MUHAMMAD

Turkey, 18th century
Ink, opaque watercolor, and gold on paper, mounted on wood, 27⅞ x 10½ in. (70.8 x 26.7 cm)
The Grinnell Collection, Bequest of William Milne Grinnell, 1920 (20.120.274)

As an intermediary who can communicate directly with the divine, the Prophet Muhammad is regarded by Muslims as the ultimate intercessor. Worshippers call upon him at times of illness, hardship, and war, but also, more importantly, to help them achieve salvation in the afterlife. Talismans and amulets that represent the Prophet's attributes, possessions, and traces have therefore functioned as protective and intercessory devices for centuries, up to the present day. Naturally, many of these talismans are textual rather than figural. The *hilya*, a textual "portrait" of the Prophet that gives a description of his physical and moral attributes, is the most widely known and used talisman of this type, particularly in Ottoman Turkey and in Iran.

In the seventeenth century, Ottoman *hilya*s developed a standardized anthropomorphic layout like the one seen here, with a "head station" (*baş makam*), a "belly" (*göbek*), and a "crescent" (*hilal*). *Hilya*s in the form of votive tablets, like this example from The Met's collection, were meant to be kept in the home. It was also customary to carry a small *hilya* on one's person as a sign of love and esteem for the Prophet. These were often folded into small squares and placed in cases, as indicated by the pattern of creases in the examples on paper (fig. 55).

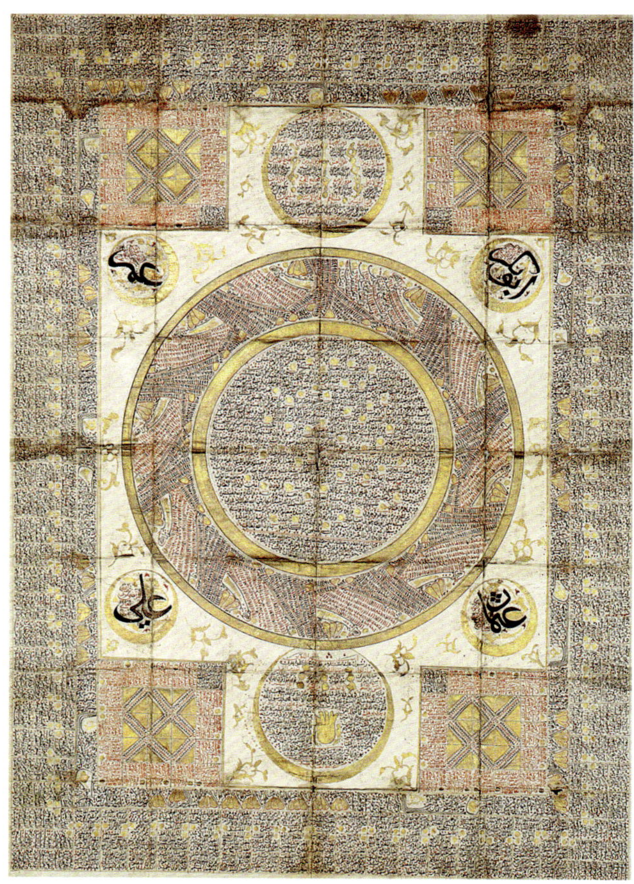

Fig. 55. Talismanic chart with a *hilya*. Turkey, Ottoman, A.H. 1124/A.D. 1712. Colored inks and gold on paper, backed with green silk, 18⅛ x 13¾ in. (46 x 34.1 cm). Khalili Collection (MSSS 079)

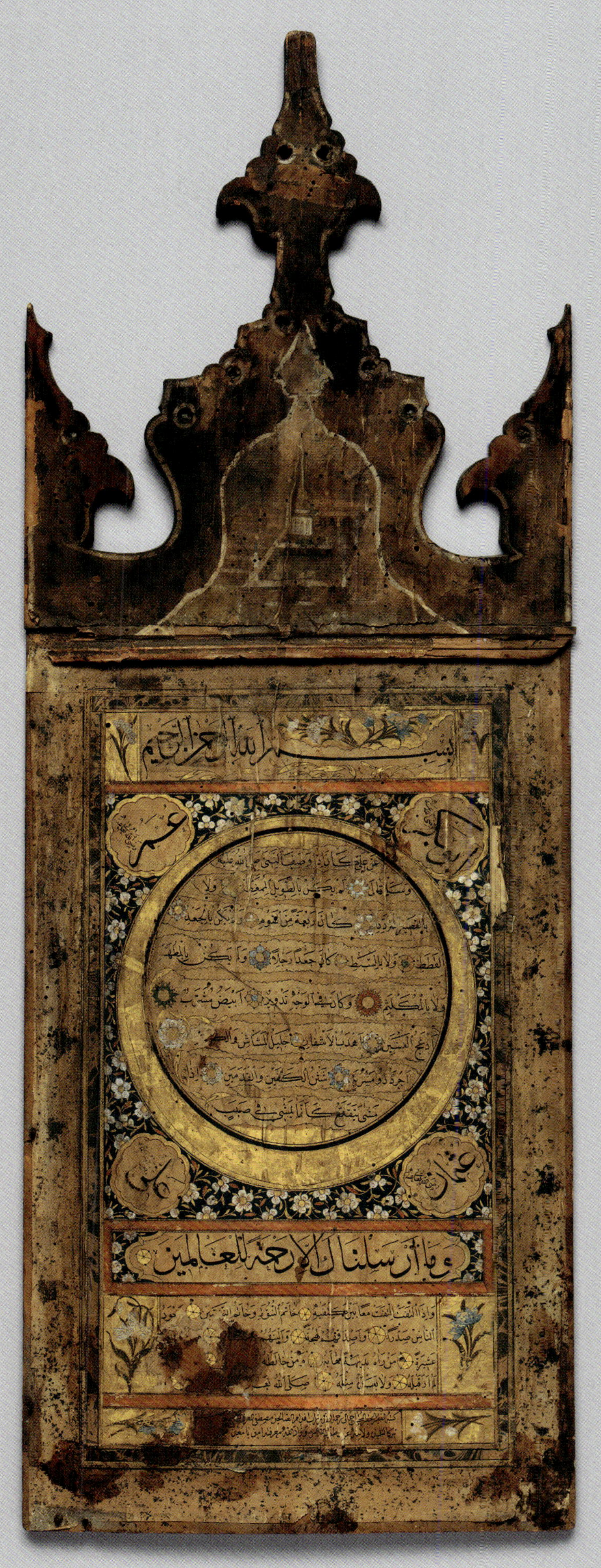

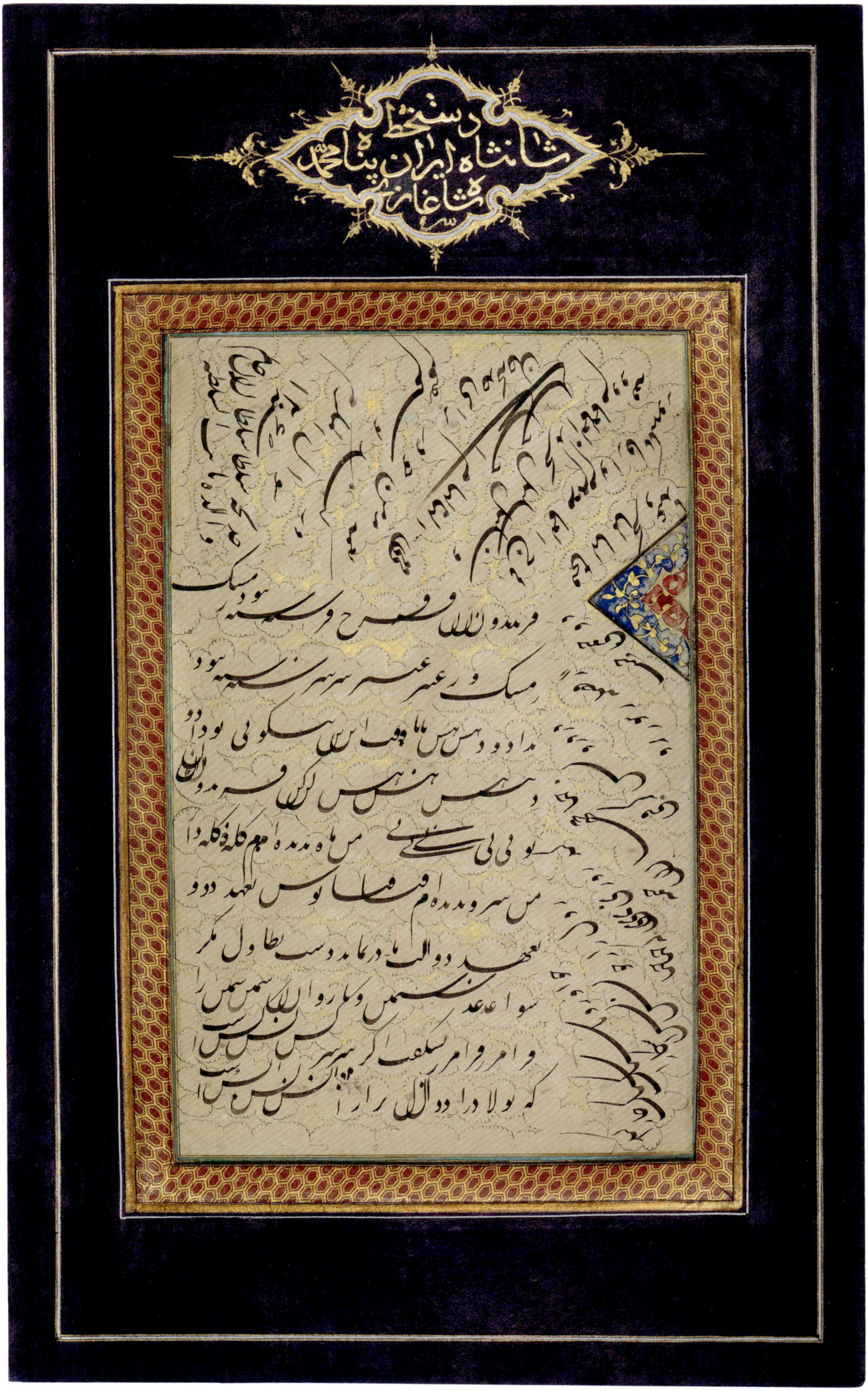

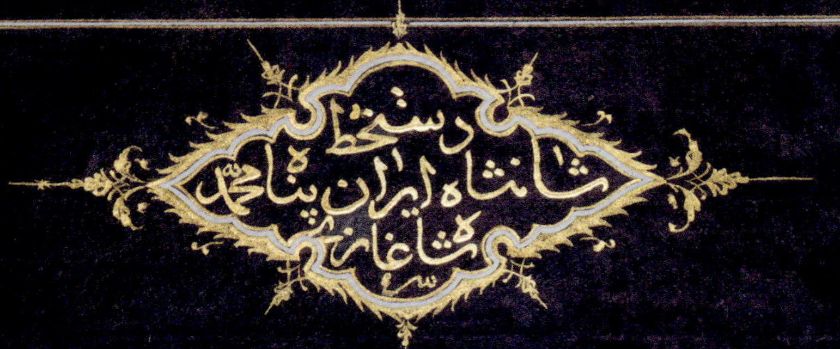
دستخط
شاهنشاه ایران پناه محمد
شاه غازی

39

CALLIGRAPHY EXERCISE (*SIYAH MASHQ*) BY A QAJAR RULER

Calligrapher: Muhammad Shah Qajar (r. 1834–48)
Iran, dated Shawwal A.H. 1260/A.D. October 1844
Ink, gold, and opaque watercolor on paper, 12 3/16 x 7 11/16 in. (31 x 19.5 cm)
Purchase, Friends of Islamic Art Gifts, 2016 (2016.535)

Two examples of the art of *siyah mashq*, one by Muhammad Shah Qajar, third ruler of the Qajar dynasty, and another by his court calligrapher, Asadullah Shirazi, illustrate that compositional practice pages were created by calligraphers from different echelons of society. In both cases, the written texts are illegible; the emphasis is not on content but on the rhythm and harmony of the letters and the lines of letters, as well as their compositional layout on the page. The literal meaning is irrelevant.

The shah's example (cat. 39) includes a dedication in the upper left corner to Khadija Sultan, one of his favorite wives. The letters and words are penned in refined and fluid *nasta'liq* script that flows in all directions on the page. To the recipient (his wife), the calligraphy was likely a special gift, for the shah's act of bestowing a *siyah mashq* in his own hand would have been equivalent to presenting her with a piece of himself. An inscription in gold on a deep purple ground says that the folio contains the "handwriting of his royal highness the Shah of Iran, Muhammad Shah Ghazi."

The second *siyah mashq* folio (fig. 56), by Asadullah Shirazi, also exhibits the lyrical quality of *nasta'liq* and was probably intended for a royal album. Here, the carefully calibrated letters are rendered in diagonal lines. In a small inscription tucked under larger letters, Asadullah signs the page and refers to himself as *katib al-hazrat al-sultani*, or "the scribe of His Royal Highness." It was a title awarded him by the shah, whose own name appears in small letters at the top of the page.

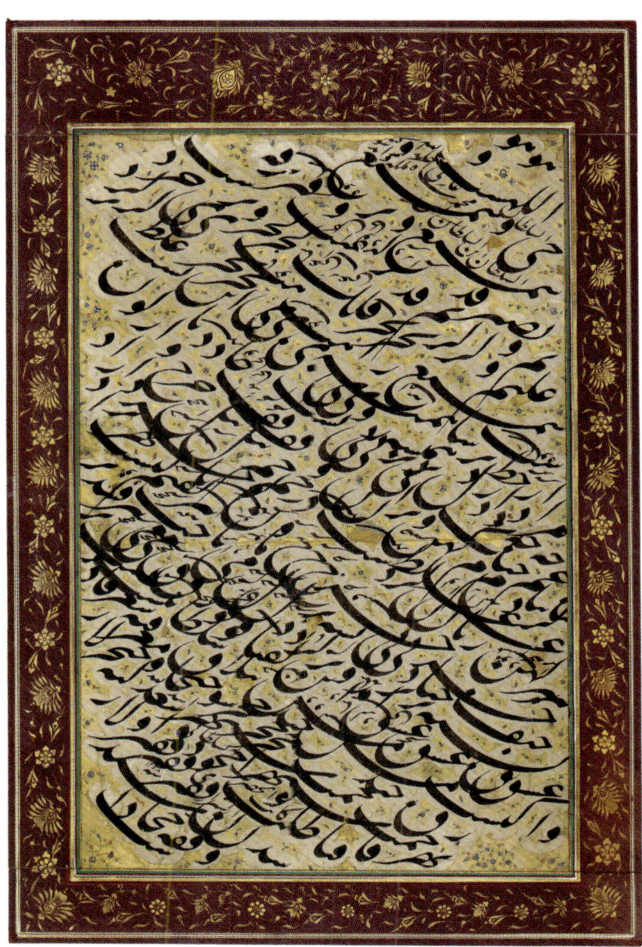

Fig. 56. Calligraphy exercise (*siyah mashq*) by a court calligrapher. Calligrapher: Asadullah Shirazi (active 1830s–50s). Iran, dated A.H. 1258/A.D. 1842–43. Ink, opaque watercolor, and gold on paper, 18 7/8 x 13 in. (48 x 33 cm). Purchase, Friends of Islamic Art Gifts, 2016 (2016.536)

POET TURNING INTO HEECH

Parviz Tanavoli (Iranian, b. Tehran, 1937)
Canada, West Vancouver, 2007
Bronze, 89 13/16 x 22 13/16 x 25 1/2 in. (228.1 x 57.9 x 64.8 cm)
Purchase, 2011 NoRuz at The Met Benefit, 2012 (2012.39)

Parviz Tanavoli made the first of his *heech* sculptures in 1964; through the decades, they have become hallmarks of Iranian modernism. *Heech* in Persian is the word for "nothing" or "nothingness." Originally, the *heeches* were a protest against the excessive commercialization, derivative nature, and westward gaze of the art scene that Tanavoli found in Iran upon his return there in 1960. But on a spiritual level, they were a sculptural realization of the Sufi notion that God creates everything from nothing. The letters in Tanavoli's *heeches* are animated and have an anthropomorphic quality, with a head, two eyes, and a body. They assume a variety of poses: they stand upright, sit on chairs, or wind around other figures.

This stunning example abstracts the figure of a poet into a cylindrical body with a polelike extension rising from its top and pseudo-inscriptions covering its upper half. *He*, the first letter of the word *heech*, winds around the poet and emerges from the front of the piece. The *heech* envelops the poet, as the two merge into one. The work illustrates Tanavoli's lifelong engagement with Persian mystical poetry and its role in sculpture. Like several of his later sculptures, this monumental *heech* was modeled on a smaller one, made in 1973 (fig. 57).

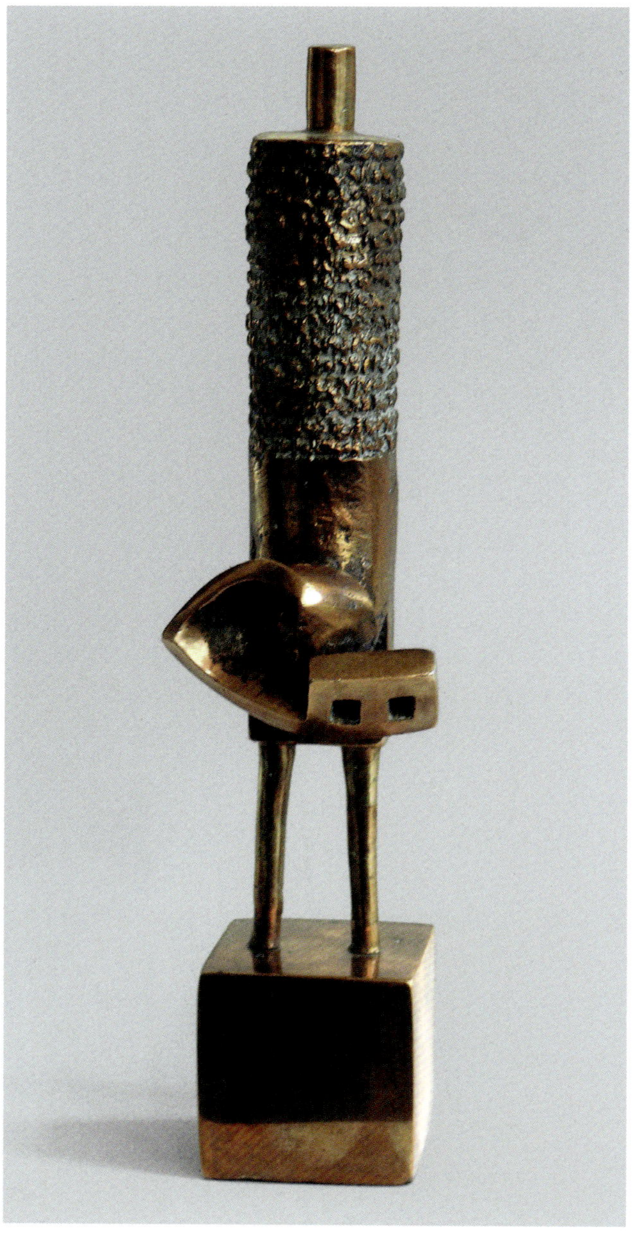

Fig. 57. Parviz Tanavoli (Iranian, b. Tehran, 1937). *Sacred Heech II*, 1973. Bronze, H. 12 in. (30.5 cm). Collection of Mrs. Manijeh Tanavoli, Tehran, Iran

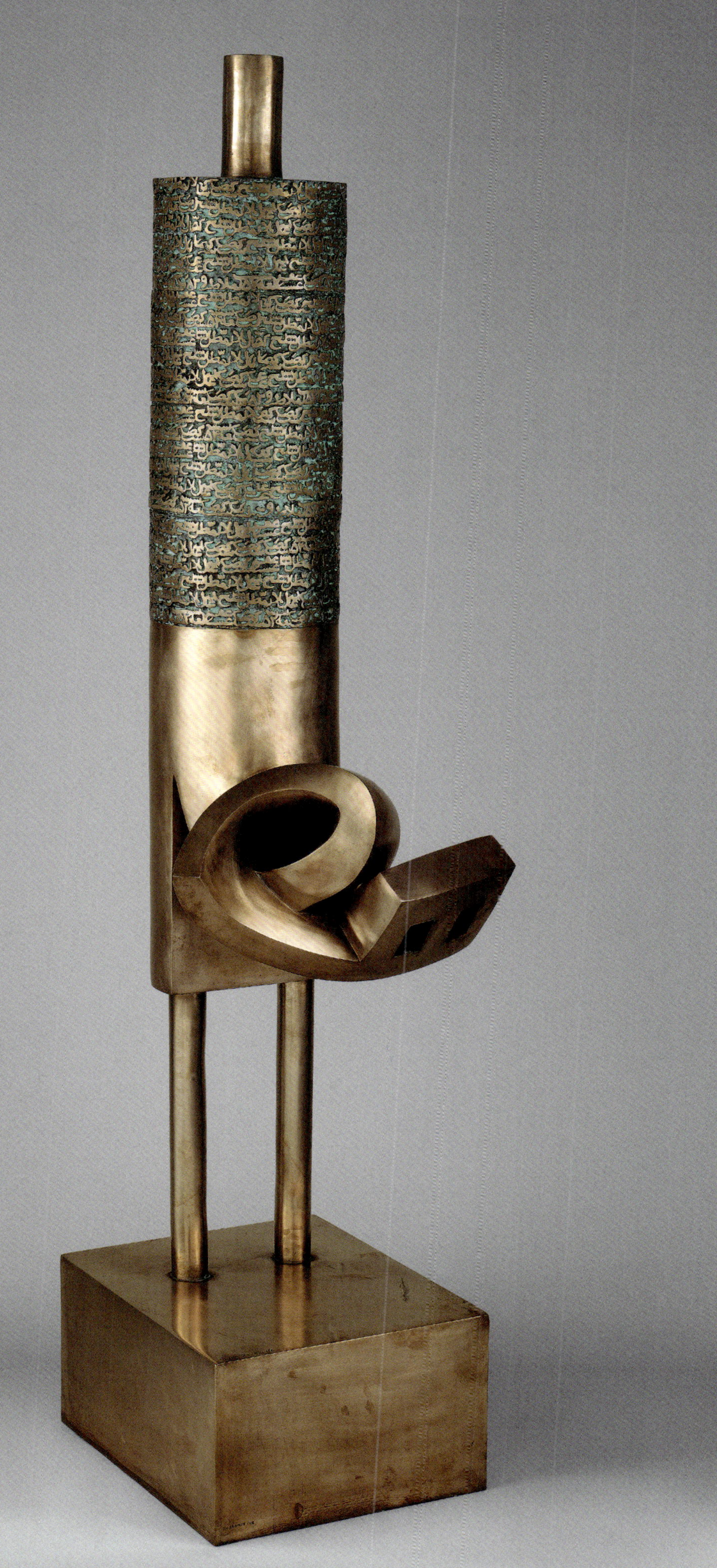

RIBBON MANIA

Burhan Doğançay (American, b. Turkey, 1929–2013)
Turkey, 1982
Acrylic on canvas, 60 x 60 in. (152.4 x 152.4 cm)
Gift of Benjamin Kaufmann, 2011 (2011.583)

Inspired by the graffiti- and poster-covered walls of New York City in the 1960s, the Turkish-born artist Burhan Doğançay mined the expressive possibilities of street art in works that span a half century. His Ribbon paintings, a series made between 1972 and 1989, are trompe-l'oeil collages in which the evocative forms of ribbons or of slashed and torn paper seem to break through the plane of a wall and project into the viewer's space, providing a glimpse into the worlds of unknown city dwellers. Here, the play of light and shadow against a pale gray ground underscores the illusion of three-dimensionality.

While the markings on the canvas suggest posters peeling from a wall, Doğançay's Ribbon paintings also recall Islamic calligraphy. A recent study by Met curator Deniz Beyazit connects the paintings to calligrams and to Ottoman calligraphy (fig. 58). Beyazit suggests that, as part of his creative process, the artist experimented with paper maquettes resembling calligraphic structures, which cast shadows that he then reinterpreted in painted form. This association with Ottoman calligraphy is particularly important, since Doğançay did not read Arabic, having been raised in the post-Atatürk era in Turkey, in an environment that rejected Ottoman and Islamic writing in favor of the Latin script.

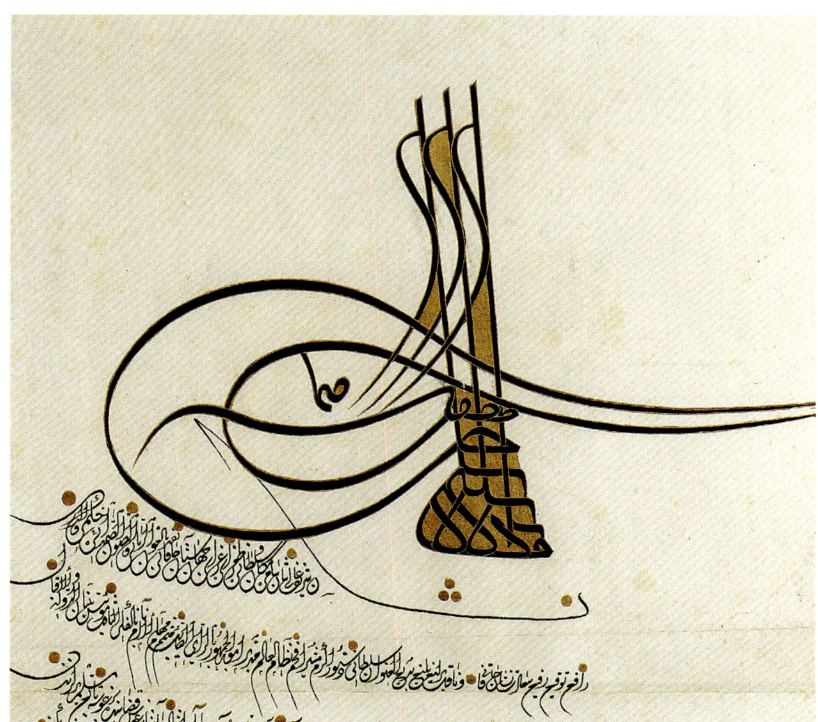

Fig. 58. *Tughra* of Sultan Murad III (r. 1574–95) (detail), dated A.H. 983/A.D. 1575. Ink and gold on paper, 55⅛ x 13½ in. (140 x 34.2 cm). Sakıp Sabancı Museum, Istanbul (160-0028-SMU)

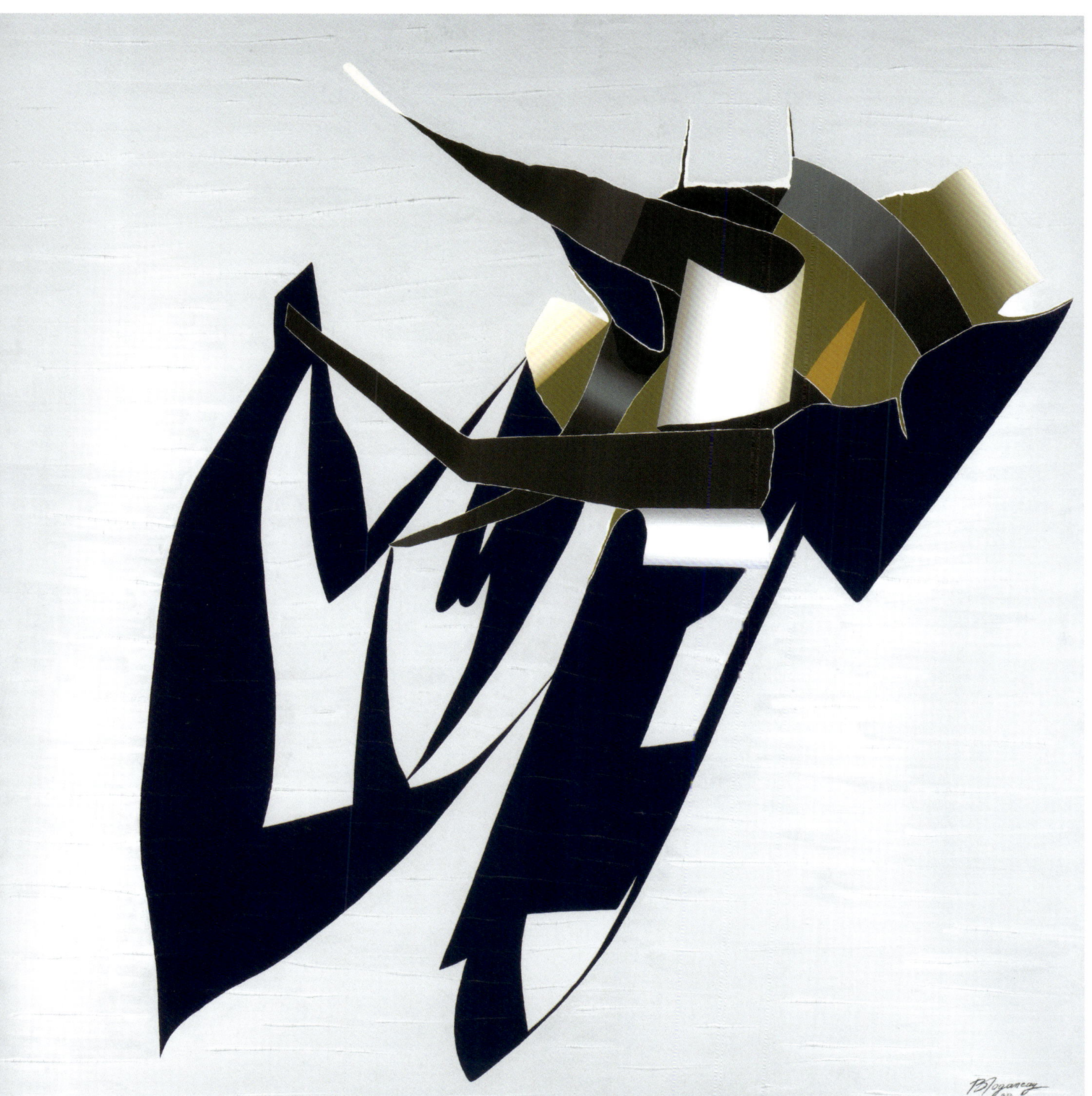

42

UNTITLED

Golnaz Fathi (Iranian, b. Tehran, 1972)
Iran, 2013
Acrylic, pen, and varnish on canvas, two panels
39⅜ x 55⅛ in. (100 x 140 cm)
Purchase, 2012 NoRuz at The Met Benefit, 2014
(2014.524a, b)

This untitled diptych by Golnaz Fathi incorporates her extensive training in classical calligraphy and graphic design (though as a painter, she is self-taught). It recalls the rhythm and movement of calligraphy practice pages (*siyah mashq*; see cat. 39), as well as the visual idioms of the digital age, such as seismographs and electrocardiograms. The work comprises two asymmetrical sections featuring markings and networks of lines, which intensify along the central horizontal axis and disperse the farther away they are from it. These marks are set against a hazy band of bright yellow that recalls warning labels for radioactive materials. On the off-center vertical axis is a thick black band of vigorous brushstrokes that extends beyond the inner frames of the two panels and wraps around the edges.

The markings recall the energetic brushwork, gestural abstraction, and "flung ink" of Asian, particularly Chinese and Japanese, calligraphy, as well as paintings by Abstract Expressionists such as Jackson Pollock and Franz Kline. Fathi, who was born and grew up in Tehran, is a classically trained calligrapher who has spent hours practicing, perfecting, and mastering her technique and manual dexterity. However, Fathi's art goes far beyond the scope of classical calligraphy, defying the rules of the canon. As a result, she frees the letters from meaning and allows them to take on a life of their own. The letters and markings move up and down, in different directions, and sometimes fall off the canvas.

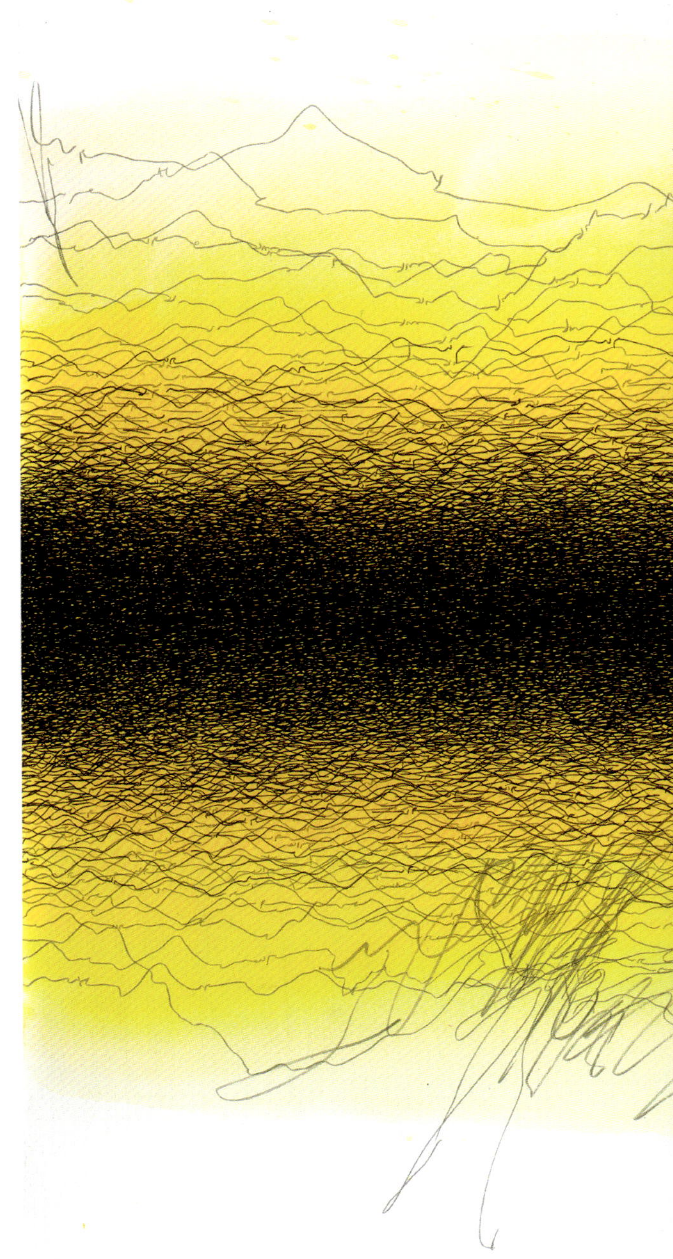

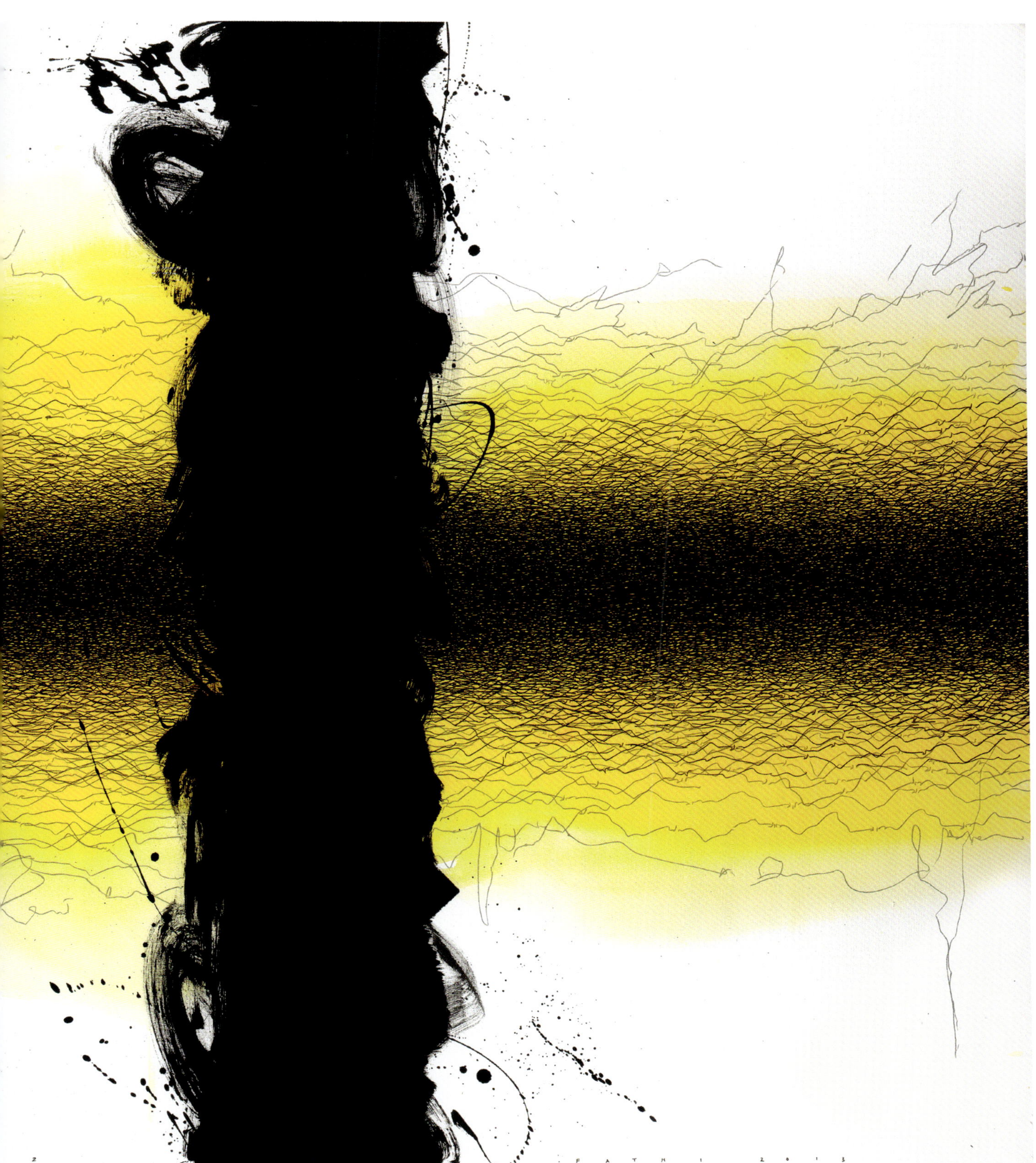
2
FATHI 2013

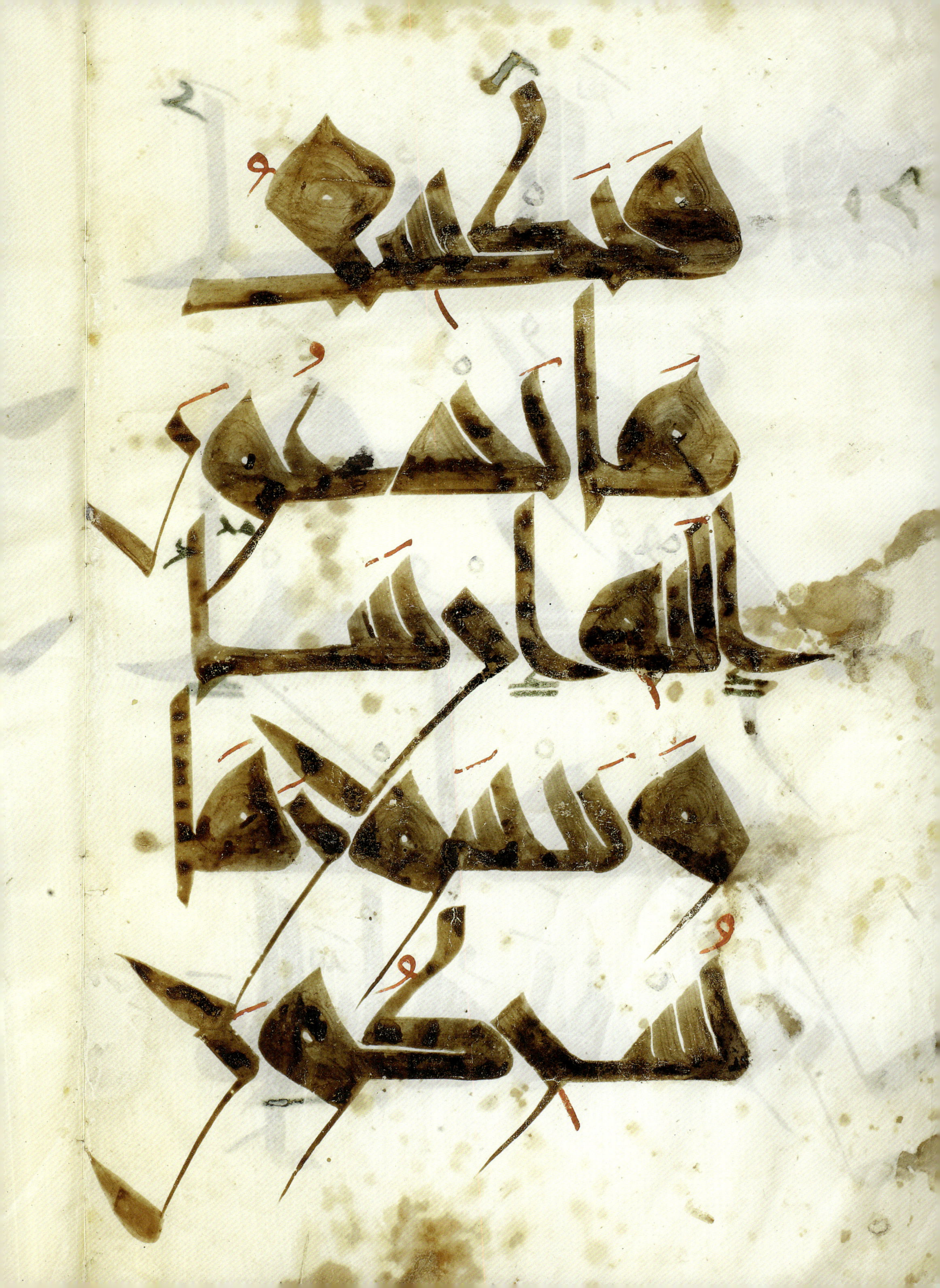

SOURCES

Introduction

Qadi Ahmad 1959, pp. 59–60, 121–22; Schimmel 1970, p. 14; Rosenthal 1971, pp. 38–39; *MMAB* 1978; Soucek 1979; Schimmel 1984; Blair 1998, p. 3; Canby and Thompson 2003, pp. 216–17; Fendall 2005; Blair 2006, pp. 57–65; McWilliams and Roxburgh 2007; Blair 2009, pp. 336–39, 344; Avinoam Shalem in Frembgen 2010, pp. 127–47; MMA 2011a; Denise Marie Teece in MMA 2011b, pp. 237–38; Glaire D. Anderson and Mariam Rosser-Owen in Landau 2015, pp. 28–51.

The Arabic Script

MMA 1975, pp. 184–86; *MMAB* 1975; Welch 1979, p. 140; Atil 1987, p. 41; MMA 1987; François Déroche in Khalili 1992–, vol. 1, pp. 58–77, 132–37; Little 1996; Blair 1998, pp. 425–30; Bloom 1999; Canby 2000, p. 72; Bloom 2001; Cardini 2001; Mack 2001; MMA 2002a; Shankland 2004; *MMAB* 2005, p. 9; Blair 2006; Ekhtiar 2006a; Blair 2008; Gully 2008; Bloom and Blair 2009; George 2010; Stefano Carboni, pp. 92–93, Walter B. Denny, p. 294, Maryam Ekhtiar, pp. 60–61, and Priscilla Soucek, pp. 90–91, in MMA 2011b; Finbarr B. Flood in MMA 2012, pp. 244–57, 265–69; George 2013; Sheila R. Canby in MMA 2016a, p. 283; Simon Rettig in Farhad and Rettig 2016, pp. 178–79.

Embellishing the Word of God

Pickthall 1930; Qadi Ahmad 1959, p. 64; MMA 1975; Welsh 1979, p. 101; Atil 1981, nos. 25–32; Nelson 1985, pp. xv, xvii, 3; MMA 1987; Whelan 1990; Khalili 1992–, vol. 4, pp. 228–57, vol. 5, pp. 74, 234, vol. 12, pp. 117–22; MMA 1992, pp. 284–86; Thackston 1994; *MMAB* 1998; James 1999, pp. 18–19; Atasoy et al. 2000, p. 297; Carboni 2002, p. 234; Carboni 2004; Lings 2005, p. 52; Blair 2006, pp. 257–81, 318, 345–49; Blair and Bloom 2006a, p. 87; Blair and Bloom 2006b, p. 223; İpek 2006; O'Kane 2006, pp. 274–75; Baker 2007, pp. 30–31; MMA 2007, pp. 253–60; Pal 2007, pp. 230–31; Roxburgh 2008; Seracettin 2008, pp. 86–89; George 2009; James 2009, p. 351; Akbarnia 2010, p. 14–15; George 2010, pp. 38–48; Christiane Gruber, pp. 117–53, and Heather Coffey, pp. 78–115, in Gruber 2010; İpek 2011; Stefano Carboni, pp. 61–62, 175–76, Paola Chadwick, p. 66, Maryam Ekhtiar, pp. 397–98, Ellen Kenney, pp. 141–42, Priscilla Soucek, pp. 27, 107–8, and Denise Marie Teece, pp. 123–24, in MMA 2011b; Eldem 2012; al-Mojan 2012; François Déroche in Blair and Bloom 2013, pp. 59–77; Suleman 2015; MMA 2015a, pp. 14, 56–59; Porter et al. 2016, p. 58; MMA 2016b; Massumeh Farhad, pp. 222–223, Jane Mcauliffe, p. 42, Simon Rettig, pp. 178–79, and Zeren Tanindidi, pp. 98–117, in Farhad and Rettig 2016.

Ornament and Abstraction

Volov 1966; *MMAB* 1968; *MMAB* 1970; Welch 1979, pp. 74–75; Baer 1983, pp. 65–72, p. 103 n. 235; *MMAB* 1983; Blair 1989, pp. 329–34; Glidden and Thompson 1989; Brosh 1991; Holly Edwards in Fisher 1991, p. 73; Frederick de Jong, pp. 228–41, and Annemarie Schimmel, pp. 73–129, in Lifchez 1992; Melikian-Chirvani 1992; Ward 1993, p. 78; Özbek 1995; MMA 1997, p. 24; Blair 1998, pp. 42–43, 106–28; MMA 1998, pp. 54–57; Roxburgh 1998; Atasoy et al. 2000; Gonzalez 2000; Philon 2000; Balaghi and Gumpert 2002; al-Moraekhi 2002, pp. 123–33; al-Mulk 2002; MMA 2002b; Porter 2006; O'Kane 2006, pp. 212–13, 217; Blair and Bloom 2006b; Ekhtiar 2006b; Brend 2007; Venetia Porter in Suleman 2007, pp. 123–34; Schick 2008; Vali 2008; Armirsadeghi 2009; Bardaouil 2009; Dadi 2010; Frembgen 2010, pp. 71–91; Heather Coffey, p. 104, and Christiane Gruber, pp. 117–53, in Gruber 2010; Philon 2010; Pocock 2010; Blair 2011; Maryam Ekhtiar, pp. 390–92, Francesca Leoni, p. 127, Venetia Porter, p. 296, and Jochen Sokoly, p. 52, in MMA 2011b; Allan 2012; Çalıkoğlu et al. 2012; Elias 2012, pp. 264–83; Daftari 2013; Diba 2013; Bier 2014, pp. 31–40; *MMAB* 2014; Eastmond 2015, pp. 1–10; Fischman and Balaghi 2015; Marika Sardar in MMA 2015b, p. 218; İrvin Cemil Schick in Bedos-Rezak and Hamburger 2016, pp. 173–97; Gumpert 2016; Leoni et al. 2016, pp. 33–66; Porter et al. 2016; Sheila R. Canby, pp. 200–201, and Martina Rugiadi, pp. 127–28, in MMA 2016a; Beyazit 2017; Ekhtiar 2017.

BIBLIOGRAPHY

Akbarnia 2010 Akbarnia, Ladan, with Francesca Leoni. *Light of the Sufis: The Mystical Arts of Islam*. Exh. cat. Museum of Fine Arts. Houston, 2010.

Allan 2012 Allan, James W. *The Art and Architecture of Twelver Shiʿism: Iraq, Iran and the Indian Sub-Continent*. London, 2012.

Armirsadeghi 2009 Armirsadeghi, Hossein, ed. *Different Sames: New Perspectives in Contemporary Iranian Art*. London, 2009.

Atasoy et al. 2000 Atasoy, Nurhan, et al. *İpek: The Crescent and the Rose. Imperial Ottoman Silks and Velvets*. London, 2000.

Atil 1981 Atil, Esin, ed. *Renaissance of Islam: Art of the Mamluks*. Exh. cat. National Museum of Natural History, Smithsonian Institution. Washington, 1981.

Atil 1987 Atil, Esin, ed. *The Age of Sultan Süleyman the Magnificent*. Exh. cat. National Gallery of Art, Washington; Art Institute of Chicago; The Metropolitan Museum of Art, New York. New York, 1981.

Baer 1983 Baer, Eva. *Metalwork in Medieval Islamic Art*. Albany, 1983.

Baker 2007 Baker, Colin F. *Qur'an Manuscripts: Calligraphy, Illumination, Design*. London, 2007.

Balaghi and Gumpert 2002 Balaghi, Shiva, and Lynn Gumpert, eds. *Picturing Iran: Art, Society and Revolution*. London, 2002.

Bardaouil 2009 Bardaouil, Sam. *Iran Inside Out: Influences of Homeland and Diaspora on the Artistic Language of Contemporary Iranian Artists*. Exh. cat. Chelsea Art Museum. New York, 2009.

Bedos-Rezak and Hamburger 2016 Bedos-Rezak, Brigitte, and Jeffrey Hamburger, eds. *Sign and Design: Script as Image in Cross-Cultural Perspective (300–1600 CE)*. Washington, 2016.

Beyazit 2017 Beyazit, Deniz. "Searching for an Artistic Identity: Doğançay and His Ottoman Heritage." In *Burhan Doğançay*, edited by Klaus Albrecht Schröder and Elsy Lahner, pp. 41–51. Munich, 2017.

Bier 2014 Bier, Carol. "Inscribed Cotton *Ikat* from Yemen in the Tenth Century CE." In *9th International Shibori Symposium*, pp. 31–40. Hangzhou, 2014.

Blair 1989 Blair, Sheila. "Legibility Versus Decoration in Islamic Epigraphy: The Case of Interlacing." In *World Art: Themes of Unity and Diversity*, edited by Irving Lavin, vol. 2, pp. 329–34. London, 1989.

Blair 1998 Blair, Sheila. *Islamic Inscriptions*. Edinburgh, 1998.

Blair 2006 Blair, Sheila. *Islamic Calligraphy*. Edinburgh, 2006.

Blair 2008 Blair, Sheila. "Transcribing God's Word: Qur'an Codices in Context." *Journal of Qur'anic Studies* 10, no. 1 (2008), pp. 71–97.

Blair 2011 Blair, Sheila. "Epigraphy III: Arabic Inscriptions in Persia." *Encyclopedia Iranica* 8, no. 5 (2011), pp. 490–98.

Blair and Bloom 2006a Blair, Sheila, and Jonathan Bloom. *Cosmophilia: Islamic Art from the David Collection, Copenhagen*. Exh. cat. McMullen Museum of Art, Boston College; Smart Museum of Art, University of Chicago. Chestnut Hill, Mass., 2006.

Blair and Bloom 2006b Blair, Sheila, and Jonathan Bloom. "Timur's Qur'an: A Reappraisal." In *Sifting Sands, Reading Signs: Studies in Honour of Professor Géza Fehérvári*, edited by Patricia L. Baker and Barbara Brend, pp. 5–13. London, 2006.

Blair and Bloom 2013 Blair, Sheila, and Jonathan Bloom. *God Is Beautiful and Loves Beauty: The Object in Islamic Art and Culture*. New Haven and London, 2013.

Blair and Bloom 2017 Blair, Sheila, and Jonathan Bloom, eds. *By the Pen and What They Write: Writing in Islamic Art and Culture*. New Haven and London, 2017.

Bloom 1999 Bloom, Jonathan. "Revolution by the Ream: A History of Paper." *Saudi Aramco World* (May/June 1999), pp. 26–39.

Bloom 2001 Bloom, Jonathan. *Paper Before Print: The History and Impact of Paper in the Islamic World*. New Haven and London, 2001.

Bloom and Blair 2009 Bloom, Jonathan, and Sheila Blair. "Calligraphy." *Grove Encyclopedia of Islamic Art and Architecture* 1 (2009), pp. 336–53.

Brend 2007 Brend, Barbara. *Islamic Art*. London, 2007.

Brosh 1991 Brosh, Na'ama, with Rachel Milstein. *Biblical Stories in Islamic Painting*. Exh. cat. Israel Museum. Jerusalem, 1991.

Çalıkoğlu et al. 2012 Çalıkoğlu, Levent, et al. *Burhan Doğançay: Fifty Years of Urban Walls*. Istanbul, 2012.

Canby 2000 Canby, Sheila R. *The Golden Age of Persian Art, 1501–1722*. New York, 2000.

Canby and Thompson 2003 Canby, Sheila R., and Jon Thompson, eds. *Hunt for Paradise: Court Arts of Safavid Iran, 1501–1576*. Exh. cat. Asia Society, New York; Museo Poldi Pezzoli and Palazzo Reale, Milan. New York, 2003.

Carboni 2002 Carboni, Stefano. *Glass from Islamic Lands*. London, 2002.

Carboni 2004 Carboni, Stefano. "Fifteenth-Century Enameled Glass and Gilded Glass Made for the Mamluks: The End of an Era, the Beginning of a New One." *Orient* 39 (2004), pp. 69–78.

Cardini 2001 Cardini, Franco. *Europe and Islam*. Hoboken, NJ, 2001.

Dadi 2010 Dadi, Iftikhar. *Modernism and the Art of Muslim South Asia*. Chapel Hill, 2010.

Daftari 2013 Daftari, Fereshteh. "Redefining Modernism: Pluralist Art Before the 1979 Revolution." In *Iran Modern*, edited by Fereshteh Daftari and Layla S. Diba. Exh. cat. Asia Society. New York, 2013.

Diba 2013 Diba, Layla S., and Golnaz Fathi. *Golnaz Fathi: Recent Works*. New York, 2013.

Fisher 1991 Fisher, Carol Garrett, ed. *Brocade of the Pen: The Art of Islamic Writing*. Exh. cat. Kresge Art Museum, Michigan State University. East Lansing, Mich., 1991.

Eastmond 2015 Eastmond, Antony, ed. *Viewing Inscriptions in the Late Antique and Medieval World*. Cambridge and New York, 2015.

Ekhtiar 2006a Ekhtiar, Maryam D. "Innovation and Revivalism in Later Persian Calligraphy: The Vesal Family of Shiraz." In *Islamic Art in the 19th Century: Tradition, Innovation and Eclecticism*, edited by Doris Behrens-Abouseif and Stephen Vernoit. Leiden, 2006.

Ekhtiar 2006b Ekhtiar, Maryam D. "Practice Makes Perfect: The Art of Calligraphy Exercises Siyah Mashq in Iran." *Muqarnas* 23 (2006), pp. 107–30.

Ekhtiar 2017 Ekhtiar, Maryam D. "Sufi Narrative: Two Works by Parviz Tanavoli." *Hali*, no. 191 (2017), pp. 67–71.

Eldem 2012 Eldem, Edhem. "Making Sense of Osman Hamdi Bey and His Paintings." *Muqarnas* 29 (2012), pp. 339–85.

Elias 2012 Elias, Jamal J. *Aisha's Cushion: Religious Art, Perception, and Practice in Islam*. Cambridge, Mass., 2012.

Farhad and Rettig 2016 Farhad, Massumeh, and Simon Rettig, eds. *The Art of the Qur'an: Treasures from the Museum of Turkish and Islamic Arts*. Exh. cat. Freer Gallery of Art and Arthur M. Sackler Galleries, Smithsonian Institution. Washington, 2016.

Fendall 2005 Fendall, Ramsey. *Islamic Calligraphy*. London, 2005.

Fischman and Balaghi 2015 Fischman, Lisa, and Shiva Balaghi. *Parvis Tanavoli*. Exh. cat. Davis Museum, Wellesley College. Wellesley, Mass., 2015.

Frembgen 2010 Frembgen, Jürgen Wasim, ed. *The Aura of Alif: The Art of Writing in Islam*. Munich, 2010.

George 2009 George, Alain F. "Color and Light in the Blue Qur'an." *Journal of Qur'anic Studies* 11, no. 1 (2009), pp. 75–125.

George 2010 George, Alain F. *The Rise of Islamic Calligraphy*. London, 2010.

George 2013 George, Alain F. *On an Early Qur'anic Palimpsest and Its Stratigraphy*. St. Andrews, Scotland, 2013.

Glidden and Thompson 1989 Glidden, Harold W., and Deborah Thompson. "*Ṭirāz* in the Byzantine Collection, Dumbarton Oaks. Parts 2 and 3: *Ṭirāz* from the Yemen, Iraq, Iran, and an Unknown Place." *Bulletin of the Asia Institute* 3 (1989), pp. 89–105.

Gonzalez 2000 Gonzalez, Valerie. "The Double Ontology of Islamic Calligraphy: A Word-Image on a Folio from the Museum of Raqqada (Tunisia)." In *M. Ügur Derman 65th Birthday Festschrift*, edited by İrvin Cemil, pp. 313–40. Istanbul, 2000.

Gruber 2010 Gruber, Christiane, ed. *The Islamic Manuscript Tradition: Ten Centuries of Book Arts in Indiana University Collections*. Bloomington, 2010.

Gully 2008 Gully, Adrian. *The Culture of Letter Writing in Pre-Modern Islamic Society*. Edinburgh, 2008.

Gumpert 2016 Gumpert, Lynn. *Global/Local: Six Artists from Iran, 1960–2015*. Exh. cat. Grey Art Gallery, New York University. New York, 2016.

İpek 2006 İpek, Selin. "Man Ravza-i Mutahhara Covers Sent from Istanbul to Medina with Surre Processions." *Muqarnas* 23 (2006), pp. 289–316.

İpek 2011 İpek, Selin. "Dressing the Prophet, Textiles from the Haramayn." *Hali*, no. 168 (2011), pp. 59–61.

James 1999 James, David. *Manuscripts of the Holy Qur'an from the Mamluk Era*. Riyadh, 1999.

James 2009 James, David. "Qur'ans and Calligraphers of the Ayyubids and Zangids." In *Ayyubid Jerusalem: The Holy City in Context, 1187–1250*, edited by Robert Hillenbrand and Sylvia Auld, pp. 348–59. London, 2009.

Khalili 1992– *The Nasser D. Khalili Collection of Islamic Art*, series edited by Julian Raby, Vol. 1, *The Abbasid Tradition: Qur'ans of the 8th to the 10th Centuries* (1992), by François Déroche; Vol. 4, *The Decorated Word: Qur'ans of the 17th to 19th Centuries* (1999), by Bayani Manijeh, Anna Contadini, and Tim Stanley; Vol. 5, *The Art of the Pen: Calligraphy of the 14th to 20th Centuries* (1996), by Nabil F. Safwat and Mohamed Zakariya; and Vol. 12, *Science, Tools, and Magic: Body, Spirit, and Mapping the Universe* (1997), by Francis Maddison and Emilie Savage-Smith. London and New York, 1992–

Landau 2015 Landau, Amy S., ed. *Pearls on a String: Artists, Patrons, and Poets at the Great Islamic Courts*. Exh. cat. Walters Art Museum, Baltimore; Asian Art Museum, San Francisco. Baltimore, 2015.

Leoni et al. 2016 Leoni, Francesca, et al. *Power and Protection: Islamic Art and the Supernatural*. Exh. cat. Ashmolean Museum. Oxford, 2016.

Lifchez 1992 Lifchez, Raymond, ed. *The Dervish Lodge: Architecture, Art, and Sufism in Ottoman Turkey*. Berkeley, 1992.

Lings 2005 Lings, Martin. *Splendours of Qur'an Calligraphy and Illumination*. Vaduz, 2005.

Little 1996 Little, Stephen. "Economic Change in 17th-Century China and Innovations at the Jingdezhen Kilns." *Ars Orientalis* 26 (1996), pp. 47–54.

Mack 2001 Mack, Rosamond E. *Bazaar to Piazza: Islamic Trade and Italian Art, 1300–1600*. Berkeley, 2001.

McWilliams and Roxburgh 2007 McWilliams, Mary, and David J. Roxburgh, eds. *Traces of the Calligrapher: Islamic Calligraphy in Practice, c. 1600–1900*. Exh. cat. Museum of Fine Arts. Houston, 2007.

Melikian-Chirvani 1992 Melikian-Chirvani, Assadullah Souren. "The Iranian *Bazm* in Early Persian Sources." *Res Orientales* 4 (1992), pp. 95–120.

MMA 1975 *A Handbook of Chinese Ceramics*, by Suzanne G. Valenstein. The Metropolitan Museum of Art. New York, 1975.

MMA 1987 *The Emperor's Album: Images of Mughal India*, by Stuart Cary Welch et al. Exh. cat. The Metropolitan Museum of Art. New York, 1987.

MMA 1992 *Al-Andalus: The Art of Islamic Spain*, by Jerrilynn Dodds. Exh. cat. The Metropolitan Museum of Art. New York, 1992.

MMA 1997 *Following the Stars: Images of the Zodiac in Islamic Art*, by Stefano Carboni. Exh. cat. The Metropolitan Museum of Art. New York, 1997.

MMA 1998 *Letters in Gold: Ottoman Calligraphy from the Sakip Sabanci Collection, Istanbul*, by Derman M. Uğur. Exh. cat. The Metropolitan Museum of Art. New York, 1998.

MMA 2002a "The Age of Süleyman 'the Magnificent' (r. 1520–1566)," by Suzan Yalman. *Heilbrunn Timeline of Art History*, The Metropolitan Museum of Art. New York, 2002. http://www.metmuseum.org/toah/hd/suly/hd_suly.htm.

MMA 2002b "The Art of the Nasrid Period (1232–1492)." *Heilbrunn Timeline of Art History*, The Metropolitan Museum of Art. New York, 2002. http://www.metmuseum.org/toah/hd/nasr/hd_nasr.htm.

MMA 2007 *Venice and the Islamic World, 828–1797*, by Stefano Carboni. Exh. cat. The Metropolitan Museum of Art. New York, 2007.

MMA 2011a *Art of the Islamic World: A Resource for Educators*, by Maryam Ekhtiar and Claire Moore. The Metropolitan Museum of Art. New York, 2011. https://www.metmuseum.org/learn/educators/curriculum-resources.

MMA 2011b *Masterpieces from the Department of Islamic Art in the Metropolitan Museum of Art*, edited by Maryam D. Ekhtiar, Priscilla P. Soucek, Sheila R. Canby, and Navina Najat Haidar. New York, 2011.

MMA 2012 *Byzantium and Islam: Age of Transition*, edited by Helen C. Evans and Brandie Ratliff. Exh. cat. The Metropolitan Museum of Art. New York, 2012.

MMA 2015a *Islamic Arms and Armor in the Metropolitan Museum of Art*, by David G. Alexander. New York, 2015.

MMA 2015b *Sultans of Deccan India, 1500–1700: Opulence and Fantasy*, by Navina Najat Haidar and Marika Sardar. Exh. cat. The Metropolitan Museum of Art. New York, 2015.

MMA 2016a *Court and Cosmos: The Great Age of the Seljuqs*, by Sheila R. Canby, Deniz Beyazit, and Martina Rugiadi. Exh. cat. The Metropolitan Museum of Art. New York, 2016.

MMA 2016b *Power and Piety: Islamic Talismans on the Battlefield*, by Maryam Ekhtiar and Rachel Parikh. The Metropolitan Museum of Art. New York, 2016. https://metmuseum.atavist.com/powerandpiety.

***MMAB* 1968** "'Pseudo-Inscriptions' in Islamic Art," by Don Aanavi. *The Metropolitan Museum of Art Bulletin* 26, no. 5 (January 1968), pp. 353–58.

***MMAB* 1970** "Valencian Lusterware of the Fifteenth Century: Notes and Documents," by Timothy Husband. *The Metropolitan Museum of Art Bulletin* 29, no. 1 (Summer 1970), pp. 11–19.

***MMAB* 1975** "Highlights of Chinese Ceramics," by Susan G. Valenstein. *The Metropolitan Museum of Art Bulletin* 33, no. 3 (Fall 1975).

***MMAB* 1978** "Islamic Art," by Richard Ettinghausen. *The Metropolitan Museum of Art Bulletin* 36, no. 2 (Fall 1978).

***MMAB* 1983** "Islamic Pottery: A Brief History," by Marilyn Jenkins. *The Metropolitan Museum of Art Bulletin* 40, no. 4 (Spring 1983).

***MMAB* 1998** "Talismanic Shirt," by Dan Walker. *The Metropolitan Museum of Art Bulletin* 56, no. 2 (Fall 1998), p. 12.

***MMAB* 2005** "Qur'an Bifolium," by Stefano Carboni. *The Metropolitan Museum of Art Bulletin* 63, no. 2 (Fall 2005), p. 9.

***MMAB* 2014** "Prayer Book (*Du'anama*)," by Maryam Ekhtiar. *The Metropolitan Museum of Art Bulletin* 72, no. 2 (Fall 2014), p. 45.

al-Mojan 2012 al-Mojan, Muhammad H. "The Textiles Made for the Prophet's Mosque at Medina: A Preliminary Study of Their Origins, History and Style." In *The Hajj: Collected Essays*, edited by Venetia Porter and Liana Saif, pp. 184–94. London, 2012.

al-Moraekhi 2002 al-Moraekhi, Moshalleh. "A New Perspective on the Phenomenon of Mirror-Image Writing in Arabic Calligraphy." In *Studies on Arabia in Honour of Professor G. Rex Smith*, edited by John F. Healey and Venetia Porter. New York and Oxford, 2002.

al-Mulk 2002 al-Mulk, Nizam. *The Book of Government; or, Rules for Kings*. Translated by Hubert Darke. London and New York 2002.

Nelson 1985 Nelson, Kristina. *The Art of Reciting the Qur'an*. Austin, 1985.

O'Kane 2006 O'Kane, Bernard. *The Treasures of Islamic Art in the Museums of Cairo*. New York, 2006.

Özbek 1995 Özbek, Yildiray. "The Peacock Figure and Its Iconography in Medieval Anatolian Turkish Art." In *10th International Congress of Turkish Art, 17–23 September 1995*. pp. 537–38. Geneva, 1995.

Pal 2007 Pal, Pratapaditya, ed. *The Arts of Kashmir*. Exh. cat. Asia Society, New York; Cincinnati Art Museum. New York and Milan, 2007.

Philon 2000 Philon, Helen. "The Murals in the Tomb of Ahmad Shah near Bidar." *Apollo* 152, no. 465 (2000), pp. 3–10.

Philon 2010 Philon, Helen, ed. *Silent Splendour: Palaces, Palaces of the Deccan: 14th–19th Centuries*. Mumbai, 2010.

Pickthall 1930 Marmaduke, Pickthall. *The Meaning of the Glorious Quran*. Flushing, N.Y., 1930.

Pocock 2010 *Parviz Tanavoli: Monograph*, by Charles Pocock; edited by Samar Faruqi. Exh. cat. Meem Gallery. Dubai, 2010.

Porter 2006 Porter, Venetia. *Word into Art: Artists of the Modern Middle East*. Exh. cat. British Museum. London, 2006.

Porter et al. 2016 Porter, Venetia, et al. *Signs of Our Time: From Calligraphy to Calligraffiti*. London, 2016.

Qadi Ahmad 1959 Qadi Ahmad ibn Mir Munshi. *Calligraphers and Painters: A Treatise by Qadi Ahmad, Son of Mir-Munshi (circa A.H. 1015/A.D. 1606)*, translated by V. Minorsky. Washington, 1959.

Rosenthal 1971 Rosenthal, Franz. *Four Essays on Art and Literature in Islam*, pp. 20–50. Leiden, 1971.

Roxburgh 1998 Roxburgh, David J. "Disorderly Conduct?: F. R. Martin and the Bahram Mirza Album." *Muqarnas* 15 (1998), pp. 32–57.

Roxburgh 2008 Roxburgh, David J. *Writing the Word of God: Calligraphy and the Qur'an*. Exh. cat. Museum of Fine Arts. Houston, 2008.

St. Laurent 1989 St. Laurent, Beatrice. "The Identification of a Magnificent Koran Manuscript." In *Les Manuscripts du Moyen-Orient: Essais de codicologie et de paléographie*, edited by François Déroche, pp. 115–24. Istanbul and Paris, 1989.

Schick 2008 Schick, İrvin Cemil. "The Iconicity of Islamic Calligraphy in Turkey." *RES: Anthropology and Aesthetics* 53/54 (Spring/Autumn 2008), pp. 211–24.

Schimmel 1970 Schimmel, Annemarie. *Islamic Calligraphy*. Iconography of Religions 22: Islam. Leiden, 1970.

Schimmel 1984 Schimmel, Annemarie. *Calligraphy and Islamic Culture*. New York, 1984.

Seracettin 2008 Seracettin, Sahin. *The Museum of Turkish and Islamic Arts: Thirteen Centuries of Glory from the Umayyads to the Ottomans*. New York, 2008.

Shankland 2004 Shankland, David, ed. *Archaeology and Heritage in the Balkans and Anatolia: The Life and Times of F. W. Hasluck, 1898–1920*. Istanbul, 2004.

Soucek 1979 Soucek, Priscilla. "The Arts of Calligraphy." In *Arts of the Book in Central Asia, 14th–16th Centuries*, edited by Basil Gray, pp. 7–34. Paris, 1979.

Suleman 2007 Suleman, Fahmida, ed. *Word of God, Art of Man: The Qur'an and Its Creative Expressions*. Oxford, 2007.

Suleman 2015 Suleman, Fahmida, ed. *People of the Prophet's House: Artistic and Ritual Expressions of Shi'i Islam*. London, 2015.

Thackston 1994 Thackston, Wheeler M. "The Role of Calligraphy." In *The Mosque: History, Architectural Development and Regional Diversity*, edited by Martin Frishman and Hasan-Uddin Khan, pp. 43–53. London, 1994.

Vali 2008 Vali, Murtaza. "Ismail Gulgee (1926–2007)." *ArtAsiaPacific*, no. 57 (March/April 2008). http://artasiapacific.com/Magazine/57/IsmailGulgee19262007.

Volov 1966 Volov, Lisa. "Plaited Kufic on Samanid Epigraphic Pottery." *Ars Orientalis* 6 (1966), pp. 107–33.

Ward 1993 Ward, Rachel. *Islamic Metalwork*. London, 1993.

Welch 1979 Welch, Anthony. *Calligraphy in the Arts of the Muslim World*. Exh. cat. Asia Society, New York. Austin and New York, 1979.

Whelan 1990 Whelan, Estelle. "Writing the Word of God: Some Early Qur'ān Manuscripts and Their Milieux, Part I." *Ars Orientalis* 20 (1990), pp. 113–47.

GLOSSARY

Abjad System in which each Arabic letter is assigned a numerical value. In Qur'ans, *abjad* letters can be used to indicate a verse number.

al-Aqlam al-Sitta Literally, "six pens"; a group of rounded cursive scripts thought to have been codified by Ibn al-Bawwab (d. 1022) and perfected by Yaqut al-Musta'simi (d. 1298).

Aya (pl. **ayat**) Literally, "sign"; verse from the Qur'an.

Baraka Blessings or bounty bestowed by God.

Bifolium Sheet of parchment or paper, folded in half.

Bismallah "In the name of God, Most Merciful, Most Compassionate"; the invocation that prefaces every *sura* in the Qur'an except *al-Tawba* ("Repentance").

Colophon Statement at the end of a manuscript that records information about it, including the date and place of production, the name of the copyist, and occasionally the name of the patron.

Diacritical mark Mark, point, or sign added or attached to a letter or character to give it a phonetic value and/or to distinguish it from another of similar form.

Divani Literally, "belonging to the imperial chancery"; a type of hanging script developed and used primarily for official documents in the Ottoman empire.

Doublure Ornamental lining on the inner face of a bookbinding.

Du'a Prayer.

Finispiece Illuminated page, or facing pages, placed after the end of a text.

Frontispiece Illuminated page, or facing pages, placed before the beginning of a text.

Ghubar Literally, "dust"; tiny script said to be as fine as dust.

Gulzar Literally, "field of roses"; a script in Iran in which the field of large letters is decorated with flowers.

Hamza Glottal stop.

Hijazi Earliest known script used to transcribe the Qur'an. The name derives from Hijaz Province, where the holy cities of Mecca and Medina are located, and where the script may have originated.

Hijra The Prophet Muhammad's flight from Mecca to Medina in A.D 622.

Hijri The Islamic calendar, the first year of which corresponds to A.D. 622 in the Christian calendar; abbreviated as A.H.

Hilya Textual description of the Prophet Muhammad in the form of a formulaic calligraphic composition

Hizb (pl. **ahzab**) One-sixtieth of the Qur'an; each can be subdivided into *maqra* (quarters). *Hizb* and *maqra* notations are found in margins of Qur'an manuscripts.

Ijaza License granted by a master calligrapher to his pupil signifying that he has mastered the scripts.

Illuminations Manuscript illustrations and decorations, usually executed in vibrant colors and gold or silver, which create a "luminous" effect.

Juz' (pl. **ajza'**) One-thirtieth of a Qur'an, permitting the complete reading of the holy book over the course of a month; the most common division of the Qur'an.

Katib Scribe.

al-Khatt al-Mansub The "proportional writing" system for rounded cursive scripts developed by Ibn Muqla (d. 940). In principle, the units for determining the proportions are the letter *alif* and the rhomboid dot placed above and below similar letter forms to distinguish one from the other.

Khattat Calligrapher.

Kufic Variety of scripts that flourished in the 8th century and emphasize horizontal strokes. The name originates from the city of Kufa, Iraq.

Maghribi Variety of scripts that developed in northwestern Africa in the 10th century and used exclusively in Spain and North Africa; letters have a consistent thickness throughout a text.

Mashq Calligraphy exercises or practice pages; also, the practice of elongating a letter.

Mastar Board with silk threads or cord tied across it in lines. When a sheet of paper is pressed against it, the lines create impressions that guide the calligrapher's hand.

Mihrab Wall niche that indicates the *qibla* (direction toward Mecca), which Muslims face while praying.

Muhaqqaq One of the "six pens"; a large script characterized by long, sharp descending letters and favored for monumental copies of the Qur'an.

Muraqqa' Literally, "patchwork"; an album of paintings and calligraphy.

Mushaf (pl. **masahif**) Written copy of the Qur'an; derived from *sahifa*, the Arabic word for folio or leaf.

Muthanna Literally, "doubled"; mirror-image writing, in which the left side of a calligraphic composition mirrors what is written on the right.

Naskh One of the "six pens"; a script notable for the contrast between its long vertical strokes and shorter descending ones. It was favored for small and mid-size Qur'ans and developed into numerous distinct regional variants.

Nasta'liq Cursive script that flourished in late 14th-century Iran; used almost exclusively for texts in Persian, particularly poetry.

New-style script Less angular than standard *kufic*, it was also called eastern *kufic*, Persian *kufic*, broken *kufic*, or broken cursive. At first (ca. 900), it was used mainly for copying Qur'ans, but after the 13th century it was used decoratively, primarily for manuscript headings.

Papyrus Support for writing or painting made by pounding the pithy stem of a water plant into sheets; used throughout Egypt and the ancient Mediterranean world.

Qalam Reed pen.

Quire Gathering of a number of folded sheets, sewn together to form a codex. Manuscripts of the Qur'an include quires composed of 5 bifolia or 10 leaves (quinions).

Rahla Wood stand, often X-shaped, used to support a Qur'an manuscript.

Rasm Basic shapes of Arabic letters, differentiated by the addition of diacritical marks; also called the "skeleton structure."

Rayhan One of the "six pens"; a smaller version of *muhaqqaq* (see above).

Riqa' One of the "six pens"; a smaller version of *tawqi'* (see below), with accentuated curvilinear strokes and unconventional ligatures.

Safina Literally, "ship"; an oblong illustrated or unillustrated manuscript of poetry bound on the short side.

Sajada Literally, "prostration." There are 14 verses in the Qur'an, usually marked by an illuminated device in the margin, that call on the reader to pause and perform *sajada*.

Sarlawh Illuminated panel that opens a text; usually positioned at the top of the page.

Shadda Sign indicating the doubling of a letter

Shamsa Sunburst illumination, sometimes bearing text, found at the beginning or end of a text.

Sukun Phonetic sign indicating that there is no vowel.

Sura (pl. **surat**) One of 114 chapters in the Qur'an.

Tajwid Rules for reciting the Qur'an.

Ta'liq Literally, "hanging"; a script used primarily by secretaries in Iran and characterized by deep curvilinear strokes, sinuous loops, and a distinct rhythm.

Tawqi' One of the "six pens"; a script resembling *thuluth* (see below), with numerous unconventional ligatures.

Thuluth One of the "six pens"; a monumental script with more curvilinear features and unconventional ligatures. It was often reserved for Qur'ans, as well as for decorative *sura* headings and architectural inscriptions.

Tughra Formulaic insignia of an Ottoman sultan; created in the imperial workshop and marked on official documents.

Unwan Illuminated heading; usually inscribed with the title of a chapter.

Vocalization System of vowels added to the Arabic consonants to aid in vocalization; initially appearing as colored dots, eventually replaced with a codified system of signs and symbols.

Waqf (pl. **awqaf**) Pious endowment or bequest to a religious foundation, mosque, or tomb. A document of a *waqf* is called a *waqfiyyah*.

MAJOR EMPIRES AND DYNASTIES OF THE ISLAMIC WORLD

Sasanian empire (224–636). Struggles with Byzantium weakened the Sasanian empire, leaving it open to defeat by Islamic armies in 642. Its capital, Ctesiphon, was based in present-day Iran.

Byzantine empire (ca. 330–1453). After the Roman emperor Constantine converted to Christianity, he made Constantinople the seat of the new Byzantine empire until its fall to the Ottomans in 1453.

Umayyad caliphate (661–750). The first major Islamic dynasty; centered at Damascus, Syria.

Abbasid caliphate (750–1258). The second major Islamic dynasty. During the second half of their rule, the Abbasid caliphs were rulers in name only, having become the puppets of other princely states, such as the the Samanids and the Seljuqs.

Spanish Umayyads (756–1031). The first Islamic dynasty to rule in Spain; established by the last Umayyad prince fleeing Syria after the Abbasid conquest.

Samanids (819–1005). The first native Persian dynasty to rule Iran after the collapse of the Sasanian empire and the Arab Muslim conquests.

Seljuqs of Iran (ca. 1040–1196). Turkic tribesmen whose dominion eventually encompassed an area extending from Central Asia to the Eastern Mediterranean. Their art is notable for its synthesis of Persian, Islamic, and Central Asian elements.

Almoravids and Almohads (ca. 1062–1147; 1130–1269). Berber dynasties that ruled southern Spain after the fall of the Spanish Umayyads. They created capitals at Marrakesh in Morocco and Seville in Spain.

Seljuqs of Rum (1081–1307). Faction of Seljuqs that established control over Anatolia, then known as "Rum," a derivation of "Rome," alluding to the Byzantine empire's legacy in that region.

Ilkhanids (1206–1353). One of the *khanates* (principalities ruled by a *khan*) established by the descendants of the Mongol conqueror Genghis Khan.

Nasrid kingdom (1232–1492). The last Islamic dynasty to rule in Spain. Centered at their capital of Granada, the Nasrids fell in 1492, when most Muslims and Jews were cast out of Spain by King Ferdinand and Queen Isabella.

Mamluks (1250–1517). Turkic military forces that served the preceding Egyptian dynasty but overthrew their masters, establishing their own rule based in Egypt.

Ottoman empire (1299–1923). One of the longest-lasting dynasties in world history, the Ottomans ruled over a vast and varied territory with the help of a highly structured bureaucracy. Many Ottoman sultans were great patrons of the arts.

Timurid empire (1307–1507). Turks who conquered much of Greater Iran and Central Asia; named for the founder of the dynasty, Timur (or Tamerlane), and renowned as great patrons of the arts.

Safavid empire (1501–1722). A Shi'i dynasty based in present-day Iran. The Safavids traced their lineage to an important Sufi mystic and were renowned for their patronage of the arts.

Mughal empire (1526–1858). Based in India, the Mughals traced their lineage to the Mongol rulers of Iran. Their art and architecture synthesized Persian, Indian, and European influences.

This publication is made possible by the Diane W. and James E. Burke Fund.

Published by The Metropolitan Museum of Art, New York
Mark Polizzotti, Publisher and Editor in Chief
Gwen Roginsky, Associate Publisher and General Manager of Publications
Peter Antony, Chief Production Manager
Michael Sittenfeld, Senior Managing Editor

Edited by Marcie M. Muscat
Production by Christopher Zichello
Designed by Miko McGinty and Rita Jules
Image acquisitions and permissions by Jessica Palinski
Map by Anandaroop Roy

Unless otherwise noted, all works are in the collection of The Metropolitan Museum of Art, New York. Photographs of works in the collection are by Katherine Dahab, Anna-Marie Kellen, and Eileen Travell, Imaging, The Metropolitan Museum of Art. Additional photography credits: Image © The Aga Khan Museum: fig. 7; © Art Directors & TRIP/Alamy Stock Photo: fig. 41; Image © Ashmolean Museum, University of Oxford: fig. 20; © Leon Barszczewski, courtesy of Igor Strojecki: fig. 38; bpk Bildagentur/Staatsbibliothek zu Berlin/Dietmar Katz/Art Resource, NY: fig. 5; Cadbury Research Library: Special Collection, University of Birmingham: fig. 30; The David Collection, Copenhagen, 86/2004, photo by Pernille Klemp: fig. 31; © Estate of Burhan Doğançay: cat. 41; © Golnaz Fathi: cat. 42; Special Collection, Fine Arts Library, Harvard University, photo by Bernard O'Kane: fig. 17; © Ismail Gulgee: fig. 50; Courtesy of the Hispanic Society of America, New York: fig. 10; Courtesy of the Khalili Collection, London: fig. 55; Courtesy of calligrapher Nuria Garcia Masip: fig. 6; © 1992 Saïd Nuseibeh Photography: fig. 14; © B. O'Kane/Alamy Stock Photo: figs. 40, 51; Calligraphy by Ahmed Fares Rizq and Abdul Rahman Mahmoud: figs. 15, 16, 18, 19, 22, 23; © RMN-Grand Palais/Art Resource, NY: fig. 39; Courtesy of Musée du Louvre Editions: fig. 12; Sadequain Foundation, USA, courtesy of Dr. Salman Ahmad: fig. 54; © Parviz Tanavoli: cat. 40, fig. 57; © Victoria and Albert Museum, London: fig. 47.

Typeset by Tina Henderson in Interstate and Documenta
Printed on FSC-certified 150 gsm Arctic Silk Plus
Printed and bound by Ofset Yapımevi, Istanbul

Front cover: Insignia (*tughra*) of Sultan Süleyman the Magnificent, ca. 1555–60 (cat. 8, detail). Back cover: Letter in *ta'liq* (hanging) script, A.H. 911/A.D. 1505–6 (cat. 10a, detail). Additional illustrations: p. 2: Folio from the "Blue Qur'an," second half 9th–mid-10th century (cat. 16, detail); p. 4: Fragmentary cenotaph cover with Qur'anic verses, 17th–18th century (cat. 28, detail); p. 6: Mihrab (detail). Iran, Isfahan, Ilkhanid, A.H. 755/A.D. 1354–55. Polychrome-glazed tiles on stonepaste, set into mortar, 135 1/16 x 113 11/16 in. (343.1 x 288.7 cm). Harris Brisbane Dick Fund, 1939 (39.20); p. 8: Stand for a Qur'an (*rahla*), A.H. 761/A.D. 1360 (cat. 22, detail); p. 14: Folio from a Qur'an in playful floriated script, 11th century (cat. 29, detail); p. 24: Colophon from the "Anonymous Baghdad Qur'an," dated A.H. 707/A.D. 1307–8 (cat. 5, detail); p. 68: Folio from a Qur'an in *maghribi* script, late 13th–14th century (cat. 20, detail); p. 106: Calligraphic galleon with the names of the Seven Sleepers, dated A.H. 1180/A.D. 1766–67 (cat. 37, detail); p. 146: Folio from the Mushaf al-Hadina ("Nurse's Qur'an"), A.H. 410/A.D. 1019–21 (cat. 4, detail)

Second printing, 2025

The Metropolitan Museum of Art
1000 Fifth Avenue
New York, New York 10028
metmuseum.org

Distributed by Yale University Press, New Haven and London
yalebooks.com/art
yalebooks.co.uk

Authorized Representative in the EU: Easy Access System Europe, Mustamäe tee 50, 10621 Tallinn, Estonia, gpsr.requests@easproject.com

Cataloging-in-Publication Data is available from the Library of Congress.
ISBN 978-1-58839-630-3